Blender 3D By Example

Design a complete workflow with Blender to create
stunning 3D scenes and films step by step!

Romain Caudron

Pierre-Armand Nicq

[PACKT] open source
PUBLISHING
community experience distilled

BIRMINGHAM - MUMBAI

Blender 3D By Example

First published: September 2015

Production reference: 1220915

Published by Packt Publishing Ltd.
Livery Place
35 Livery Street
Birmingham B3 2PB, UK.

ISBN 978-1-78528-507-3

www.packtpub.com

Credits

Authors
Romain Caudron

Pierre-Armand Nicq

Reviewer
Fernando Castilhos Melo

Acquisition Editor
Tushar Gupta

Content Development Editor
Athira Laji

Technical Editor
Menza Mathew

Copy Editor
Kausambhi Majumdar

Project Coordinator
Bijal Patel

Proofreader
Safis Editing

Indexer
Rekha Nair

Production Coordinator
Aparna Bhagat

Cover Work
Aparna Bhagat

About the Authors

Romain Caudron is a French 2D/3D artist. He is a cofounder and CG artist of Main Digitales, a new video game studio in Montpellier in the south of France, and he specializes in virtual reality. Also, he is an assistant to Patrice Stellest, the Swiss contemporary artist.

Romain has had a mostly self-taught career, but he received a master's degree in cinema and game design from Paul Valery University, Montpellier III, France. Then, he studied 3D animation using CGTrainer. His interest in hacker culture and open source software led him to start working with Blender in 2012.

Before this book, in 2014, he was a reviewer on *Blender Cycles: Materials and Textures Cookbook* by Enrico Valenza.

Pierre-Armand Nicq started learning how to generate 3D images with Blender 2.4x at a young age. He is really passionate about all types of multimedia creation and uses Blender for projects such as 3D images/animations and games. He codes in different programming languages, such as C/C++, C#, AS3, JavaScript, and PHP, to create games and other kinds of programs. Pierre-Armand loves to share his knowledge. This is why he founded a French YouTube channel (http://www.youtube.com/ToutApprendre). It has more than 9,500 subscribers and 200 tutorials about 3D and programming. Currently, he is in his fifth and last year of school at IIM (Paris/La Défense). During his free time, he loves to play jazz music, participate in GameJams, and perform card tricks.

I would like to thank my family and all my friends for supporting me in my passion. Also, I would like to thank my coauthor, Romain. Moreover, I am really grateful to the entire Packt Publishing team for believing in our project and helping us throughout the creation of this book. Last but not least, I hope you will have fun mixing tons of ingredients in your Blender.

About the Reviewers

Fernando Castilhos Melo lives in Caxias do Sul, Brazil, and works in a software company as a software developer and systems analyst. In his spare time, he works on 3D modeling using Blender. He has been using Blender since 2009. He has given several lectures on Blender and 3D modeling at several Brazilian free / open source software events, such as FLISOL and TcheLinux. Fernando holds a degree in computer science from UCS (University of Caxias do Sul).

This is the second book on Blender that he has worked on. The first one was *Blender Cycles: Lighting and Rendering Cookbook* in 2013. He had developed an integration between Blender and Kinect named "Kinected Blender" to generate 3D animation. This project is currently in the alpha version. For more information, you can go to his web page at http://www.fernando.melo.nom.br/.

I want to thank my wife, Mauren, my parents, Eloir and Miriam, and all my friends for their support during the review of this book.

www.PacktPub.com

Support files, eBooks, discount offers, and more

For support files and downloads related to your book, please visit www.PacktPub.com.

Did you know that Packt offers eBook versions of every book published, with PDF and ePub files available? You can upgrade to the eBook version at www.PacktPub.com and as a print book customer, you are entitled to a discount on the eBook copy. Get in touch with us at service@packtpub.com for more details.

At www.PacktPub.com, you can also read a collection of free technical articles, sign up for a range of free newsletters and receive exclusive discounts and offers on Packt books and eBooks.

https://www2.packtpub.com/books/subscription/packtlib

Do you need instant solutions to your IT questions? PacktLib is Packt's online digital book library. Here, you can search, access, and read Packt's entire library of books.

Why subscribe?

- Fully searchable across every book published by Packt
- Copy and paste, print, and bookmark content
- On demand and accessible via a web browser

Free access for Packt account holders

If you have an account with Packt at www.PacktPub.com, you can use this to access PacktLib today and view 9 entirely free books. Simply use your login credentials for immediate access.

Table of Contents

Preface

Welcome to the wonderful world of Blender! This book will guide you through the majority of the 3D tools and techniques by creating four concrete projects. Blender is a very powerful and Open Source software, that is, it is totally free. You can even sell your productions with this! This is a very good alternative to other famous 3D solutions.

One of Blender's strengths is that it can cover any multimedia productions such as animation movies, games, or commercials. Moreover, Blender is very stable, frequently updated, available anywhere around the world with an internet connection, and it is lightweight. The Blender Foundation, which is in charge of the official development of the software, often produces short films that are entirely made with Blender. The last one was the amazing film, Cosmos Laundromat, which proved us again that Blender is capable of meeting the needs of an ambitious professional production. During the production of these short films, the software evolved with new tools and optimizations.

Despite the fact that Blender is an amazing program with tremendous possibilities, it is nothing more than a tool that will help you to realize an idea or a project. It is important to work on the artistic aspect of your creations. That's why this book will not just cover the technical dimensions of the software.

With a little bit of practice, Blender will be very efficient in terms of productivity and artistic freedom, so don't worry, you have made a good choice! This book will give you everything you need to start creating your own 3D projects.

We hope that you will enjoy reading this book as much as we have enjoyed writing it.

Good reading and trust yourself!

What this book covers

Chapter 1, Straight into Blender!, discovers the fundamentals of 3D creation and covers how to navigate in the Blender user interface.

Chapter 2, Robot Toy – Modeling of an Object, teaches the basic polygonal modeling tools of Blender. In this chapter, you will model a complete Robot Toy starting from a 2D concept.

Chapter 3, Alien Character – Base Mesh Creation and Sculpting, helps you to understand the sculpting tools of Blender while sculpting an alien character. In order to have the best result, this chapter provides an introduction to anatomy as well.

Chapter 4, Alien Character – Creating a Proper Topology and Transferring the Sculpt Details, covers how to create a clean version of the sculpted model that can be used for animation or game. Moreover, this chapter explains how to unwrap UVs so that a normal and ambient occlusion map can be baked.

Chapter 5, Haunted House – Modeling of the Scene, covers more advanced modeling tools such as curves, in order to model a full haunted house scene.

Chapter 6, Haunted House – Putting Colors on It, improves the haunted house scene using the texturing tools of Blender. Some techniques to produce hand painted tiled textures are explained as well.

Chapter 7, Haunted House – Adding Materials and Lights in Cycles, explains how lights work in order to light the scene. This chapter also provides a basic comprehension of the Cycles render engine and its node-based material creation process.

Chapter 8, Rat Cowboy – Learning to Rig a Character for Animation, covers the creation of a full bipedal rig by hand using bones, constraints, shape keys, and custom shapes.

Chapter 9, Rat Cowboy – Animate a Full Sequence, covers the preproduction stage of animation. Then after explaining the principles of animation, this chapter dives into the animation of a full sequence using the different tools that Blender has to offer.

Chapter 10, Rat Cowboy – Rendering, Compositing, and Editing, covers more advanced techniques to create a fur or a skin material. Then it explains how to polish and edit the sequence using the nodal compositing and the editing tools of Blender.

What you need for this book

The only necessary thing to have is the last official release of Blender (2.75, at the time of writing). You can download it from `http://www.blender.org/download`. A pen tablet is highly recommended for *Chapter 3, Alien Character – Base Mesh Creation and Sculpting*.

Who this book is for

This book will provide beginners with the necessary skills and knowledge to create their own 3D projects with Blender. You don't need to have any previous experience in 3D in general, but if you do, then this book is a great way get you started with Blender. This book is for anyone who wants to learn Blender by creating concrete projects.

Conventions

In this book, you will find a number of text styles that distinguish between different kinds of information. Here are some examples of these styles and an explanation of their meaning.

Code words in text, database table names, folder names, filenames, file extensions, pathnames, dummy URLs, user input, and Twitter handles are shown as follows: "We will rename this shader `HouseRoof1`."

New terms and **important words** are shown in bold. Words that you see on the screen, for example, in menus or dialog boxes, appear in the text like this: "We will click on the **Use node** button in order to work in the Node editor."

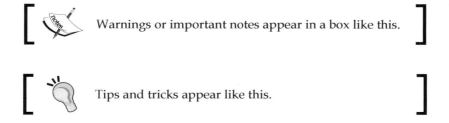

Warnings or important notes appear in a box like this.

Tips and tricks appear like this.

Reader feedback

Feedback from our readers is always welcome. Let us know what you think about this book—what you liked or disliked. Reader feedback is important for us as it helps us develop titles that you will really get the most out of.

To send us general feedback, simply e-mail feedback@packtpub.com, and mention the book's title in the subject of your message.

If there is a topic that you have expertise in and you are interested in either writing or contributing to a book, see our author guide at www.packtpub.com/authors.

Customer support

Now that you are the proud owner of a Packt book, we have a number of things to help you to get the most from your purchase.

Downloading the color images of this book

We also provide you with a PDF file that has color images of the screenshots/ diagrams used in this book. The color images will help you better understand the changes in the output. You can download this file from https://www.packtpub.com/sites/default/files/downloads/5073OS_ColoredImages.pdf.

Errata

Although we have taken every care to ensure the accuracy of our content, mistakes do happen. If you find a mistake in one of our books—maybe a mistake in the text or the code—we would be grateful if you could report this to us. By doing so, you can save other readers from frustration and help us improve subsequent versions of this book. If you find any errata, please report them by visiting http://www.packtpub.com/submit-errata, selecting your book, clicking on the **Errata Submission Form** link, and entering the details of your errata. Once your errata are verified, your submission will be accepted and the errata will be uploaded to our website or added to any list of existing errata under the Errata section of that title.

To view the previously submitted errata, go to https://www.packtpub.com/books/content/support and enter the name of the book in the search field. The required information will appear under the **Errata** section.

Piracy

Piracy of copyrighted material on the Internet is an ongoing problem across all media. At Packt, we take the protection of our copyright and licenses very seriously. If you come across any illegal copies of our works in any form on the Internet, please provide us with the location address or website name immediately so that we can pursue a remedy.

Please contact us at copyright@packtpub.com with a link to the suspected pirated material.

We appreciate your help in protecting our authors and our ability to bring you valuable content.

Questions

If you have a problem with any aspect of this book, you can contact us at questions@packtpub.com, and we will do our best to address the problem.

1
Straight into Blender!

Welcome to the first chapter, in which you will start getting familiar with Blender.

Here, navigation within the interface will be presented. Its approach is atypical in comparison to other 3D software, such as Autodesk Maya® or Autodesk 3DS Max®, but once you get used to this, it will be extremely effective.

If you have had the opportunity to use Blender before, it is important to note that the interface went through changes during the evolution of the software (especially since version 2.5).

We will give you an idea of the possibilities that this wonderful free and open source software gives by presenting different workflows. You will learn some vocabulary and key concepts of 3D creation so that you will not to get lost during your learning.

Finally, you will have a brief introduction to the projects that we will carry out throughout this book.

Let's dive into the third dimension! The following topics will be covered in this chapter:

- Learning some theory and vocabulary
- Navigating the 3D viewport
- How to set up preferences
- Using keyboard shortcuts to save time

An overview of the 3D workflow

Before learning how to navigate the Blender interface, we will give you a short introduction to the 3D workflow.

The anatomy of a 3D scene

To start learning about Blender, you need to understand some basic concepts. Don't worry, there is no need to have special knowledge in mathematics or programming to create beautiful 3D objects; it only requires curiosity. Some artistic notions are a plus.

All 3D elements, which you will handle, will evolve in to a scene. There is a three-dimensional space with a coordinate system composed of three axes. In Blender, the x axis shows the width, y axis shows the depth, and the z axis shows the height. Some softwares use a different approach and reverses the y and z axes. These axes are color-coded, we advise you to remember them: the x axis in red, the y axis in green and the z axis in blue.

A scene may have the scale you want and you can adjust it according to your needs. This looks like a film set for a movie. A scene can be populated by one or more cameras, lights, models, rigs, and many other elements. You will have the control of their placement and their setup.

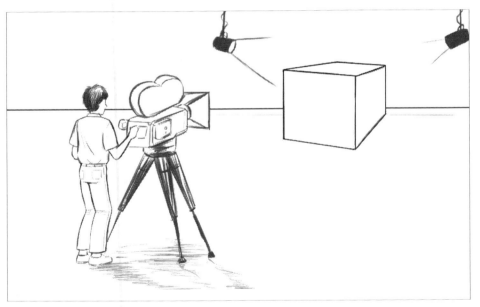

A 3D scene looks like a film set.

A mesh is made of vertices, edges, and faces. The vertices are some points in the scene space that are placed at the end of the edges. They could be thought of as 3D points in space and the edges connect them. Connected together, the edges and the vertices form a face, also called a polygon. It is a geometric plane, which has several sides as its name suggests.

In 3D software, a polygon is constituted of at least three sides. It is often essential to favor four-sided polygons during modeling for a better result. You will have an opportunity to see this in more detail later.

Your actors and environments will be made of polygonal objects, or more commonly called as meshes. If you have played old 3D games, you've probably noticed the very angular outline of the characters; it was, in fact, due to a low count of polygons.

We must clarify that the orientation of the faces is important for your polygon object to be illuminated. Each face has a normal. This is a perpendicular vector that indicates the direction of the polygon. In order for the surface to be seen, it is necessary that the normals point to the outside of the model. Except in special cases where the interior of a polygonal object is empty and invisible. You will be able to create your actors and environment as if you were handling virtual clay to give them the desired shape.

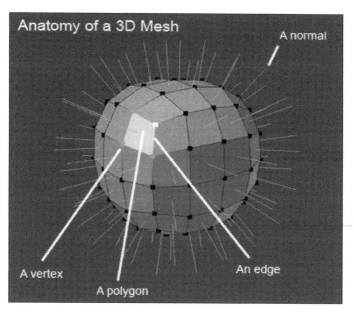

Anatomy of a 3D Mesh

To make your characters presentable, you will have to create their textures, which are 2D images that will be mapped to the 3D object. UV coordinates will be necessary in order to project the texture onto the mesh. Imagine an origami paper cube that you are going to unfold. This is roughly the same. These details are contained in a square space with the representation of the mesh laid flat. You can paint the texture of your model in your favorite software, even in Blender.

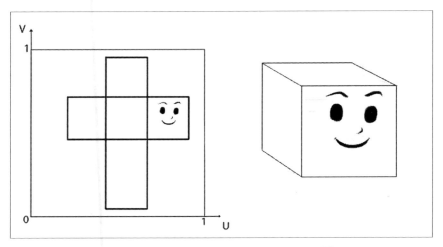

This is the representation of the UV mapping process. The texture on the left is projected to the 3D model on the right.

After this, you can give the illusion of life to your virtual actors by animating them. For this, you will need to place animation keys spaced on the timeline. If you change the state of the object between two keyframes, you will get the illusion of movement—animation. To move the characters, there is a very interesting process that uses a bone system, mimicking the mechanism of a real skeleton. Your polygon object will be then attached to the skeleton with a weight assigned to the vertices on each bone, so if you animate the bones, the mesh components will follow them.

Once your characters, props, or environment are ready, you will be able to choose a focal length and an adequate framework for your camera.

In order to light your scene, the choice of the render engine will be important for the kind of lamps to use, but usually there are three types of lamps as used in cinema productions. You will have to place them carefully. There are directional lights, which behave like the sun and produce hard shadows. There are omnidirectional lights, which will allow you to simulate diffuse light, illuminating everything around it and casting soft shadows. There are also spots that will simulate a conical shape. As in the film industry or other imaging creation fields, good lighting is a must-have in order to sell the final picture. Lighting is an expressive and narrative element that can magnify your models, or make them irrelevant.

Once everything is in place, you are going to make a render. You will have a choice between a still image and an animated sequence. All the given parameters with the lights and materials will be calculated by the render engine. Some render engines offer an approach based on physics with rays that are launched from the camera. Cycles is a good example of this kind of engine and succeed in producing very realistic renders. Others will have a much simpler approach, but none less technically based on visible elements from the camera.

All of this is an overview of what you will be able to achieve while reading this book and following along with Blender.

What can you do with Blender?

In addition to being completely free and open source, Blender is a powerful tool that is stable and with an integral workflow that will allow you to understand your learning of 3D creation with ease. Software updates are very frequent; they fix bugs and, more importantly, add new features.

You will not feel alone as Blender has an active and passionate community around it. There are many sites providing tutorials, and an official documentation detailing the features of Blender.

You will be able to carry out everything you need in Blender, including things that are unusual for a 3D package such as concept art creation, sculpting, or digital postproduction, which we have not yet discussed, including compositing and video editing. This is particularly interesting in order to push the aesthetics of your future images and movies to another level.

It is also possible to make video games. Also, note that the Blender game engine is still largely unknown and underestimated. Although this aspect of the software is not as developed as other specialized game engines, it is possible to make good quality games without switching to another software.

You will realize that the possibilities are enormous, and you will be able to adjust your workflow to suit your needs and desires.

Software of this type could scare you by its unusual handling and its complexity, but you'll realize that once you have learned its basics, it is really intuitive in many ways.

Getting used to the navigation in Blender

Now that you have been introduced to the 3D workflow, you will learn how to navigate the Blender interface, starting with the 3D viewport.

An introduction to the navigation of the 3D Viewport

It is time to learn how to navigate in the Blender viewport. The viewport represents the 3D space, in which you will spend most of your time. As we previously said, it is defined by three axes (x, y, and z). Its main goal is to display the 3D scene from a certain point of view while you're working on it.

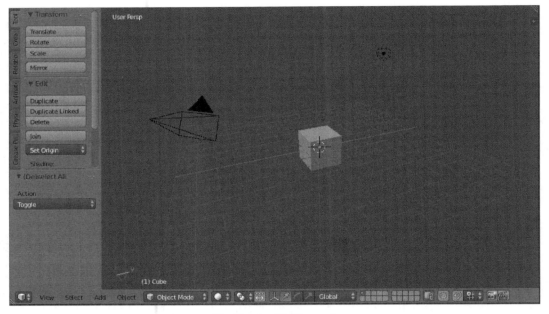

The Blender 3D Viewport

When you are navigating through this, it will be as if you were a movie director but with special powers that allow you to film from any point of view.

The navigation is defined by three main actions: pan, orbit, and zoom. The pan action means that you will move horizontally or vertically according to your current point of view. If we connect that to our cameraman metaphor, it's like if you were moving laterally to the left, or to the right, or moving up or down with a camera crane.

By default, in Blender the shortcut to pan around is to press the *Shift* button and the **Middle Mouse Button (MMB)**, and drag the mouse.

The orbit action means that you will rotate around the point that you are focusing on. For instance, imagine that you are filming a romantic scene of two actors and that you rotate around them in a circular manner. In this case, the couple will be the main focus. In a 3D scene, your main focus would be a 3D character, a light, or any other 3D object.

To orbit around in the Blender viewport, the default shortcut is to press the MMB and then drag the mouse.

The last action that we mentioned is zoom. The zoom action is straightforward. It is the action of moving our point of view closer to an element or further away from an element.

In Blender, you can zoom in by scrolling your mouse wheel up and zoom out by scrolling your mouse wheel down.

To gain time and precision, Blender proposes some predefined points of view. For instance, you can quickly go in a top view by pressing the numpad *7*, you can also go in a front view by pressing the numpad *1*, you can go in a side view by pressing the numpad *3*, and last but not least, the numpad *0* allows you to go in **Camera** view, which represents the final render point of the view of your scene.

You can also press the numpad *5* in order to activate or deactivate the orthographic mode. The orthographic mode removes perspective. It is very useful if you want to be precise. It feels as if you were manipulating a blueprint of the 3D scene.

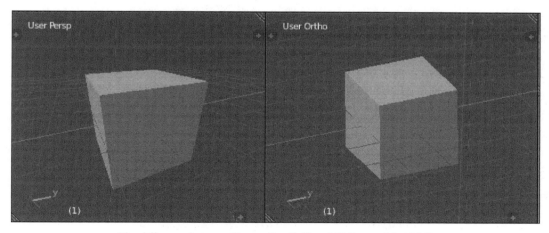

The difference between Perspective (left) and Orthographic (right)

If you are lost, you can always look at the top left corner of the viewport in order to see in which view you are, and whether the orthographic mode is on or off.

Try to learn by heart all these shortcuts; you will use them a lot. With repetition, this will become a habit.

What are editors?

In Blender, the interface is divided into subpanels that we call **editors**; even the menu bar where you save your file is an editor. Each editor gives you access to tools categorized by their functionality. You have already used an editor, the 3D view. Now it's time to learn more about the editor's anatomy.

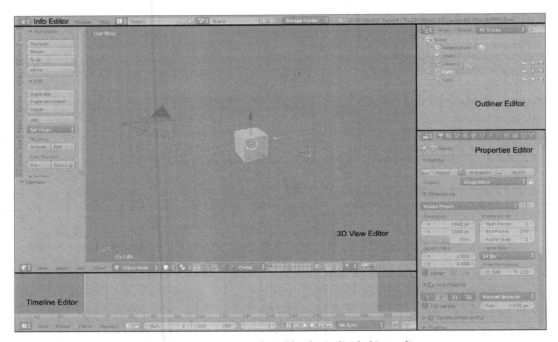

In this picture, you can see how Blender is divided into editors

The anatomy of an editor

There are 17 different editors in Blender and they all have the same base. An editor is composed of a **Header**, which is a menu that groups different options related to the editor. The first button of the header is to switch between other editors. For instance, you can replace the 3D view by the **UV/Image Editor** by clicking on it. You can easily change its place by right-clicking on it in an empty space and by choosing the **Flip to Top/Bottom** option.

The header can be hidden by selecting its top edge and by pulling it down. If you want to bring it back, press the little plus sign at the far right.

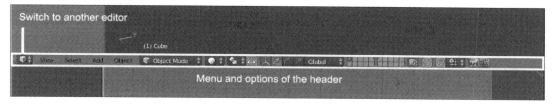

The header of the 3D viewport. The first button is for switching between editors, and also, we can choose between different options in the menu

In some editors, you can get access to hidden panels that give you other options. For instance, in the 3D view you can press the *T* key or the *N* key to toggle them on or off. As in the header, if a sub panel of an editor is hidden, you can click on the little plus sign to display it again.

Split, Join, and Detach

Blender offers you the possibility of creating editors where you want. To do this, you need to right-click on the border of an editor and select **Split Area** in order to choose where to separate them.

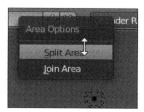

Right-click on the border of an editor to split it into two editors

The current editor will then be split in two editors. Now you can switch to any other editor that you desire by clicking on the first button of the header bar. If you want to merge two editors into one, you can right-click on the border that separates them and select the **Join Area** button. You will then have to click on the editor that you want to erase by pointing the arrow on it.

Use the **Join Area** option to join two editors together

You then have to choose which editor you want to remove by pointing and clicking on it.

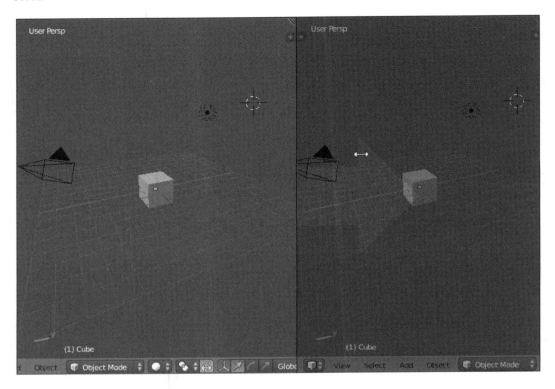

We are going to see another method of splitting editors that is nice. You can drag the top right corner of an editor and another editor will magically appear! If you want to join back two editors together, you will have to drag the top right corner in the direction of the editor that you want to remove. The last manipulation can be tricky at first, but with a little bit of practice, you will be able to do it closed eyes!

The top right corner of an editor

If you have multiple monitors, it could be a great idea to detach some editors in a separated window. With this, you could gain space and won't be overwhelmed by a condensed interface. In order to do this, you will need to press the *Shift* key and drag the top right corner of the editor with the **Left Mouse Button** (**LMB**).

Some useful layout presets

Blender offers you many predefined layouts that depend on the context of your creation. For instance, you can select the Animation preset in order to have all the major animation tools, or you can use the UV Editing preset in order to prepare your texturing. To switch between the presets, go to the top of the interface (in the **Info** editor, near the **Help** menu) and click on the drop-down menu. If you want, you can add new presets by clicking on the plus sign or delete presets by clicking on the X button. If you want to rename a preset, simply enter a new name in the corresponding text field. The following screenshot shows the Layout presets drop-down menu:

The layout presets drop-down menu

Setting up your preferences

When we start learning new software, it's good to know how to set up your preferences. Blender has a large number of options, but we will show you just the basic ones in order to change the default navigation style or to add new tools that we call add-ons in Blender.

An introduction to the Preferences window

The preferences window can be opened by navigating to the **File** menu and selecting the **User Preferences** option. If you want, you can use the *Ctrl + Alt + U* shortcut or the *Cmd* key and comma key on a Mac system.

There are seven tabs in this window as shown here:

The different tabs that compose the Preferences window

A nice thing that Blender offers is the ability to change its default theme. For this, you can go to the **Themes** tab and choose between different presets or even change the aspect of each interface elements.

Another useful setting to change is the number of undo that is 32 steps, by default. To change this number, go to the **Editing** tab and under the **Undo** label, slide the **Steps** to the desired value.

Customizing the default navigation style

We will now show you how to use a different style of navigation in the viewport. In many other 3D programs, such as Autodesk Maya®, you can use the *Alt* key in order to navigate in the 3D view. In order to activate this in Blender, navigate to the **Input** tab, and under the **Mouse** section, check the **Emulate 3 Button Mouse** option. Now if you want to use this navigation style in the viewport, you can press *Alt* and LMB to orbit around, *Ctrl + Alt* and the LMB to zoom, and *Alt + Shift* and the LMB to pan. Remember these shortcuts as they will be very useful when we enter the sculpting mode while using a pen tablet. The **Emulate 3 Button Mouse** checkbox is shown as follows:

The Emulate 3 Button Mouse will be very useful when sculpting using a pen tablet

Another useful setting is the **Emulate Numpad**. It allows you to use the numeric keys that are above the QWERTY keys in addition to the numpad keys. This is very useful for changing the views if you have a laptop without a numpad, or if you want to improve your workflow speed.

The Emulate Numpad allows you to use the numeric keys above the QWERTY keys
in order to switch views or toggle the perspective on or off

Improving Blender with add-ons

If you want even more tools, you can install what is called as add-ons on your copy of Blender. **Add-ons**, also called **Plugins** or **Scripts**, are Python files with the .py extension. By default, Blender comes with many disabled add-ons ordered by category. We will now activate two very useful add-ons that will improve our speed while modeling. First, go to the **Add-ons** tab, and click on the **Mesh** button in the category list at the left. Here, you will see all the default mesh add-ons available. Click on the check-boxes at the left of the **Mesh: F2** and **Mesh: LoopTools** subpanels in order to activate these add-ons. If you know the name of the add-on you want to activate, you can try to find it by typing its name in the search bar. There are many websites where you can download free add-ons, starting from the official Blender website. If you want to install a script, you can click on the **Install from File** button and you will be asked to select the corresponding Python file.

The official Blender Add-ons Catalog

You can find it at http://wiki.blender.org/index.php/Extensions:2.6/Py/Scripts.

The following screenshot shows the steps for activating the add-ons:

Steps for Add-ons activation

Where are the add-ons on the hard-disk?

All the scripts are placed in the add-ons folder that is located wherever you have installed Blender on your hard disk. This folder will usually be at Your Installation Path\Blender Foundation\Blender\2.VersionNumber\scripts\addons.

If you find it easier, you can drop the Python files here instead of at the standard installation.

Don't forget to click on the **Save User Settings** button in order to save all your changes!

A brief introduction to the projects

You will now be introduced to the fun projects that we will do together during each of the later chapters. You will need practice to improve your skills.

The Robot Toy

In this project, you will follow step by step the modeling of a little Robot Toy, starting from a simple cube primitive. This old school mechanic robot will make you re-live your childhood. The goal of this chapter is to teach you the modeling process in Blender. You will gain a good overview of the main modeling tools, such as extrude or loop cut. On the other hand, you will discover what a good workflow is by creating your model according to a reference.

The Alien Character

This project will be exciting! We think you will have enough experience to start learning how to create your own alien character using the sculpting tools of Blender. During the project, you will encounter a new modeling process by creating a base mesh for sculpting. After this, you will understand how to retopologize and keep the details of that sculpt. It will be divided into two parts: the sculpting and the retopology process.

The Haunted House

The Haunted House is a nice but scary little house in the middle of the Pennsylvania... Booooohhhhhhhhooooohhh! The legend says that it is haunted by thousands of spectrums. In this project, divided into three parts, you will start by modeling the house and its environment while discovering new modeling techniques, such as the array modifier. After completing the modeling, you will learn how to use the powerful Blender texturing and UV tools in order to add colors to your meshes. Finally, you will use the **Cycles** nodal editor in order to create materials with the textures previously made. After reading the corresponding chapters, you will have a good understanding of how a full 3D scene is constructed and how to organize yourself for such a big task.

The Rat Cowboy

The Rat Cowboy and the story of the holes in the cheese will be your first animated sequence. It will be a nice starting point to learn more about rigging and animation. The Rat will face a piece of cheese pinched under a rat trap, and he will unsheathe his gun to shoot the cheese. The Gruyère cheese is born. In order to produce a polished final shot, you will learn some compositing tricks and how to render the sequence with Cycles.

Summary

In this chapter, you have learned the steps behind 3D creations. You know what a mesh is and what it is composed of. Then you have been introduced to navigation in Blender by manipulating the 3D viewport and going through the user preference menu. In the later sections, you configured some preferences and extended Blender by activating some add-ons.

You are now ready to start the 3D modeling of our Robot Toy project.

2
Robot Toy – Modeling of an Object

In this chapter, we will start our first project in order to discover the fundamental modeling tools of Blender. We will create a little robot that is inspired by vintage toys with a drawing image reference. You will learn polygonal modeling workflow, which will be useful for your future 3D productions. The head will be created with a simple cylindrical primitive that we will modify to give it the right shape. Then, in the same way, starting from a primitive, we will model the rest of the body, always with a good topology in mind. Indeed, we are going to maximize the number of quads (polygons with four faces) and organize them so that they best fit the shape of each part. In the end, we will do a quick render with the Blender internal render engine. Without further ado, let's enter the marvelous world of 3D modeling! In this chapter, we will cover the following topics:

- Adding and editing objects
- Using the basic modeling tools
- Understanding the basic modifiers (such as mirror and subsurface)
- Modeling with a proper topology
- Creating a quick preview with Blender Internal

In the following screenshot, on the right, you can see the 3D robot modeled using a sketch, shown on the left as a reference, with Krita, which is another open source tool for 2D art:

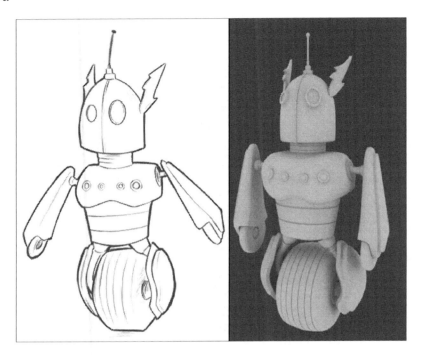

Let's start the modeling of our robot toy

We will now start the modeling of the robot toy by adding the first object to the scene. The robot will be modeled from a simple cylinder.

Preparing the workflow by adding an image reference

In order to start the modeling of the robot, let's have a look at the following procedure:

1. We will add the robot image reference in a new **UV/Image Editor**.

2. After dividing the view and selecting the right editor (by clicking on the RMB on the edge of an editor and selecting **Split Area**), go to the **UV/Image Editor** header and select **Open Image** to choose the corresponding reference in the file browser.

3. To pan or zoom in this editor, use the same shortcuts as the 3D view. This reference will serve as a guide during the modeling process. Refer to this in order to get the main shape right, but don't rely on its details.

Adding the head primitive

When you start modeling an object, you need to start with a basic 3D shape that is close to the shape you want to model. In our case, we will use a cylindrical primitive to start modeling the head. To do this, follow these steps:

1. First we will need to remove the 3D cube that is placed by default in any Blender starting file. The cube is selected if it has an orange outline. If this isn't the case, you can right-click on it. This is the main selection method in Blender. If you want to select or unselect all the objects present in the 3D view, you can press the *A* (All) key.

2. You can now remove the selected cube by pressing the *X* key or the *Delete* key. It's now time to add the cylindrical primitive.

3. All the primitives are going to spawn at the 3D Cursor location. We will ensure that the cursor is at the center of the scene by pressing *Shift + C*.

4. We can now use the *Shift + A* shortcut, and select **Mesh | Cylinder** to create the primitive at the center of the scene.

5. Our new object has too many details, so we will decrease the number of vertices in the left 3D view panel. If you can't see this panel, press the *T* key. At the bottom of this, you can see the preferences of the currently active tool (the mesh creation, in our case), and you can change the number of vertices of our cylinder to **16**.

6. We will now set the 3D view focus on the newly created object by pressing the dot numpad key or by selecting **View | View Selected** in the 3D view header.

About naming shortcuts

Most of the shortcuts correspond to the first letter of the tool's name. For instance, the Grab tool can be activated by the *G* key and the Scale tool can be selected by the *S* key.

If you want to explore all Blender's shortcuts, visit http://www. shortcutsheaven.com/.

The cylinder located at the cursor position (center of the world) that we will use as a base for the head of the robot.

The Edit Mode versus the Object Mode

Currently, we cannot access the components (vertices, edges, and faces) of our cylinder because we are in the **Object Mode**. This mode allows you to do basic things on objects such as moving, rotating, or scaling them. Let's perform the following set of steps:

1. If you want to edit an object, you need to use the **Edit Mode**. To switch between these modes, press the *Tab* key or go to the **Modes** drop-down menu in the 3D view header while any object is selected. In the **Edit Mode**, you can choose the type of components to select by pressing *Ctrl* + *Tab* or by selecting the component type in the 3D view header.

2. Let's go into the **Face Mode** and select the top face of the cylinder by right-clicking on it. As you can see, in Blender, faces (or polygons) are represented by a little square in the middle.

3. Now you can go into the orthographic front view (the *3* numpad key and *5* numpad key for perspective/orthographic views respectively), and use the *z* axis of the Gizmo tool to move the selected face a little bit down.

In Blender, we don't encourage you to use gizmos as there is a much faster method to move, rotate, or scale your selection. To move a selection, press the *G* (Grab) key and, if you want to constrain your move to a certain axis, press the corresponding *X*, *Y*, or *Z* keys. You can even hide the Gizmo tool by pressing *Ctrl + Space*.

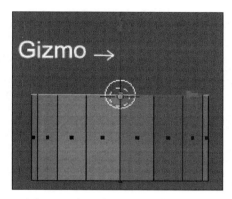

The top face moved down in the **Edit Mode** with the z axis of the Gizmo tool or by pressing the *G + Z* shortcut.

Using the basic modeling tools

In the following, you will learn the powerful usage of the main modeling tools of Blender, such as the Extrusion, Bevel, or Loop Cut tool, while creating your little robot toy.

Modeling the head

We will now use the basic modeling tools in order to form the shape of the head. As you may have understood, we are going to add new geometry gradually to approximate the shape in 3D. One of the useful tools is called **Extrusion**.

What is an extrusion?

This is the process of creating new geometry by extending (and optionally transforming) selected components.

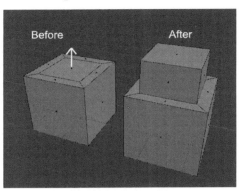

1. While the top face of the cylinder is selected in the **Edit Mode**, we will press the *E* key in order to create a new geometry from that face. Then, we will need to position and validate the extrusion.

2. We now have two choices in order to confirm the extrusion. If you want, you can move the extruded geometry, and after this, press LMB in order to validate its position. The other choice is to press RMB, in order to place the extruded geometry at the same position as that of the selected component(s). In our case, we will place the extrusion just over the selected face.

3. We can now scale our extrusion by pressing the *S* key, and repeat the process of extruding the top face and scaling it three times in order to have a bell shape. We can always go back by pressing *Ctrl + Z* and redo these steps.

4. We can also go into the **Edge** component mode (*Ctrl + Tab*), and select the edge loops that came from the different extrusions by placing the mouse pointer over them and pressing *Alt* and RMB.

5. After this, we can move them along the volume by tapping the *G* key twice.

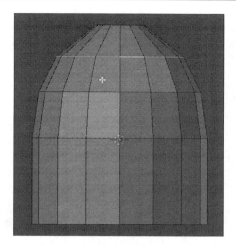

Shaping the head with extrusions.

What is an Edge Loop?

An Edge Loop is a set of edges that are connected together and form a loop. You can also get face loops to follow the same principle but with faces. They are essential to construct the shape of an object.

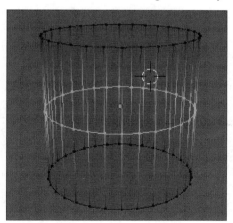

Modeling the antenna

In order to create the antenna, we will start from the head and detach it later. Follow these steps to create the antenna:

1. In the head **Edit Mode**, we will select the top face and extrude it a little bit to make the base of the antenna.

2. Then we will make an inset from the top face of the base by pressing the *I* key.

What is an inset?

An inset allows you to add some padding on a face:

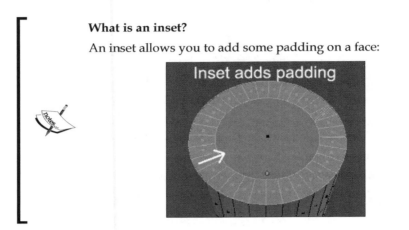

3. With the inner face of the inset selected, we are going to repeat the process one more time (extrusion + inset).

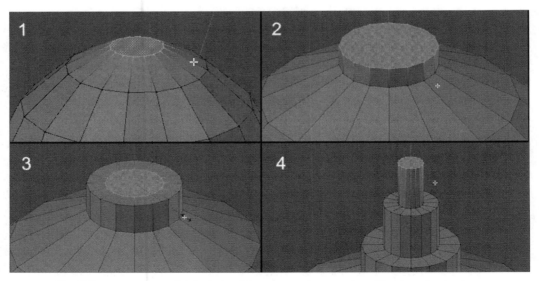

The different steps to model the base of the antenna. A succession of insets and extrusions.

4. After this, we will add the stem of the antenna by moving the cursor to the top of the antenna's base, selecting the top face, pressing *Shift + S*, and selecting **Cursor to Selected**.

5. Now we can add a cylinder in the **Object Mode** that will pop up on the cursor. This cylinder will represent the stem, so scale it accordingly and end it with some extrusions that you will form in a sphere shape by scaling them and following the same process as that of head modeling.

6. You can also select the top part of the stem and use the smooth option (by pressing the *W* key and selecting **Smooth**) to relax the geometry.

The stem with the different extrusions that we have shaped like a sphere with the Smooth tool

7. We now have an **N-Gon** at the top of the stem. An N-Gon is a polygon that has more than four edges. It is considered a bad practice to have these kinds of polygons in a 3D object. We are going to solve this by going into the top view (the *7* numpad key) and by doing a small inset on the object in order to maintain the border.

8. After this, we will connect some vertices together in order to have only quads (polygons that have four sides).

9. Then, we select the two opposite vertical vertices by right-clicking on the first one and pressing *Shift* and right-clicking on the second one. Pressing *Shift* and invoking any selection method allows you to add new items to your current selection.

10. After this, we join them to a new edge with the *J* key (to connect the vertex path tool) to separate the N-Gon into two equal parts.

11. Now we ought to select the two opposite horizontal vertices and join them to form a cross. If you look closely, we haven't resolved the N-Gon problem yet, because we have four more of them.

12. As we can't leave them in the mesh, we are going to repeat the process by joining the other facing vertices in order to have only quads. If you want, you can also use the Knife tool in order to cut in the geometry by pressing *K*. With the knife we will have to click on the vertices that we want to connect together and when we finish, we can press the *Return* key in order to validate.

13. At this point, we can use the **LoopTool** add-on that we installed in the first chapter. We can select the four middle faces (in **Face Mode**) and use the **LoopTool** circle option (press *W* then select **LoopTool | Circle**). This allows us to form a circle with the selected components.

14. It's time to detach the antenna. In order to do this, we select the loop at the base of the antenna (press RMB and *Alt*) and press *V* to rip the loop. Blender will give us the choice of moving the ripped part, but we won't. So we cancel the move by clicking the RMB.

15. Now, we will detach the geometry of the antenna to form a new object. First we deselect all the components (*A*), then we move our mouse pointer over the antenna and press *L* to select the linked geometry.

16. After pressing the *P* key and choosing **Selection** in the pop-up menu, the selected part will be separated to form another object.

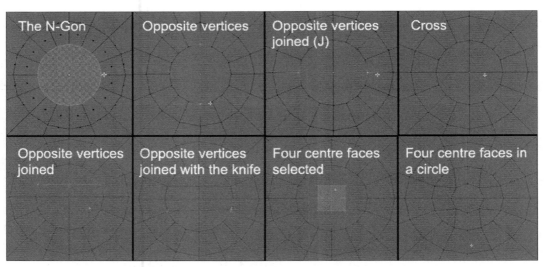

N-Gon correction with the Join tool and the Knife

17. We will have to clear three N-Gons: one at the bottom and at the top of the head, and one at the top of the base of the antenna. We have decided to resolve them with the previously explained method.

An introduction to the Subdivision Surface modifier

We will now smooth the geometry of the robot head and the antenna using the following steps:

1. First we go to the left 3D view panel (*T*), and with both objects selected in the **Object Mode**, we click the **Smooth** button under **Shading**. This will create a blend between the faces but not round our objects. In order to round our geometry, we will need to use a modifier called **Subdivision Surface**.

2. Let's go into the Properties editor and select the adjustable wrench. Then, we choose a **Subdivision Surface** modifier in the **Add Modifier** drop-down menu. All we need to do now is repeat the process with each object.

What is a modifier?

A modifier is a tool that applies to the entire object. You can push new modifiers on the modifier stack of the object where the top modifier will take effect before the bottom one. You can also reorganize their order using the up and down arrows. You may hide a modifier using the Eye button. If you want to collapse a modifier, use the left-hand side horizontal arrow. You can also apply the behavior of the modifier with the **Apply** button. Always save your work before doing this.

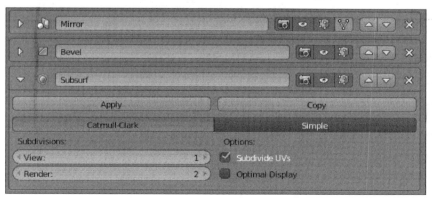

The stack of three object modifiers. The **Subdivision Surface** applies over the Mirror and the Bevel modifier.

3. As you may have seen, the subdivision divides all the polygons by four and tries to do an interpolation by smoothing them. If you want more divisions, you can increase the View slider under Subdivisions.

4. The shape looks better but needs to be sharp at some points. In order to do this, we will maintain a border by adding edge loops with *Ctrl + R*. The LoopCut tool is very useful; it allows us to add edge loops where we want and as many as we want.

About the LoopCut tool

To add an edge loop, use the *Ctrl + R* shortcut and move your mouse cursor perpendicular to where you want to add a new edge loop. You will see a preview of the new cuts. You can add multiple loops at the same time by scrolling your mouse wheel or by pressing the + or – keys. After you have validated the cuts, you will need to position them and validate their location by left-clicking or right-clicking. The later will center the cuts.

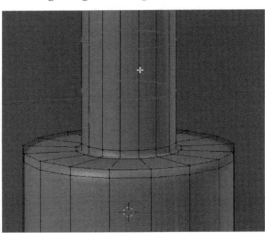

5. We can also sharpen the edges by selecting them and using the Bevel tool. Remember that the nearer the edge loops are, the sharper the result will be.

About the Bevel tool

The Bevel tool allows you to split one edge into multiple edges. When you activate it with *Ctrl + B*, you can choose the number of splits that you want by scrolling your mouse wheel or by pressing the + or – keys. You can also decrease the speed of the tool by pressing the *Shift* key. As always, you can validate your placement by left-clicking or cancel it by right-clicking.

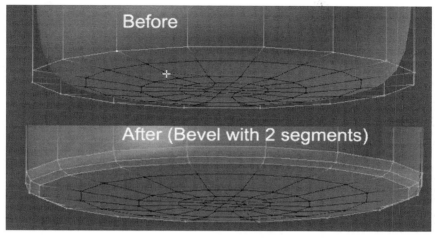

Improving the head shape

Let's select the head and go into the **Edit Mode**.

1. From the front view, we will now select the central edge loop. One way to do this is to use the wireframe mode by pressing the *Z* key. This mode allows us to see through the mesh and the selected components that are behind it.

2. We can now use the Box Selection tool with the *B* key in order to draw a rectangle area around the vertices that we want to select. If you want, you can hide the antenna and the stem by selecting them and pressing *H* (Hide). The Bevel tool will help you to create a thin base in the middle of the head. This bevel will be maintained with two new cuts. To do this, we can do an extrusion without moving it (cancel the move with RMB).

3. We can now scale the newly extruded faces on the *x* axis using the *S + X* shortcut. The thickness is added by selecting the inner face loop and extruding it at the same place.

4. In order to push the extrusion according to the normals, we use the *Alt + S* shortcut.

5. We will also have to maintain the shape of the head by adding multiple edge loops (with *Ctrl + R*, for instance).

Save your work!

After all the work you've done, it's very important to save it! To write your blend file to your hard disk, go to the **File** menu and press the **Save** option or use the *Ctrl + S* shortcut. You can now choose which directory you want to place it in. A nice trick is to press the **+** or **–** key to add or remove one unit from the name of your file.

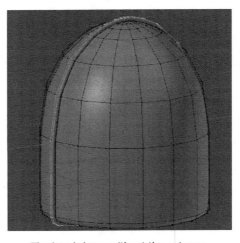

The head shape without the antenna.

6. You can unhide the antenna and the stem in the **Object Mode** by pressing *Shift + H*.

Modeling the thunderbolts

It's now time to start modeling the thunderbolts; let's have a look at the following steps:

1. We will start by going into the Side Orthographic view (the 3 numpad key) and by placing the cursor next to the head with a simple left-click.

2. Then we will add a plane and in the **Edit Mode** we will remove all the vertices with the *X* key.

3. In the **Edit Mode**, we are going create a chain of vertices that matches the thunderbolt shape of the image reference.

4. Pressing *Ctrl* and LMB, we will add new vertices and create the silhouette of the thunderbolt.

5. In order to close the shape, we select the first and last vertices and press the F key to fill them with an edge.

6. If you want to add more details to the shape, select two connected vertices and with the LoopCut tool (*Ctrl + R*), place a new vertex in the middle of both the connected vertices.

7. We can then select all the vertices (*A*) and fill the shape with an N-Gon (F) that we are going to resolve later.

8. We can now add an inset (I) in order to keep an outline.

9. After we've done this, we will have to clean the mesh by replacing the N-Gon with quads using the join tool (J) or the knife tool (K). If you have one triangle or N-Gon, it's not a problem for now as it could be solved later.

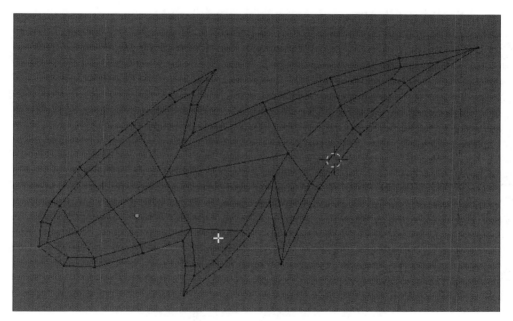

The thunderbolt shape.

10. We can now add a **Subdivision Surface** modifier in the **Object Mode**.

11. We will have to sharpen the spikes using tight bevels.

12. Of course, we will have to clean the mesh by removing the N-Gons.

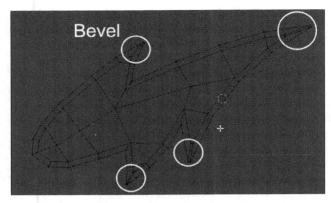

Maintaining the spikes with bevels.

13. It's now time to extrude the whole thunderbolt by selecting all the faces (*A*). You may get a lighting error with black faces. It means that the normals are pointing inward and can't catch the light. You can verify this by opening the right panel of the viewport (*N*) and, under Normals, you can check the face icon. If the normals are not pointing outward, then you will need to recalculate their direction by selecting all the components and pressing the *Ctrl + N* shortcut.

14. We can now select the inner faces on the outside of the thunderbolt with either *Shift* + RMB or using the *C* key, which allows you to paint and select the components that you want according to the current view. With these faces selected we can create a small inner extrusion, and maintain the shape with the LoopCut tool (*Ctrl + R*).

The finished thunderbolt with a view 2 **Subdivision Surface**.

15. In order to mirror the thunderbolt on the other side of the head, we will use a **Mirror** modifier with the head as the center of a pivot. Place and rotate the thunderbolts according to the image reference.

The Mirror modifier

This is an easy way to make a symmetry from your 3D model. The basic symmetry is based on the positioning of the pivot point and the *x* axis. All of these are configurable by changing the axis. It is strongly advised you use the **Clipping** option if you want to weld the components that are on the symmetry axis of your geometry. By doing this, you will avoid holes. With the **Mirror Object** option, you can choose to base the symmetry axis on the pivot point of another object in your scene.

16. The last thing we may want to do at this stage is to correctly name our objects in the outline editor that is situated in the top-right corner of the interface by default.

The outliner

The outliner displays a list of all the entities that make up the current scene. When you select an object in the 3D view, it will be highlighted in the outliner and conversely. You can rename any item in the list by double-clicking on its name. The outliner also gives you control of the visibility of any object with the Eye icon button. The mouse cursor button can be toggled on or off to allow the selection of the corresponding object in the viewport.

Modeling the eyes

It's time to finish the head of our robot by adding a pair of eyes on it. This is done with the following steps:

1. In the **Edit Mode** of the head, we select the edge that is roughly positioned at the eye location.

2. We use a bevel to add more geometry.

3. It is now possible to slide the top and bottom edges of the bevel according to the volume by selecting them in the **Edge Mode** and pressing G twice to form an ellipsoidal shape.

4. After this, we can use the *F* key to fill the eye. It will remove the two vertical edges that come from the bevel.

5. Now we can do a series of insets and extrusions to pop out the eye.

6. Applying the same method to the other side, we will add a little cartoon effect.

7. As always, we now need to clear the geometry by removing N-Gons using the knife.

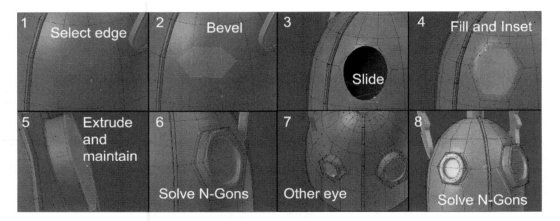

Modeling the chest

It is time to model the chest. The following steps will help you do so:

1. Now we put the 3D cursor at the center of the space (*Shift + S*), then we add a box (*Shift + A*) for the base shape of the chest.

2. We can adjust the position under the head (*G + Z*) in the front view, and switch to the **Edit Mode** to start the modeling.

3. It is much faster to work with the symmetry, so we are going to cut the cube at its center with an edge loop (*Ctrl + R*). We select all the vertices on the left-hand side with the box select tool (*Ctrl + B*) in the wireframe shading mode (*Z*) and we delete them (*X*).

4. In the object mode (*Tab*), we add a mirror modifier to work with symmetry.

5. More polygons can be added to create the basic shape of the chest. We, therefore, add two vertical edge loops (*Ctrl + R* and scroll the mouse wheel up) from the side view and slide these on the *y* axis (*S + Y*).

6. Next, we move the polygon situated at the center of the chest from the side view (*G + X*) and add another vertical edge loop from the front view.

7. In the orthographic (*5*) front view (*1*), and with Wireframe (*Z*) Shading activated, we can easily work the shape by moving (*G*) and rotating (*R*) the selected vertices (refer to **2** and **3** in the following screenshot). Then we move the top face up a little (*G + Z*).

8. We can see that our central edge loop is not very well aligned in the front view. Therefore, we select and replace it by applying a zero scale on the *x* axis (*S + X + 0* on the numeric keypad), which perfectly aligns our selected vertices.

9. In order to have a less angular shape, we are going to activate the edge mode and select the edges at the top and bottom of the chest (press *Shift + Alt* and the LMB) to finally do a bevel (*Ctrl + B*) (refer to **5** in the following screenshot).

10. To balance the polygon flow of the mesh, we add a horizontal edge loop to the center (*Ctrl + R*) that we will extend with the Scale tool on the *y* axis (*S+Y*) (refer to **6** in the following screenshot). The goal is to use the maximum area of the drawing as a reference. Always remember to check the silhouette of your object.

11. For a more curved shape, we will use **Proportional Editing** that can be activated by the small circle icon located at the header of the 3D view.

12. The **Proportional Editing** tool will help us to shrink the side of the bust. Be careful to check the behavior of the clipping option of the mirror modifier for the vertices located on the axis of symmetry. They don't have to be merged at the center. To smooth the model, we will add a **Subdivision Surface** modifier and will check the **Smooth Shading** option in the **Transform** panel (*T*) in order to remove the flat aspect of the polygons.

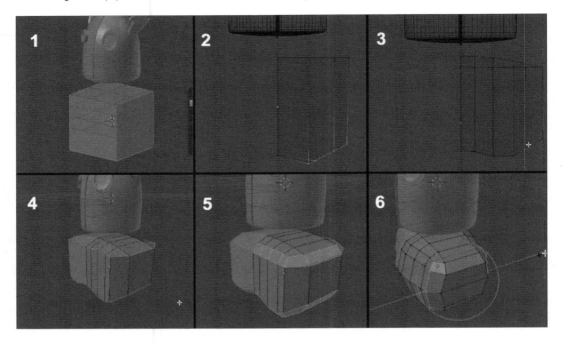

The Proportional Editing tool

This allows you to change the shape of an object in the **Edit Mode** in a smooth manner. It acts like a magnet for unselected components that are inside a circle of influence that you can adjust by scrolling the mouse wheel. This is perfect when you want to move a set of components and when the geometry is too compact.

The **Connected** option allows you to limit the scope to the geometry connected to the selection.

The **Falloff** option offers a series of attenuation curve profiles.

13. With some bevels and additional edge loops, we will just sharpen some curves (refer to **7** and **8** in the following screenshot).

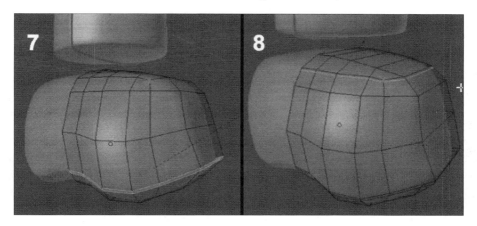

14. To flatten the top a little, we will select the highest faces and scale them on the Z axis with the **Proportional Editing** tool turned on. (S+Z and O).

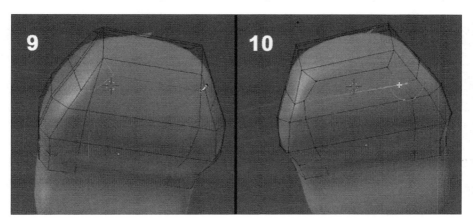

15. From the bottom view, we use the Knife Topology tool (*K*) to change the organization of our vertices, edges, and faces (refer to **9** and **10** in the preceding screenshot). The process of arranging the components in the order that they best fit the shape is called "searching for a good topology". An easy way to grasp good topology is to remember that the edge loops are going to wrap around the object you want to create. Another thing that we already talked about is using only quads because they are easier to manage.

16. We form a loop to allow a better subdivision of the surface. Other edge loops can be added again horizontally and vertically to add details.

17. Then we switch to **Face Mode** and select six faces on the side of the bust in order to round them off with the LoopTools **Circle** feature (press *W* and select **LoopTool | Circle**) (refer to **11** in the following screenshot). We can choose the influence of this tool at the bottom of the left panel (*T*). A value of 80 percent will best fit here.

18. Then we adjust the angle of these faces with a rotation on the X axis (*R* + *X*). To quickly select polygons, we advise you to use the Circle Select (press *C* and the LMB) tool, which is used like a brush.

19. We do a small inset (*I*) to sharpen the geometry at the location of the shoulders.

20. We continue to move some vertices (*G*) here and there to gradually round the shape, and we adjust sets of vertices by rotating them (*R*). It is important to always navigate around your object to have the correct silhouette from different points of view. This is the essence of 3D modeling.

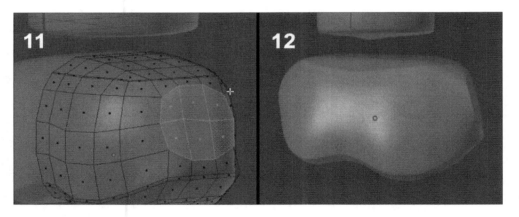

21. If you want more sharp edges, you can add a few edge loops (*Ctrl* + *R*) around them. Remember to use the smoothness parameter of the LoopCut tool (a value ranging from 0 to 1) in the left panel (*T*).

Modeling the neck

Still working on the bust in the **Edit Mode**, we will again flatten the top part of the bust and more precisely the area.

1. We start with the neck by selecting six polygons and scaling them on the *z* axis (*S* + *Z* + *0* on the numeric keypad).

2. These faces will be arranged in a circle with the LoopTool Circle (by pressing *W* and selecting **LoopTools | Circle**) (refer to **1** in the following screenshot).

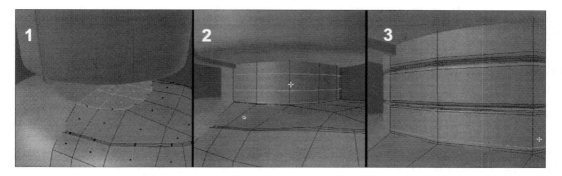

3. Then we make a very light extrusion (*E*) to hold the lower part of the neck.

4. Afterwards, we continue with another extrusion that penetrates in to the head.

5. In the Wireframe Shading mode, we remove the nonvisible face that is inside the head, which is useless.

6. Then we add two loops cuts (*Ctrl + R* and press MMB) (refer to **2** in the preceding screenshot) that we will divide into thinner edge loops with a slight bevel (*Ctrl + B*). These newly created face loops will be extruded (E) and scaled on the *x* and *y* axes (*S + Shift + Z*) (refer to **3** in the preceding screenshot).

7. As always, we will maintain the shape by adding edge loops with the LoopCut tool (*Ctrl + R*).

8. We end with a small extrusion (*E*) at the bottom to get the neck demarcation.

Modeling the torso

We will now work on the torso, which shares essentially the same modeling techniques as the neck. This will be done as follows:

1. We now snap the cursor on a vertex that lies on the symmetry axis of the lower part of the chest by opening the Snap floating menu with *Shift + S*. We select the fourth option.

2. We add a new cylinder (*Shift + A*) with 16 vertices (the number of vertices could be changed in the left panel by pressing *T*). By choosing this number of vertices, we get a cylinder that can be mirrored at its center and that has enough faces. We place the cylinder under the chest and we remove the top face that is not visible.

3. Next, we select the top edge loop and we change its scale on the *x* axis (*S* + *X*) and the bottom one on the *y* axis (*S* + *Y*).

4. We add two edge loops (*Ctrl* + *R*), add a bevel (*Ctrl* + *B*) to each of them, and finally, extrude (*E*) them inside (refer to the neck section).

5. We will round the lower part of the torso with a series of extrusions.

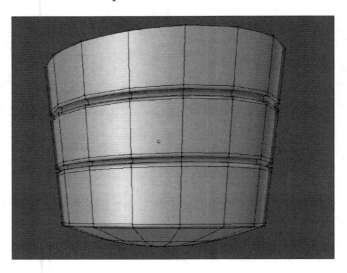

6. To get a smooth surface, we again need a **Subdivision Surface** modifier with the **Smooth Face Shading** option (Left panel: *T*).

7. We sharpen the edges with some edge loops (*Ctrl* + *R*).

8. Then, we clear our topology by solving the N-Gon with the same technique that we've used for the head.

Modeling the buttons

If you have followed the techniques used previously, the buttons are quite easy to make. The following steps are used to create the buttons:

1. We add a cylinder (with 16 vertices again), which we adjust in size and rotation with the Scaling (*S*) and Rotating tool (*R*). You can have a Free Rotation in all axes by pressing the R key twice. Don't forget this tool; it is very useful for aligning objects from a certain point of view!

2. We define the shape with a bevel at the top and an inward and outward extrusion.

3. We sharpen the shape with the LoopCut tool (*Ctrl + R*) and the Bevel tool (*Ctrl +B*).

4. The basic shape of one button can be achieved with only these tools (Extrusion, Bevel, and LoopCut).

5. In the **Object Mode**, we duplicate this with the Duplicate Linked tool (*Alt + D*).

The Duplicate Object (*Shift + D*) and the Duplicate Linked (*Alt + D*) tools

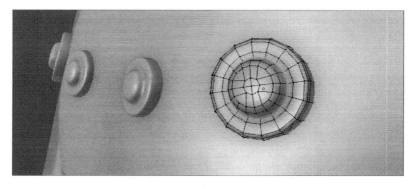

These both duplicate objects or components. The Duplicate Linked tool creates an instance of the object while in the **Object Mode**. The mesh data are connected. It means that, in the **Edit Mode**, any change of geometry will be reflected on the linked objects. However, the transformations done in the **Object Mode** are not reflected. If you want to break the link between two linked objects, press *U* (in the **Object Mode**) – **Make Single User** – **Object & Data**.

6. We will add a mirror modifier on each button. In the **Mirror Object** option, we select the torso. It will serve as the origin for the symmetry.

Modeling the fork

Now that we have finished the body, we will model the fork that covers the wheel, with the following steps:

1. In order to do this, we place the cursor to the right in the front orthographic view and add a cylinder (*Shift + A*).

2. In the **Active tool** options, we change the **Cap Fill Type** to **Nothing**. Our cylinder will have holes at the bottom and at the top.

3. Then we scale it in the **Object Mode** and rotate it with the *R* key, always in the front view for greater precision.

4. We can now add a **Subdivision Surface** modifier and apply **Smooth Shading**.

5. As always, we will maintain the shape with edge loops in the **Edit Mode**.

6. We select the outer edge loop and, pressing *Ctrl* and LMB, we extrude the fork in a twisted arch manner. This is the same tool that was used for the thunderbolt creation.

7. The last edge loop should be flattened on the *x* axis. To do this, we select it and press the *S + X* and *0* numpad key shortcut to constrain our scaling on the *x* axis and give it a value of 0.

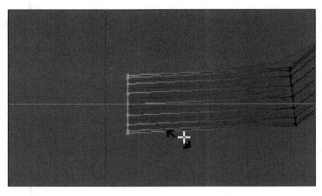

Flattening the last (inner) edge loop.

8. We will mirror the half fork to the other side using a mirror modifier. But if we do it right now, we will have a problem with pivot point placement. We have to move the pivot of our object to the same location as our body. To do this, we select the body and using the *Shift + S* command, we select the fourth option, **Cursor to Selected** (Note that, in any floating menu, you can choose the option that you want by typing the corresponding key on your numpad).

9. Now that the cursor is placed at the pivot point of the body, we will map the origin (also called pivot) of our fork by selecting it and going to the **Object** menu in the 3D view header and selecting **Transform | Origin to 3D Cursor**. You can also get a pop-up menu with the same options as that of the **Transform** menu with the *Ctrl + Alt + Shift + C* shortcut (one of the longest in Blender's history). Our origin is at the same location as that of the body.

10. Now, we apply the rotation by pressing *Ctrl + A* and selecting **Rotation**. Applying the rotation is important here because we changed it in the **Object Mode**.

11. We can now safely add a **Mirror** modifier.

12. At this point, we will add a temporary cylinder that will represent the wheel. This will help us to correctly place the fork.

13. If you want to adjust the thickness of the fork tube, use the *Alt + S* shortcut to push the polygons along the normals.

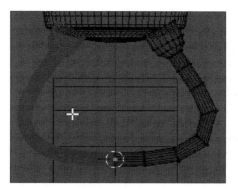

The fork in the **Edit Mode**, with its mirror modifier and the temporary wheel.

About the origin/pivot

The origin, also called the pivot, is represented with a small origin circle in Blender. It determines the center of the mass of an object. Any rotation or scale modifications will take the origin into account by default. You can change the way these transformations work by using the **Pivot Point** drop-down menu in the 3D View header (next to the **Shading** drop-down menu).

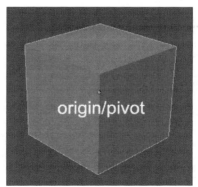

We will revisit the fork later. It's now time to create protections that cover it.

Modeling protections for the fork

In order to model this piece, we go inside the view by pressing the 3 numpad key and perform the following set of operations:

1. We add a plane, and in the **Edit Mode**, do an inset.

2. After this, we add a loop cut in the middle with *Ctrl + R* and scale it on the *z* axis by pressing *S + Z*.

3. With the two outer vertices of the top selected, we do a scale constrained on the *x* axis. This will give us a pointed shape.

4. After this, we do a bevel of the center edge loop and add loop cuts horizontally and vertically.

5. We will then round the lower part of the shape. While the two middle edge loops are selected, we go inside the orthographic view and, with **Proportional Editing** (*O*) using a sphere curve, we move the vertices back to round the shape.

6. We can now place the piece near the fork in the **Object Mode** and, with the wireframe shading activated (*Z*) in the **Edit Mode**, we can adapt its silhouette by following the fork shape.

7. It's now time to use **Smooth** shading and the **Subdivision Surface** modifier in the **Object Mode**. We will add a new modifier that will add thickness to the object as if we were extruding it entirely. This modifier is called the **Solidify** modifier. You can tweak its **Thickness** slider to change the amount of thickness that you want. This modifier will be placed under the **Subdivision Surface** in order to be applied to it. If you now go into the **Edit Mode**, you will see that it has added a new geometry.

8. You can maintain the newly added thickness with loop cuts.

9. We added some details on the side using the Inset tool and by extruding the created faces.

10. We will now combine protections with the fork. To do this, we first select the protection and then the fork, and by pressing *Ctrl + J* we will join them in one mesh. As a result, the protection is mirrored because it is inside an object that has a mirror modifier. Note that, if you reverse the order of selection, you will join the fork in the protection. That's not what we want.

11. Going back to the fork, we can add decorations to it by adding two edge loops near the top.

12. We can extrude the face loop between these edge loops and scale them according to the normals with *E* and *Alt + S*.

13. Of course, we can sharpen the edges with the LoopCut tool.

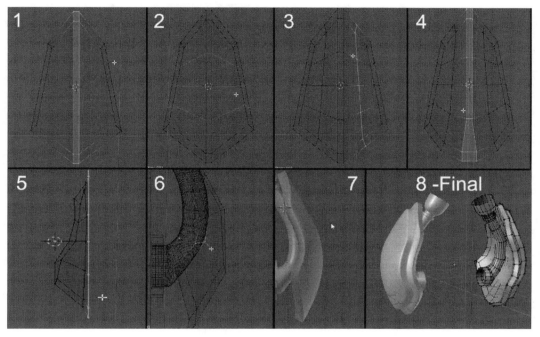

The process of modeling the protections and the final result with the fork.

Modeling the main wheel

We will start modeling the wheel with the temporary cylinder that we have placed in the fork section. There are many methods to do this. We will do this here with the same tools that we introduced to you before.

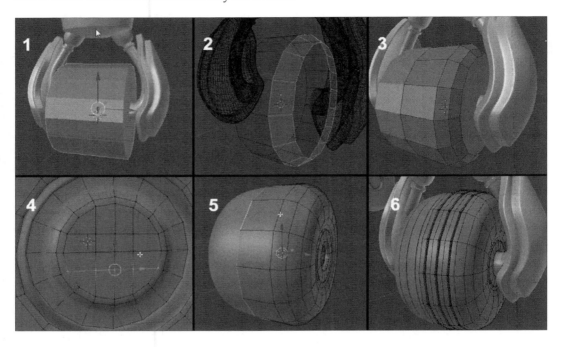

1. We will resize the wheel by enlarging it on the y and z axes (press S + *Shift* + X). When you press *Shift* and click on any axis during a transformation (rotation, scale, or grab), it will remove the constraint on that axis.

2. We then place our cylinder at the center of the forks.

3. Before you enter the **Edit Mode**, consider applying the rotation and the scale (press $Ctrl$ + A and select **Scale and Rotate**) to avoid unpleasant surprises.

4. In the **Edit Mode**, we add an edge loop at the center ($Ctrl$ + R) and remove the faces on the left-hand side (press **X** and select **Delete faces**).

5. Then we can add a mirror modifier with the clipping option activated.

6. In the **Edges Mode**, we add several loop cuts using a **Bevel** (press $Ctrl$ + B and scroll the mouse wheel up) on the outer edge of the wheel (refer to **2** in the following screenshot), then a succession of insets and extrusions to form the side of the wheel. To work more easily on this, we will enter the **Local Mode** by pressing the slash key (/). This is like hiding all the other objects. If you want to leave the **Local Mode**, press the slash key again.

7. A **Subdivision Surface** can be added.

8. The N-Gon will also be transformed in quads on the side with the Vertex Connect Path (*J*) (refer to **4** in the preceding screenshot).

9. We will round the wheel by adding an edge loop to the center of it from the front view.

10. After this, we will add some grooves. For this, we will add five edge loops vertically on the front of the wheel (refer to **6** in the preceding screenshot). We will set the smoothness option to **1** in the last active tool panel in order to place the grooves without destroying the curve profile of the wheel.

11. Then we add a **Bevel** (*Ctrl + B*) and push its resulting faces by doing an **Extrude** (*E*) with a scale based on the normals (*Alt + S*).

12. Then we accentuate every stripe with the LoopCut tool (*Ctrl + R*).

Modeling the arm

The arm is composed of four objects: the shoulder, the articulation ball, the arm, and the wheel. We will review the previous techniques by always focusing on the topology. Let's begin with the shoulder.

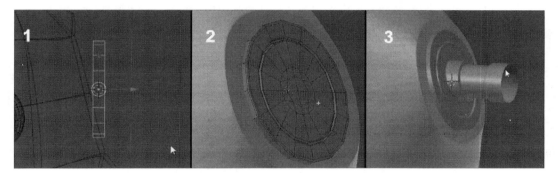

1. We will start with the arm articulation. For this, we simply add a cylinder that will be placed at the right shoulder location (refer to 1 in the preceding screenshot). It must be correctly oriented with a rotation (*R*) and flattened in the **Object Mode** with the Scale tool (*S*). When doing this, remember to constrain on the correct axis of transformation. To do these manipulations, it is better to be in orthographic view. Whenever we transform an object in the **Object Mode**, we don't forget to apply these transformations (*Ctrl + A*).

2. Then, we do a series of extrusions (*E*) in the **Local Mode** (*/*) and remove the face that enters the chest and thus will not be visible. Avoiding polygons that are not displayed is a good practice. Not doing this might lead to wastage of your computer resources and this is especially true for complex scenes with many polygons.

3. We can add details by digging a face loop (extrude and scale on the normals with *Alt* + *S*), which can be created with two edge loops (refer to **2** in the preceding screenshot).

4. We add a **Subdivision Subsurface** modifier and we apply **Smooth Shading**.

5. Then we extrude the tip that will hold the articulation ball. This extrusion will be flattened on the *x* axis (*S* + *X* + *0* numpad key) (refer to **3** in the preceding screenshot).

6. We add a sphere by placing the cursor in the middle of the last edge loop right at the tip of the articulation (press *Shift* + *S* and select **Cursor to Selected**).

7. The cursor is in the right place within the **Object Mode**, so we add a UV sphere (*Shift* + *A*). We lower the number of segments to **16** and the number of rings to **8** in the last active tool panel.

8. We add a **Subdivision Surface** and apply a **Smooth Shading**.

9. We can delete the two vertices that are located on either side of the sphere as they will be hidden by other objects (press *X* and select **Delete vertices**).

10. We place the cursor at the center of the sphere and add a cube.

11. We need to resize the cube and then, in the **Edit Mode**, we move the top and bottom faces on the *z* axis (*G* + *Z*) to set the height of the arm (refer to **4** in the following screenshot).

12. With the bottom face selected, we make a scale on the Y axis (refer to **5** in the following screenshot).

13. We select the external edge of the top face and slightly move it on the *x* axis (refer to **6** in the following screenshot).

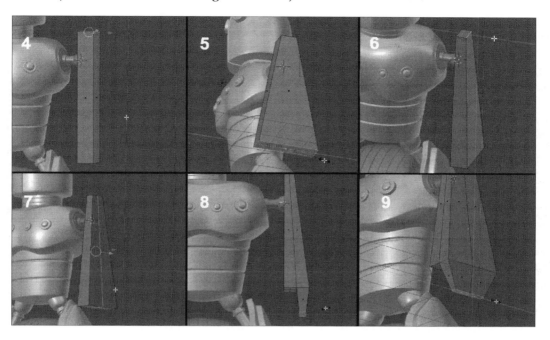

14. We add an edge loop to the center (refer to **7** in the preceding screenshot) in the side view and round the shape by slightly moving it upwards.

15. Then, we add a vertical edge loop in the front view in order to add the needed geometry for the protection of the wheel with an extrusion (refer to **8** in the preceding screenshot).

16. We now select the two right faces from the bottom view (*Ctrl + 7*).

17. We scale the faces slightly.

18. We will round the profile of the arm by selecting the middle edge loop and by pushing it along the normals (*Alt + S*).

19. It's time to add our lovely **Subdivision Subsurface** modifier and remove the flat shading. As always, we will maintain the sharp angles with a couple of edge loops.

20. We will then select the four inner faces of the hand and do an inset. This will create a face loop delimiting the inner part of the hand. These inner faces will then be extruded inward in order to create the hole that will keep the wheel.

21. We will then do an inset of the external faces of the arm.

22. These faces will then be extruded to create a small thickness.

23. It's now time to add the cylinder primitive of the hand.

24. We place it at the right location and change its size. As always, we will apply the transformation (*Ctrl + A*).

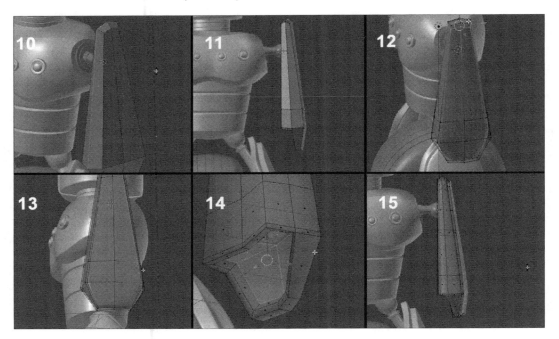

25. It will be easier to model the wheel with a mirror modifier. So we will cut the cylinder into two equal parts (*Ctrl + R*), and we will remove the left side of it to add the Mirror modifier with the clipping option checked on.

26. With multiples insets and extrusions, we then construct the wheel while in the Local view (*/*) (refer to **18** in the following screenshot).

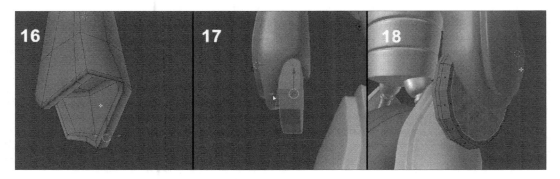

27. We will again use the subsurface modifier with the **Smooth Shading** option.

28. After we have shaped the silhouette of the wheel, we will add asymmetric details on its left-hand side by applying the mirror modifier. Add a hole here with your best friends: the Inset and Extrude tools.

29. We will then fix the hand to encapsulate the wheel in it with precision. For this, we will use **Proportional Editing**.

30. Maybe you've seen that there are bad tensions in the right-angle form of the hand and the arm due to the **Subdivision Surface** modifier. These kind of artifacts warns you of a bad topology. So we will, of course, find a way to correct this. To do this, we use the Knife tool (*K*) and we cut by following the hand outline (refer to **16** in the preceding screenshot).

31. We can use the Merge tool (press *Alt + M* and select **At center**) in order to merge the two vertices that are part of the newly created triangle.

32. We will also close the newly created N-Gon with the Vertex Connect Path tool (*J*).

33. The **Bevel** tool will be useful to maintain the inner border of the hand.

34. We will now mirror the arm, its clip, and its wheel in the **Object Mode** with the mirror modifier using the chest as the mirror object.

35. You can always push your modeling further by adjusting the transformation of each part and by adding details with the tools that we have introduced you to (such as the LoopCut tool, Extrude, and Scale along the normals).

All the parts of the robot are done now! Congratulation!

Using Blender Internal to render our Robot Toy

We will now select the camera of our scene, and in a new 3D editor, we will see through it. To do so, we'll perform the following set of steps:

1. We will split the 3D view, and in the newly created editor (which should be 3D view), we will press the 0 numpad key.

2. We can move or rotate the camera like a normal object. Notice that the camera is shaped like a triangle. This represents the field of the view of your camera. If you want to place your camera while navigating around the robot, you can press the *Ctrl + 0* shortcut.

3. Now that our camera is correctly placed (that is, focusing on our robot), we can try to render the scene. We will do a very basic render by activating **Ambient Occlusion** in the **Additive Mode**. This option is located under the World icon button in the Properties editor. You just need to check the corresponding check box.

4. In order to do a render, we will press the *F12* key or go to the Camera icon button in the Properties editor and press the big **Render** button. Blender will automatically switch your current 3D View to a **UV/Image Editor** that will show you the calculated image. You can, of course, switch it back to a 3D view as we showed you in the first chapter.

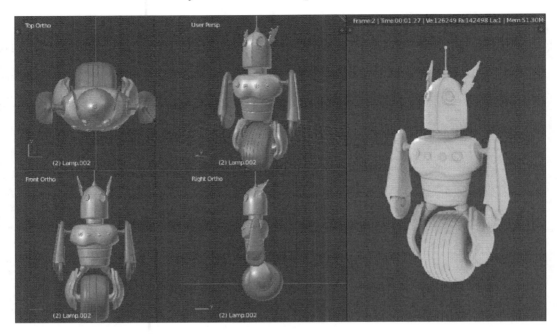

You've now completed the Robot Toy project!

Summary

In this chapter, you learned to use the main modeling tools in Blender. You will keep learning about the other ways of modeling in the next chapters. Polygons can be seen as virtual clay. There are some rules to follow, but as soon as you know them, you will be free to model everything you wish

3
Alien Character – Base Mesh Creation and Sculpting

In this chapter, you will discover a new way of modeling 3D objects with the powerful sculpting tools of Blender.

We will start with an overview of the sculpting process including brush settings and how to optimize the viewport. We will then create a base mesh with an amazing tool that Blender offers called the Skin modifier, which follows the concept art of an alien character.

Afterwards, we will sculpt the character using the tools that we had previously introduced and learn more about their usage in the different cases that are required for our character.

As sculpting is an artistic process, you will also learn about proportions and anatomy.

Let's jump to another planet! This chapter will cover the following topics:

- Understanding the sculpting process
- Optimizing the viewport
- Learning about and using brushes
- Creating a base mesh with the Skin modifier
- Using Dyntopo
- Understanding the basics of anatomy and proportions

You will start the sculpting of the following alien character (shown on the right) using a sketch as a reference (shown on the left). This is done with **Krita** (an open source tool for 2D art).

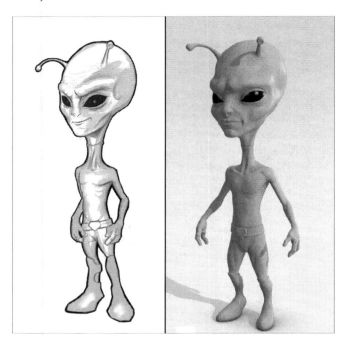

Understanding the sculpting process

Before starting to sculpt our alien, we will take some time to understand what this means and what the advantages are of using this modeling method. We will then give an overview of the basic tools that Blender has to offer.

An introduction to sculpting

Before the introduction of sculpting in the 3D world, there was only the polygonal modeling method (the method that we've used in the second chapter) that takes more time when creating organic shapes. The goal of sculpting is to have more freedom while modeling. The process looks a little bit like real sculpting art, but in this case we sculpt over a 3D mesh (our digital clay). When sculpting in Blender, we use brushes as tools that act on the mesh. There are many brushes that have different behaviors such as digging, moving, or pinching.

Choosing sculpting over poly modeling

Sculpting allows us to think more about the shape of the object and less about its technical part, such as its topology. So, the goal of this method is to really concentrate on the design part of the object. We won't see the vertices, edges, or polygons. The technique is more efficient when the goal is to reach an organic object. When you model with the tools that we have previously shown to you (the poly modeling method) you need to keep the topology in mind while researching the shape, and it is even more complicated when you have finer details. So what if we want to have a good topology with a sculpture? We have to do a retopology, but you'll see this in the next chapter

Using a pen tablet

When we modeled the Robot Toy in the previous chapter, we used a mouse. While we are sculpting, it's pretty hard to use a mouse because it is not precise according to the process. This is why we use a pen tablet that gives the sensibility needed to get the right shape. It takes some time to get used to this, but with practice you will have more control over your sculpture.

In order to navigate with the pen tablet in the 3D viewport, go to the **User Preferences** panel (*Ctrl + Alt + U*) and check the **Emulate 3 Button mouse** option. We will now be able to use the *Alt* key to navigate. Refer to *Chapter 1, Straight into Blender!* for more precise details.

It's also a good thing to check the **Emulate Numpad** option in order to be able to switch views with the keys that are above the QWERTY keys.

A pen tablet with its stylus

The sculpt mode

In order to access all the tools needed for sculpting we need to go into the **Sculpt Mode**. The **Sculpt Mode** won't let us access the components of our mesh as in the **Edit Mode**, and we also won't be able to apply transformations on our objects as in the **Object Mode**. To switch to the **Sculpt Mode**, we select it in the drop-down menu located in the header of the viewport. As you can see, it is in the same place as the **Edit Mode** and the **Object Mode**.

Optimizing the viewport

Sculpting usually takes more resources than poly modeling because the number of polygons will quickly increase each time you want to add details. This is why we need to activate some settings that will boost our viewport. This is done as follows:

1. The first setting that we will check is located under the **System** tab in the **User Preferences** window (*Ctrl + Alt + U*) and it is called **VBOs**. It is used by **OpenGL** (the rendering API used by Blender) to better organize the data displayed on the screen.

2. In the **Options** tab, under the **Options** subpanel in the left panel of the viewport (in the **Sculpt Mode**), we will activate the **Fast Navigate** option.

3. We will also ensure that the **Double Sided** option is turned off. To do this, we can use a nice little add-on called **Sculpt Tool**. After the add-on is installed, on the **Sculpt** tab of the left panel of the viewport we now have the **Double Sided Off** option. Note that you can always access any option by pressing the Space key in the viewport and by typing the name of the tool that you want.

4. Later, when we sculpt our objects, we don't want to have something else other than our objects in the viewport. So we will deactivate the grid, the gizmos, and any other viewport information that we don't need.

5. In order to do this, we will go to the right panel of the viewport. We can open this by pressing the *N* key, and under the **Display** subpanel we will check the **Only Render** option.

6. By checking this option, we will simply deactivate all the options that are below the **Only Render** option, such as **Outline Selected** that consumes a lot of resources of the viewport. Remember this option as we will toggle it on or off depending on our needs.

Anatomy of a brush

As previously mentioned, we will use a lot of brushes that behave differently in order to sculpt our alien. In this section, we will take our hands over the settings that are shared between all the brushes with the **Sculpt/Draw** brush as an example. Let's perform the following set of steps:

1. In order to do our experimentation, we will use a Cube primitive. In the **Object Mode**, we place our cursor at the center of the scene (*Shift* + *C*) and we add a Cube (*Shift* + *A*). Note that you can use the one placed by default in any new scene if you want.

2. The Cube has a low polygonal resolution so we will have to subdivide it by going in to the **Edit Mode**, select all its components, and use the **Subdivide Smooth** option under the **Specials** menu (the *W* key). We will repeat this action six times in order to have a good density of polygons.

3. In the **Sculpt Mode**, we will then select the **Standard** brush (if not already selected) in the left panel of the 3D viewport by clicking on the brush icon button under the **Tools** tab (refer to **1** in the following screenshot).

4. We can now draw on the subdivided cube. As you can see, it pushes the geometry. This is because our brush has the **Add** option activated by default. If we want to go deeper, we will need to switch to the **Subtract** mode. The **Subtract** option simply reverses the behavior of the brush. Both the options are placed under the **Brush** subpanel in the **Tools** tab (refer to **2** and **3** in the following screenshot). It's not very convenient to click on buttons in order to do such a simple manipulation, so we encourage you to use the *Ctrl* key while sculpting on your mesh to switch between these modes.

5. As you may have seen, we are not really precise because of the size of our brush.

6. In order to change the size, we will use the corresponding slider under the brush icon called **Radius** (refer to **4** in the following screenshot). We can (and recommend this to you) use the *F* key as a shortcut.

7. Now that we have more control over the size of our brush, we will change its **Strength** under the **Radius** slider (refer to **5** in the following screenshot). We can use the *Shift + F* key as a shortcut. As you can see, on the right-hand side of both sliders (Strength and Radius), there is a little icon that allow us to use the pen tablet sensitivity in order to dynamically change these options. We will only use this for the Strength option, so when we lightly press on the pen tablet, we will have less strength than if we were pressing it harder.

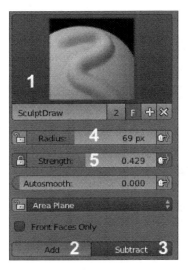

Brush options

8. Another interesting thing that we can set for our brushes is **Texture** (also called an **alpha**). An alpha is usually a black and white image that is useful while adding details such as skin pores or patterns to an object. When an alpha is added to a brush, the black pixels will remove the brush behavior during sculpting. To import an alpha, we will first need to go in the **Textures** subpanel of the Properties panel (on the far left of the interface, by default) and click on the third icon (a checker pattern) (refer to **1** in the following screenshot).

9. We can now add a new texture, and under the **Image** subpanel, we can open an image. We can now go under the **Textures** subpanel of the **Tools** tab in order to select our newly imported texture (refer to **2** in the following screenshot).

10. If we want, we can also change the repetition of our alpha by changing the **X**, **Y**, and **Z** size sliders (refer to **3** in the following screenshot).

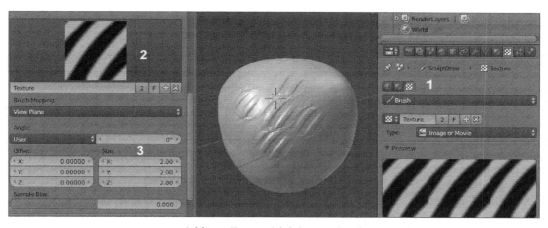

Adding a Texture (alpha) to our brush

11. The last setting that we will test is the **Curve** profile of our brush. The curve of the brush is located under the **Curve** subpanel in the **Tools** tab. Changing the curve profile allows us to change the behavior of the brush. For instance, with our current brush, **Sculpt/Draw**, if we click on the last icon (the flat curve) under the curve, we can see that the brush is harder while sculpting over our cube.

12. To understand this setting better, imagine that this is half of the profile of a real brush (see the following screenshot). We can select each point that composes the curve and move it to change the curve profile. We can also add a new point on the curve by clicking anywhere on it. When a point is selected, we can remove it by clicking on the **X** button. This curve is called a Bezier curve, so we can also change the smoothness of a point using the Tool icon and choosing the handle type that we want.

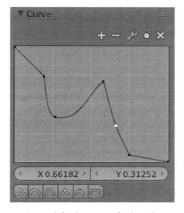

A modified curve of a brush.

Dyntopo versus the Multires modifier

In order to test our brush settings, we subdivided our cube by hand but it's not practical while sculpting an object because we didn't have enough control over the subdivision. In order to have control over our mesh, Blender gives us two main methods, the **Multires** (a.k.a. Multiresolution) modifier and **Dyntopo**.

First touch with the Multires modifier

The Multires modifier is added to the modifier stack of an object and allows us to maintain subdivision levels of sculpture. For instance, we can sculpt at a low level (with a low resolution), and the details will be transferred to the higher levels and vice versa. We will test it right now! This is done as follows:

1. We will first create a new Blender file (by navigating to **File | New**) and then with the default cube selected, we will go to the Properties panel in order to add a Multires modifier.

2. We will subdivide our cube six times with the **Subdivide** button (refer to **1** in the following screenshot). If we were using a **Subdivision surface** modifier, our cube will be rounder. To test this out, we can go into the sculpt mode and start sculpting our cube with the Draw brush.

3. We can now move between the different subdivision levels with the **Sculpt** slider of the **Multires** modifier (refer to **2** in the following screenshot). As you can see, we don't lose our sculpted information while changing levels, we are just changing the amount of details of the object. Of course, when you are at a lower level, you won't have as much detail as at the higher levels. The goal of all of this is to give you the possibility of changing the main shape of your sculpture at a low resolution without overwhelming yourself with all the details that you have sculpted at the higher levels. So don't try to add details too early in order to get the shape right and progressively increase the subdivisions.

The Multires modifier with an example of three different levels of subdivisions

First touch with Dyntopo

The Dyntopo method will generate details according to the amount that we choose. The geometry will be subdivided when we sculpt an object and will be located where we have placed our mouse pointer. We will be using this method for our alien soon, so let's test this to get used to it:

1. We will first create a new Blender file (by navigating to **File | New**).

2. The cube is a little bit low in resolution, so we will subdivide it twice with the **Subdivide Smooth** option (the *W* key).

3. In the **Tools** tab, under the **Dyntopo** subpanel, we can activate Dyntopo by clicking on the **Enable Dyntopo** button. Our cube will now be converted to triangles (this is not a problem because remember, while sculpting an object, we don't care about its topology, we care about its shape). If you want to look at the wireframe of the object, use the *Z* key or simply go into the **Edit Mode**.

4. By default, we are in **Relative Details** as you can see in the second drop-down menu. This option means that the amount of detail will be proportional to the distance of your working camera view. If we sculpt near the object, the amount of detail will be much more important than if we sculpt far from the object.

5. This method is nice, but there is another method that allows us to control the amount of detail without caring about our distance from the object. This is the constant details option (we will use this one for the alien). We can change from **Relative details** to **Constant Details** in the Sculpt details drop-down menu.

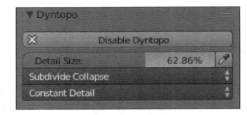

The **Dyntopo** settings

6. As you can see, we now have the detail size slider expressed by a percentage that allows us to change the amount of detail that our brush will generate on our mesh. With a small percentage, we will have finer details and vice versa.

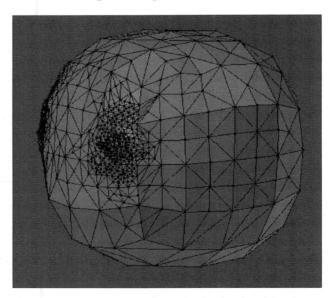

A Dyntopo mesh with different levels of sculpted details.

Creating a base mesh with the Skin modifier

Before we sculpt our alien, we need to have a base mesh that has roughly its proportions. If you want, you can use the methods that you've learned in the previous chapter in order to model it, but here we are going to use a cool modifier that Blender has to offer: the **Skin** modifier. Its goal is to create a geometry around each vertex. We can simply extrude some vertices as if we were doing a real wire armature, and the Skin modifier will add volume around it. For each vertex, we have control over the volume size. Let's start our base mesh:

1. We will start by entering in to the **Edit Mode** of our default cube. Then we will select all the vertices (*A*) and merge them to a sole vertex at the center (press *Alt* + *M* and click on the center). We now have our root vertex that will be the pelvis of our alien.

2. It's now time to add a **Skin** modifier to our object in the modifier stack. As you can see, our vertex is controlling a new geometry around it. The geometry is low, so we will add a **Subdivision surface** modifier on top of the Skin modifier in order to have a smoother look. As you may have seen, the vertex has a red circle around it. This means that it is the root of our armature.

3. We can now extrude our vertex (**E**) on the *Z* axis in order to start the torso of our alien.

4. Now we will add a **Mirror** modifier with the **Clipping option** turned on. This modifier needs to be placed before the Skin and **Subdivision Surface** modifier (use the up and down arrows to move it to the first place). Ensure that the vertices that are on the symmetry axis are merged.

5. We can now select the top vertex (the base of the neck) and extrude it by pressing *Ctrl* and LMB to the right in order to create the shoulder. Be careful with the position of your vertex as the topology generated could be bad. Always try to move your vertices a little bit in order to see whether you can't have a better topology.

6. We will now change the size of the volume that has been generated around the shoulder vertex. To do this, we will use the *Ctrl* + *A* shortcut and we move our mouse to adjust it.

7. We will then extrude the arm. In order to give a more dynamic shape, we will bend it at the elbow. We then adjust its size. At this point, it is very important to match the proportions of the concept. Proportions means the length and size of the different members with respect to each other. If you need to constrain the size or change the volume on a certain axis, you can press *Ctrl* + *A* + *X*, *Y*, or *Z*.

8. Let's extrude the long neck of our alien.

9. It's now time to add the legs of our alien. We will do this by extruding the pelvis vertex at a 45 degree angle (press *Ctrl* and LMB). Then we extrude the leg and adjust its profile by changing the size of the different vertices (*Ctrl* + *A*). As we did for the arm, we will bend the leg a little bit at the knee location. Note that the pelvis vertex should be always marked as the root of the armature. If this is not the case, select it and in the **Skin modifier**, press the **Mark Root** button.

10. The foot will be then extruded and resized. We can create the heel by simply extruding the ankle vertex to the back. The ankle vertex needs to be marked as **Loose** in order to have a nice transition with the front and the heel of the foot. To do this, we select it and use the **Mark Loose** button in the Skin modifier.

11. It's now time to create the hand by extruding the wrist vertex. From the new vertex, we will extrude three fingers that will be rescaled appropriately. Note that the thumb is at a 45 degree angle from the other fingers. To add a more dynamic feeling to the hand, we will slightly bend the fingers inwards.

12. We will then extrude the base of the neck. From the newly created vertex, we can extrude the head vertex that will then be the base for the chin and the cranium.

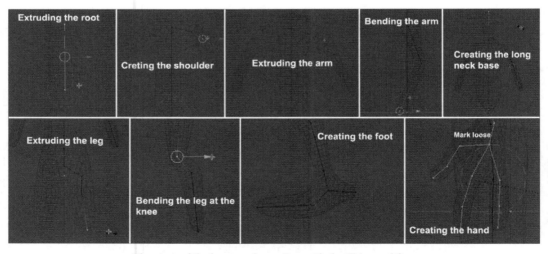

The steps of the base mesh creation with the **Skin** modifier.

13. We can now apply all our modifiers from the top to the bottom of the stack.

14. If we enter in the **Edit Mode**, we can see that some parts are very dense. This is why we are going to remove some edge loops from certain parts such as the fingers. However, rather than doing this for both sides of the model, we are going to split the mesh in two and add a mirror modifier. To do this, we first need to ensure that there is a symmetry axis in the middle of our mesh. If this not the case, you can use the knife tool (*K*) to create it. Then we can delete half of our model and add a mirror modifier as we did in the previous chapter. We can now select some edge loops where there is a lot of condensed geometry by pressing *Shift + Alt* and the RMB, and by pressing *X* we can delete them (delete the **edge loops**, not the vertices or faces).

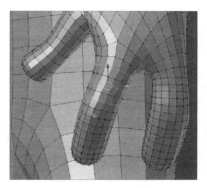

Removing some edge loops of the dense parts.

15. The base mesh is now ready to be sculpted.

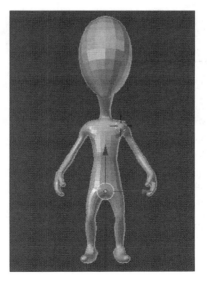

The final base mesh

Visual preparation

While sculpting, it's nice to use Matcap. It is simply an image that will be projected on your mesh in the viewport and that looks like a material. For instance, you can use a Matcap that reminds you of clay. Let's begin with our sculpting:

1. To set up a Matcap for our mesh, we will have to set up the default material of our mesh in the Properties panel under the **Material** tab (refer to **1** in the following screenshot). Note that if you can't see a material, you can press the **New** button.

2. Now we will check the **Shadeless** option under the **Shading** subpanel (refer to **1** in the following screenshot).

Creation of a new material with the Shadeless option.

3. As we have said before, a Matcap is an image, so we will import our image as the texture of our material. To do this, we go to the **Texture** tab (refer to **3** in the following screenshot) and we add a new texture by clicking on the **New** button. In the image subpanel, we will click on the **Open** button (refer to **4** in the following screenshot) and we choose our Matcap image.

4. A Matcap is mapped to a mesh according to its normals, so in the **Mapping** subpanel change the **Coordinates** from **UV** to **Normals** (refer to **5** in the following screenshot). We will also adjust the size of our projection by decreasing the **X**, **Y**, and **Z** size sliders to 0.95 (refer to **6** in the following screenshot).

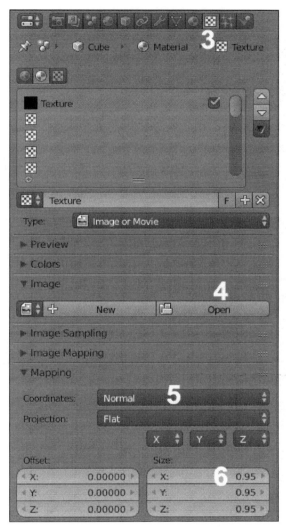

Setting the Matcap image texture for our material

5. In order to see our Matcap in the viewport, we will replace the **Multitexture** display mode with **GLSL** in the right panel of the 3D view (*N*) under the **Shading** subpanel.

6. Last but not least, we will go into the **Shading** mode under **Texture Viewport** using the corresponding drop-down menu in the 3D view header. You can also use the *Alt + Z* shortcut to quickly switch to this mode. Our Matcap is now perfectly set up!

Setting the **GLSL** display mode in the right panel of the viewport (*N*).

An introduction to artistic anatomy

Before continuing with the alien creation, some basic knowledge of anatomy can be very useful. It is a basic discipline for a character artist. Don't worry, we will clarify the concerned parts of the body for each step with illustrations.

Of course it is an alien, so we can accept the fact that we don't always have to respect human anatomy for specific parts. He has a huge head, only two fingers and a thumb, and very different feet. His humanoid appearance imposes some anatomical likelihood. This is especially useful if you plan to animate it later on. Improving your knowledge of this topic will help you to understand the movements and postures better.

In the early 16th century, Leonardo Da Vinci was one of the first artists who tried to understand the human anatomy. While religious obscurantism prohibited the examination of corpses, he dared to defy this. By dissection and observation, he did many illustrations detailing the positioning of muscles, joints, nerves, and organs.

It won't be necessary in our case to know the scientific names by heart. It's rather important to know and understand their general forms. Overall, it's more about the comprehension of human body mechanisms.

Many good books treat this subject. For more information, you can have a look at these websites:

- `http://md3dinc.com/`
- `https://www.anatomy4sculptors.com/`
- `http://www.3d.sk/`

Sculpting the body

We are continuing the modeling of our alien using Dyntopo as we had previously mentioned. This will allow the creation of the antennae very easily while they are not yet present in the base mesh.

The following is the preparation of our environment before sculpting:

1. We will set the optimizing options that were previously explained.
2. We can adjust the lens parameter in the right panel of the 3D viewport (*N*). A high value lessens the focal deformations.
3. We must check the mirror options in the left panel of the 3D viewport (*T*) to Symmetry/Lock by choosing the axis of symmetry. It is very important in order to save time.
4. We will then activate the **Dyntopo** option in the left panel of the viewport. A detail size of around 25 percent is enough to start. It depends on the size of your model.

For a better understanding, we are going to start sculpting by adding details by iteration.

The head

We start defining the jaw and chin with the **Clay Strips** brush (refer to **1** in the following screenshot). It is unnecessary to have too many details for the moment. While sculpting, always remember to define the main shapes (the volumes) and then gradually move towards the details.

We then accentuate the delimitation between the jaw and neck without exaggeration. A strength of **0.5** is enough.

The Clay Strips brush

The **Clay Strips** brush is a very useful brush to define muscles, dig or add polygons in a straight direction with pretty sharp outlines. It is the equivalent of the Clay Buildup in Zbrush.

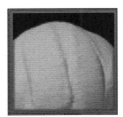

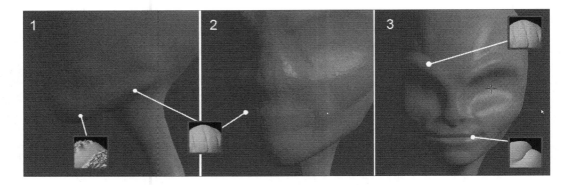

1. In order to dig into the polygons, we press *Ctrl* while sculpting. It allows us to switch to the **Subtract** mode on the fly.

2. Then we slightly smooth the added geometry with the **Smooth** brush for a better blend of the created shape. You need to remember to smooth the shape very often in order to avoid having something too grainy.

The Smooth brush

This is often a very useful brush. It allows you to soften and smooth your shapes. This brush is so useful that there is a special shortcut that you absolutely need to know. Hold the Shift key while sculpting in order to use it. It works while using any brush. When you use it over a big density of polygons, it will be harder to smooth your shape, so it will be mainly useful before working on the details.

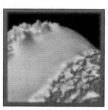

3. Now that the jaw is sketched, we will go to the side view. Then we have to adjust the silhouette of the neck, as well as the skull with the **Grab** brush. Our alien has a very curved neck.

4. We will adjust the shape of our model little by little by turning it around. It's very important to observe your model from different points of view.

    Do not hesitate a moment to look at the reference sketch and position the alien in a very similar pose. You can also create a new 3D view editor to keep an eye on the view of your choice (in our case, we've used the orthographic side view).

The Grab brush

This is often a very useful brush when you start a new model. It works a little bit in the same way that the **Proportional Editing** tool does. If you have any difficulties using it, you can go to the **Curve** options in the left panel of the viewport and modify the curve to decrease its profile.

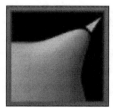

In our case, we are going to use a very soft curve for the **Smooth** brush.

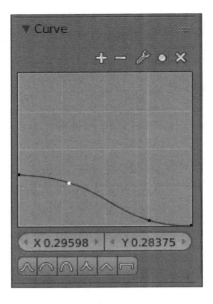

1. Again, we will take the **Clay Strips** brush to keep going on the face of the alien in order to dig the orbits and accentuate the eyebrows by adding matter (refer to **2** and **3** in the previous screenshot). Be careful to not add too much volume at this place. Do not hesitate to decrease the strength (*Shift + F*) of your brush, if necessary.

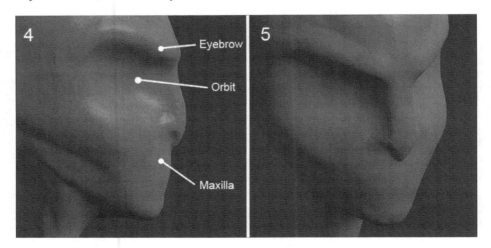

2. We will also start to sketch the nose and the mouth (refer to **3** in the previous screenshot). Before detailing the lips, we need to start adding some new volume. We form a rounded edge created by the maxilla and the jaw. Remember that the front of a set of teeth has almost a semi-cylindrical shape. It's easier to create the mouth rounded volume from the bottom view.

3. Once this is done, we can start sketching the opening of the mouth with the **Crease** brush, which allows us to draw a mined line. Consider the fact that the geometry is dynamic, so don't hesitate to add some resolution and pinch your shapes in order to make them more accentuated.

The Crease brush

This brush will allow you to draw lines by digging or adding some volume to your shapes while being pinched. It is perfect to accentuate muscles and make them well visible. It is the equivalent of the Dam Standard in Zbrush.

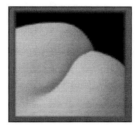

4. We will again use the **Clay Strips** brush in order to give some volume to the lips.

    Remember to leave a little gap between the lower lip and the top lip. The top lip is a little bit more forward than the lower lip from a profile view.

5. In the face view (refer to **5** in the previous screenshot), we will go back to the **Object Mode** (*Tab*) and place the 3D cursor where we want the eye at the middle of the orbit. It doesn't matter if the orbit is not completely dug.

6. We will add **UVSphere** (*Shift + A*). We will resize this with the **Scale Tool** (*S*), and we will position it (*G*) in the front view (*1*) just as in the side view (*3*). For a good placement of the eye, looking at the wireframe can be helpful. You only need to go to the Object Data tab and then to the **Group** in the Properties editor, and check the **Wire and Draw all Edges** option.

7. Then, we can sculpt around the eyelids with the **Clay Strips** brush by being careful to accentuate the outside and inside corner (the lacrimale caruncle) (refer to **7** in the following screenshot).

8. In order to accentuate the eyes, let's pinch the upper and lower eyelids with the Crease brush (refer to **8** in the following screenshot).

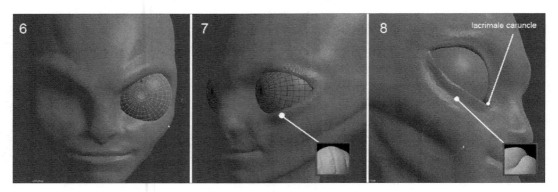

Finding a good position of the eye is not an easy task. You can move the facial structure with the **Grab** brush if you have problems. The top eyelid must be slightly forward. Conceptually, the eyes are inordinately big, so be careful that they don't touch each other.

9. Now that the face begins to take shape, we will continue with the neck. We adjust the shape a little bit more with the **Grab** brush, then we start sculpting the muscles and bones of the neck. We carve the clavicles with the **Clay Strips** brush.

10. Then we will move on the sterno-mastoid muscles. It is a muscle group that starts from the mastoid near the ear and attaches to the sternum and the clavicle. We keep working with the **Clay Strips** brush (refer to **9** and **10** in the following screenshot).

11. In the side view, we can polish the silhouette of the neck with the **Grab** brush (refer to **11** in the following screenshot).

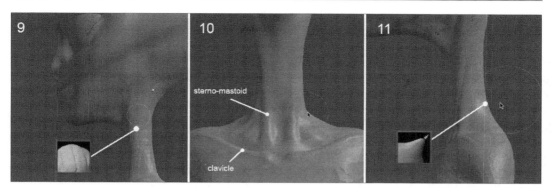

Now let's refine the face:

1. We will come back to the mouth by adding some volume to accentuate the circular muscles around the mouth. Be careful to adjust the level details of Dyntopo to around 10 percent (refer to **13** in the following screenshot). As you may have seen, when you are sculpting an object, you don't directly get the shape that you want, so you always need to go back and forth over the different parts.

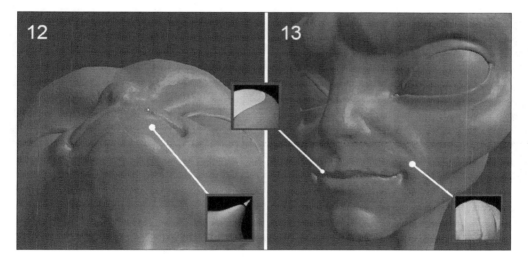

2. This brings us to accentuating the wrinkles that make the junction with the cheeks.

3. Then we will go and pinch the upper lips with the **Pinch/Magnify** brush. The lower lip doesn't need to be as pinched like the upper one. Again, you can increase the level detail of Dyntopo to around 7%.

The Pinch/Magnify brush

This brush allow us to pinch the polygons outwards or inwards (in the **Subtract** mode). It is perfect in our case to detail the lips, the wrinkles, or accentuate the contour of muscles. It is often used to get a cartoon style or for a hard surface modeling where you need to sculpt angular surfaces.

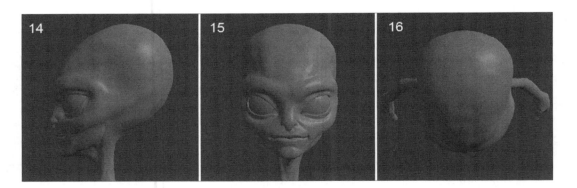

4. We will take a moment to turn the head, including the top view (**16**); then we adjust the round shape of the skull with the **Grab** brush.

5. Now, it's time to add the antennae (refer to **17** in the following image). For this, we are going to use the **Snake Hook** brush with a Dyntopo level detail of around 14%. The difficulty will be to find a good point of view of the head because we can't move the view while extracting the geometry with the **Snake Hook** brush. We must be positioned on the side in order to be able to extract the matter from a little area on the top of the forehead and stretch it outwards in a good direction. Do not hesitate to make several tries if this does not suit you. You can always adjust the size of the brush and the level of detail.

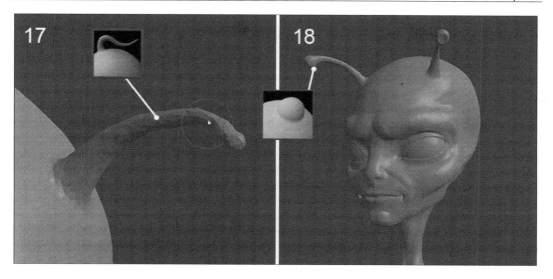

Undo while being in the Sculpt Mode

Unfortunately, the Undo function of Blender is not very optimized for the moment in the **Sculpt Mode**. It can be very slow, so do not use it too often. In many cases, you can probably quickly fix your mistakes without Undo.

The Snake Hook brush

This is very useful to sculpt horns or tentacles. This brush is more interesting with Dyntopo. The problem with a mesh that uses a Multires modifier is that topology problems quickly appear with a lack of geometry. As long as the topology is dynamic, we can easily create an arm, a leg, or anything else. We can extend this as long as we wish the shape of our model to be.

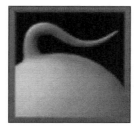

6. Once the antennae are sculpted, we will add some polygons with the **Clay Strips** brush, then we will smooth them with the **Smooth** brush. We will magnify the extremity with the **Inflate/Deflate** brush (refer to **18** in the preceding screenshot).

7. We will end this by digging forward a little bit with the **Clay Strips** brush in order to break the rounded shape.

The Inflate/Deflate brush

This brush will allow you to inflate volumes by pushing the polygons in the normal's direction, or the inverse in the opposite direction in the **Subtract** mode. It can be very useful for meshes with closely spaced surfaces that are difficult to sculpt. This gives a very fast volume that makes it much more comfortable for sculpting.

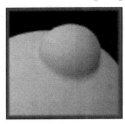

So our little alien has now its telepathy organs. We are going to sculpt the torso.

The torso

We will start the torso by sketching the pectoralis major muscle:

1. We will start by smoothing the surface and adding enough details.
2. With the **Clay Strips** brush, we will dig the dividing lines with the clavicle and the shoulder. (refer to **19** in the following screenshot).
3. Then gradually, we will add some volume accentuating the muscle fibers. The brush strokes start from the bottom of the shoulder at the clip with the biceps and go to the center of the chest (refer to **20** in the following screenshot). Get used to guiding your brush movements in the direction of the muscle.

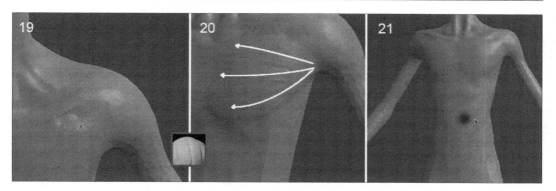

4. Once the pectoral is sculpted, we will slightly accentuate the bottom of the chest and the abs with very light touches of the **Clay Strip** brush. This is to suggest forms rather than showing them (refer to **21** in the preceding screenshot).

5. We will then work on the back part of the alien. It is a complex part of the body. So we will start to draw the muscles (refer to **22** and **23** in the following screenshots) to gain visibility with the **Crease** brush. We can soften and smooth the muscle shapes. Then we will accentuate the spine with the **Pinch/Magnify** brush.

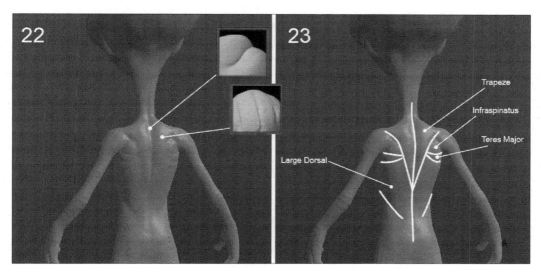

6. Now we will sculpt the buttocks. Avoid putting too much volume here. Turn the model around and observe the side view a moment, if necessary adjust the silhouette. Remember to draw a pinch line to accentuate the bottom of the buttocks with the **Pinch/Magnify** brush. This forms a fold between the buttock and the thigh (refer to **24** in the following screenshot).

7. We will add a few folds to show that it is a combination.

8. We will use the **Pinch** brush to accentuate the lower abdomen and pelvic bones (refer to **25** in the following screenshot). Unless you desire a different sexual orientation for our alien, feel free to add some volume to his crotch, it brings a little more realism. Don't be shy.

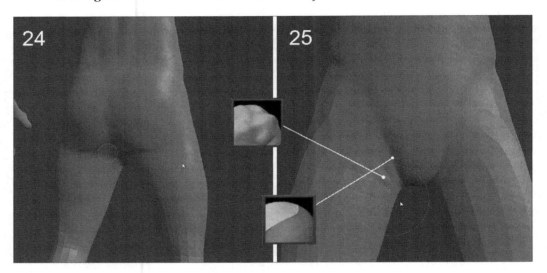

The Clay brush

This brush allows you to add planar relief with a few soft edges. It is quite close to the **Clay Strip** brush that you already know but with a less sharp effect. It adds volume by raising with a low intensity. It is very good to refine organic shapes with precision.

The arms

Now, let's start the arms. We can see in the drawing that they are pretty fine and not very muscular. His hands have two fingers and a thumb.

We won't need a lot of muscle details. We will be just interested in the major forms.

Let's begin the process:

1. We will start by digging the part between the shoulder and the biceps with the **Clay** brush (refer to **26** in the following screenshot). This accentuates the shoulders.

2. We will smooth a little, and then add some volume to the biceps (refer to **27** in the following screenshot). Slightly, we mark the outline of the muscles with the **Crease** brush and adjust the shape with the **Grab** brush.

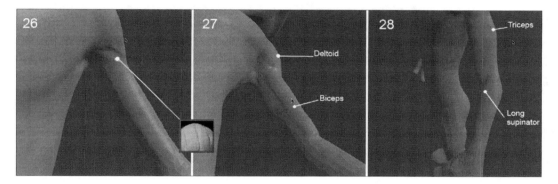

3. Then we will work on the triceps that is located at the back of the arm. It is a muscle connected to the deltoid and covers the entire rear portion of the upper arm. We give it some volume by drawing the muscle fibers with some touches of the **Clay Strips** brush.

4. The forearm is a complex area of human anatomy. It is usually quite difficult to sculpt. It consists of several muscles that twist to ensure the mobility of the hand and the fingers. For our alien, we simplified it by lessening the muscle visibility. With the **Clay Strips** brush, we will draw the long supinator that emerges because it forms the junction with the end of the biceps (refer to **28** in the preceding screenshot) near the elbow. We will then add some volume to the elbow.

5. We will start from the elbow, and we mark a slight stroke of the **Clay Strips** brush in the direction of the wrist.

6. The wrist is reinforced by slightly accentuating the bones on the sides of the upper part.

7. We go and dig and slightly flatten the lower part of the wrist. (Refer to **30** in the following screenshot.)

The hand is also a fairly complex part of the body. We will not detail the anatomy here. We will try to focus on the main forms that compose it. Observe your own hands for better understanding of the forms.

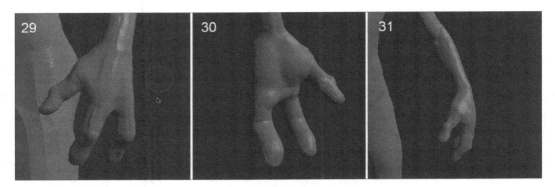

Now, we will begin forming gristle on the upper part of the hand with the **Clay Strips** brush.

1. We have placed a bit of volume to the different phalanges in order to accentuate them. (Refer to **29** in the preceding screenshot.)

2. There is some skin between the two fingers and between the index finger and thumb that we will dig. This skin allows the flexibility and elasticity of finger movements.

3. We will take the **Crease** brush and mark the lower part of the phalanges where the folds of fingers will be.

4. We will keep working with the **Crease** brush and draw the lines of the hands. The three main lines are enough to give the appearance of a palm (refer to **30** in the preceding screenshot).

The legs

We continue our sculpture with the legs. We can see that he has quite muscular thighs. The feet have a dynamic style that reflects the legs of a rabbit.

1. As with other parts of the body previously created, we will adjust the silhouette of the legs with the **Grab** brush before detailing the shapes.

2. We will slightly dig a line from the hip to the inside of the thigh that allows us to accentuate the adductor muscles (refer to the following screenshot).

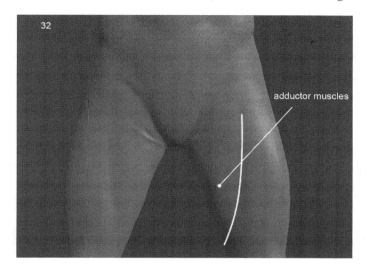

3. Now it is time to use the **Mask** brush that will be only shown without our Matcap activated, that's why you can't see the Matcap in the following screenshots. The boots are up to the knees and have a window over the calves (refer screenshot **34**). It is necessary to have enough polygons in order to get the mask contour sharp.

4. In order to highlight the edges of boots, we will reverse the mask with the shortcut *Ctrl + I* (refer to **35**).

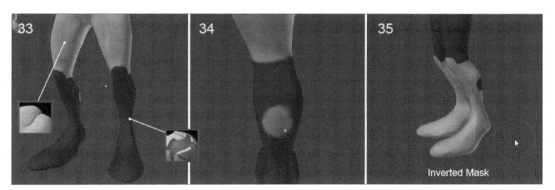

The Mask brush

This is a quite special brush. It allows us to mask an area of the mesh. It means that this area stays unchanged when any other brush is used as long as it is masked. Thus, we can create shapes that would be impossible to do otherwise. The uses are many. It is very useful for extruding surfaces.

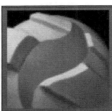

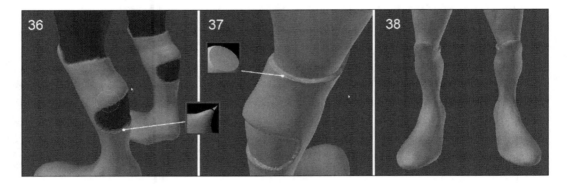

5. With the **Grab** brush, we will pull the polygons at the edge of the masking. Then we slightly raise them (refer to screenshot **36**).

6. We increase the level of detail to enhance the edges of the boots. We mark the separation with the **Flatten/Contrast** brush. We need to zoom enough and adjust the brush size (*F*) accordingly.

The Flatten/Contrast brush

In the **Flatten** mode, this brush allows us to smooth over a surface while digging slightly, or otherwise in the **Contrast** mode, it greatly increases the height of the relief. These two very different functions make it an even more interesting brush.

By using the same technique, we can sculpt the collar in the neck area.

The belt

The belt needs to be treated separately because it's not about sculpting. We are going to use more the traditional tools that we saw in the previous chapter. But as you'll see, it is very interesting to mix the different techniques that you've learned in this chapter with polygonal modeling tools. That's why we are going to use the **Grab** brush in order to wrap the belt around his waist.

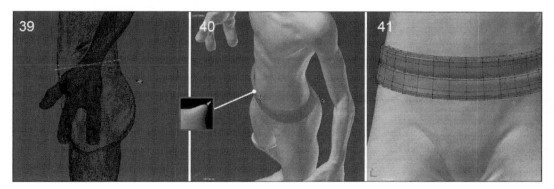

We will start the modeling of the belt with a primitive circle. After this, we will then place our cursor at the center of the character in the **Object Mode** from the top view in order to add a new circle with 32 vertices.

1. In the **Edit Mode** (*Tab*), and with the **Wireframe** option of **Viewport Shading** on, we will adjust the size of the circle by scaling on the Y axis (*S* + *Y*). We then rotate it a little bit in order to match with the shape of the alien (refer to **39** in the preceding screenshot).

2. We will then extrude the circle to form the height and the thickness of the belt. As we said before, we can now use the **Grab** brush (in the **Sculpt Mode**) in order to stick the belt to the waist. In our case, it's as if we were using the **Proportional Editing** tool (refer to **40** of the preceding screenshot).

3. Then we will go back to the **Edit Mode** in order to add more resolution with the Loop Cut tool (*Ctrl* + *R*). We will also place a loop cut in the middle of the belt on which we will add a little **Bevel** (*Ctrl* + *B*).

4. In the middle of the bevel, we will add a new edge loop that we will scale along the normals (*Alt* + *S*) (refer to **41** in the preceding screenshot).

5. We can now switch back to the **Sculpt Mode**, and with the X symmetry option off, we can move the right-hand side down a little with the **Grab** brush.

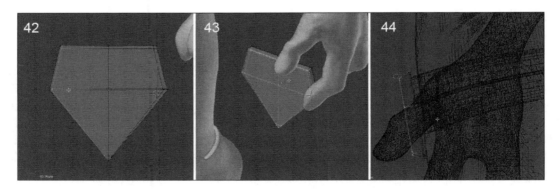

Now that we've finished the belt, it's now time to add the belt buckle as follows:

1. In the **Object Mode**, we will add a new plane.

2. Then we will go in the **Edit Mode** (**Tab**) and add a horizontal and a vertical edge loop (*Ctrl* + *R*).

3. We will then resize these edge loops so that they form a diamond shape (refer to **42** in the preceding screenshot).

4. It's now time to add a **Subdivision Surface** modifier.

5. We will then add some edge loops on both sides in order to maintain the diamond shape.

6. In order to add thickness to the buckle, we will do some extrusions of the whole geometry (*A* and *E*). As always, we will maintain the shape with the Loop Cut tool (*Ctrl + R*).

7. We will also scale the front polygons of the buckle.

8. Finally, we can place our belt buckle at the right place in the **Object Mode**.

There you go! Our little alien is ready for crazy galactic adventures!

A render of the final alien sculpt with Blender Internal Renderer

Summary

In this chapter, you've learned a new modeling technique that is best suited for your organic models. By mixing this method with polygonal modeling techniques you will be able to create awesome characters in a very short time! If you have a powerful computer, you can go into further details such as skin pores and wrinkles using alphas, for instance. For now, the alien character doesn't have a good topology, so we will learn how to create a new topology over the model and extract the details of our sculpting in the next chapter.

4
Alien Character – Creating a Proper Topology and Transferring the Sculpt Details

This chapter will be more technical than the previous one. We will see how to create a production-ready character with a nice topology, starting with the sculpture of our little alien. Of course, we can't go through all every possible techniques to reach our goal but you will have a solid understanding of what a good organic topology is. You will also learn how to retrieve the details of a sculpture with a normal map. Furthermore, you will learn how to enhance the look of the alien with an ambient occlusion. These maps could be a good starting point to create a more complex and rich texture later. As you learn more and more tools, you will be able to have more possibilities to express your imagination. What you really need to grasp in this chapter is the logical way of doing a good topology, because each object needs one topology according to your needs. So, let's dive in!

This chapter will cover the following topics:

- Understanding the retopology process
- Using the UV unwrapping tools
- Baking normal maps and Ambient Occlusion
- Displaying the baked maps in the 3D viewport
- Making a good topology

We will now create a retopology of our sculpture by using some of the tools that you've already encountered during the robot toy modeling, and some new tools. But, wait a minute, why are we remodeling our alien if we have already sculpted it?

Why make a retopology?

The main goal of doing a retopology is to have a clean version of the sculpture with a good topology. It means that the mesh geometry needs to follow the shapes of the sculpture by defining proper edge loops. A good topology is also a must-have when you want to animate an object, and it's even more important when you are dealing with organic shapes. The muscles need to correctly bend, so this is why we are following them with edge loops. But, of course, we can't delimit each of the muscles, so we are thinking more about their overall form, treating them as groups, such as the pectorals muscles.

Another goal of a retopology is to have a less dense object. I don't know whether you have already made the mistake of entering into the **Edit Mode** of the alien sculpture, but if this is the case, you have seen a tremendous amount of polygons organized in a fancy way. Technically, the process will be as easy as adding new geometry that snaps to the sculpture. However, it could quickly turn out to be a puzzle if you don't know what you are doing.

Possibilities of arranging polygons

As we have mentioned before, we will be using pretty much all of the poly modeling tools that we've learned previously, such as the grab, rotate, or face creation tool. But what really matters while doing a retopology is the arrangement of the polygons through the loops that defines the shape. In this section, we will give you some useful techniques in order to help you rework the flow of your topology. Before reading further, we advise you to train yourself on a subdivided plane:

1. Create a new plane (*Shift* + *A*).

2. Select it in the **Edit Mode** and under the **Specials** menu (*W*), select the **Subdivision** option.

3. Redo step 2 thrice.

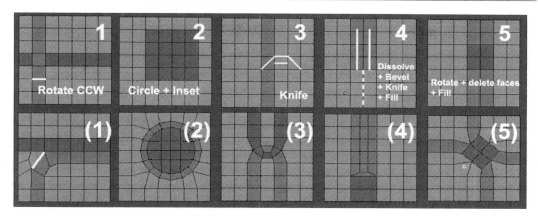

Five topology cases you may encounter

We will now go through the five cases presented in the preceding screenshot.

In many cases, you will need to change the direction of a loop. As you can see in the first case of the preceding screenshot, we have two colored face loops. We will rearrange them so that the blue one doesn't cross the red one. Remember that in order to select a face loop, we will use the *Alt* + RMB shortcut.

1. To resolve the first case, we will select the bottom edge of the blue face situated below the cross intersection.

   We will then select the **Rotate Edge CCW** (Counter Clock Wise) in the **Edge** menu (*Ctrl* + *E*).

   Now, we can rearrange the polygons to get a nice round corner.

   Sometimes, you may want to have a circular shape in your topology. This occurs mainly in hard surface modeling.

2. In order to resolve the second case, we will select the piece of geometry that will be of circular shape and use the Mesh Loop add-on (by pressing *W* and selecting **LoopTools | Circle**) to form a circle. You can also move your vertices one by one if you don't want a perfect circle.

   Now, we will maintain the geometry by doing an inset of the selected faces. As you can see, our circle perfectly incorporates the flow of our geometry.

   Another situation that you may encounter is when two face loops forming an arc are stuck together. This technique can be useful when defining muscles or articulations. We will later use this for the knee of the alien.

3. For the third case, we will start with the Knife tool by cutting the three edges that form an arc.

    As you may have seen, we now have two triangles that we need to resolve in quads. So, we will add a cut in the middle of both of them with the Knife tool or the Loop Cut tool.

    You will often need to reduce the number of polygons at some location. For instance, there could be lot of condensed polygons behind the head, so in order to have less of them for the back, we will make a U shape.

4. So, our goal for the fourth case is to make a U shape with blues faces that leaves us with only one face under it:

    1. To do this, we will first dissolve all the vertical vertices that are in the middle of, and below, the blue faces (the dashed line in the screenshot).

    2. Now we can do a bevel of the edges that separates the two vertical lines of the face.

    3. We can now use the *J* key to join the two vertices that form the base of the U shape (the one marked in the screenshot).

5. We will now show you one last technique, but you need to keep in mind that there are many other methods that we can't show you here because it would require a whole book! Sometimes you need to rotate some polygons in the geometry, but you don't want stretches after rotating them.

    If you look at the last case of the preceding screenshot, the red square of the polygons has been simply rotated with the *R* key.

    At this point, the geometry around it should be stretched. The best way to solve this is to simply remove the parts that are causing you problems and recreate the geometry in a better way. In our case, we've done this by bridging the square outline back to the rest of the geometry with the *F* key.

Errors to avoid during the creation of retopology

We will now talk a little bit about the main problems that you should avoid while creating a proper topology. The first thing that we have already expressed before is that we need to try to have as few triangles possible. Triangles are bad because they break the face loops, and they can cause some rendering artifacts with the lighting, and the topology could be harder to maintain.

Some people may think that this is not a problem because triangles are used a lot in the video game industry, but usually, the triangles that we see in a game model result from a tessellation made by the game engine after the model was created. They are also needed in cases where there is a lack of performance, especially in mobile games where the amount of geometry needs to be lowered. But the performance of smart phones are doing better with time, so this is not going to be a problem in the future. Sometimes, triangles can be placed at a position that doesn't bend a lot. For instance, the ear of a human rarely deforms, so it's not a problem to place a triangle here. When you add triangles, do it in such a way that it doesn't bother the silhouette of your object.

Another thing that you want to avoid is poles. A pole is a vertex that connects a minimum of four edges. Usually, poles are useful to redirect face loops, so they are usable but they need to be carefully managed. You can create poles if, and only if, you need to change the flow of your face loops and if you are in a place where the geometry won't bend a lot during animation. For instance, on the human face, we can place poles on the cheekbone because we need to redirect the topology. You will encounter this with the alien's head.

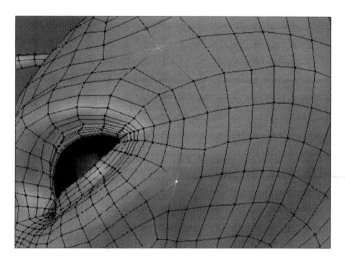

An example of two selected poles

Don't be discouraged if you don't get the topology right the first time, come back later and you'll have a clear mind to try to figure out the problem again. Another thing to keep in mind while doing a retopology is that if you want to have a certain loop, create it without waiting because you'll be quickly overwhelmed by polygons, and you could face problems when you need to remove a lot of geometry in order to connect the loop back. Creating a good topology is like solving a puzzle—it always has a solution!

Density of polygons

While doing a retopology, you need to think about the general flow of your topology. If you've done this right, you'll be able to quickly add or remove edge loops in order to increase or decrease the density of the mesh. The more geometry you have, the more you will be able to be precise in the approximation of the sculpted shape. Of course, you need to take into account the eventual constraints that you will have. For instance, if you are creating a mobile game character, it's best to try to reach the minimum number of polygons that gives you the global silhouette. Choosing the right number of polygons is more of a decision that you'll take on the fly.

Making the retopology of the alien character

Now that we have seen a few basic techniques, we are going to see a practical case by working on our little alien character sculpture.

Preparing the environment

Before starting the retopology of our little character that came from distant worlds, we must prepare the working environment for the method that we will use. There are several possibilities in Blender to do a retopology, including with very good add-ons (Retopology MT and Retopology Tools, for example). We will not use them here; instead we will focus mainly on internal Blender tools.

1. We will start by placing the cursor at the center of our sculpted mesh. For this, we will select the mesh and press *Shift + S* to open the snap menu. Then, we will choose the **Cursor to Selected** option.

2. We will then create a plane in the **Object Mode** (pressing *Shift + A* and selecting **Mesh | Plane**) that we will place in front of the eyes. This new object that has been created is going to be the new mesh for our character. We rename it as `Alien_Retopo`.

3. In the **Edit Mode**, we will bisect the plane, delete the vertices on the left-hand side, and then we will add a **Mirror Modifier**. Don't forget to check the **Clipping** option.

4. We need to make a transparent shader that will allow us to work comfortably in order to visualize the mesh. In the **Material** menu, we will check the **New** button. It's also good to name this; in our case, it is `M_Retopo`. This way, we can look through our polygons and check the **Transparency** option with an **Alpha** value of `0.208`.

5. We will then go in the **GLSL** mode in the **Shading** menu of the right panel of the 3D viewport (*N*). This allows us to visualize the new material that has been created.

6. We will also check the **Backface Culling** option just below the **Shading** menu to avoid being too bothered by the rear faces.

7. We switch to the **Texture shading** mode in the corresponding drop-down menu located in the 3D view header.

8. After this, we need to add a **Hemi** light (by pressing *Shift + A* and selecting **Lamp | Hemi**) that is to be placed just above the 3D model in the direction of the ground. We will set its energy value to **1**.

9. We will activate **Xray** in the Properties editor in the **Object** tab under the **Display** subpanel.

10. For our comfort, we need to change the size of the vertices. For this, we will go to **File | User Preferences | Theme | 3DView | Vertex Size**. We will enter a value of **6**.

11. In the **User Preferences** menu, we will check that the **F2 add-on** is activated.

12. In the 3D viewport header bar, we will activate **Snap** (it looks like a little magnet) in **Face Mode** (just on the right-hand side of the snap icon).

13. We still have to activate the buttons located a little more on the right-hand side called as **Project Individual Elements** on the surface of other objects and **Snap onto itself**. Let the mouse hover over a button for a moment so that you can see its tooltip appear.

Now we can start to build the new topology.

The head

Let's start our retopology with the head of our alien character:

1. In the **Edit Mode**, we will snap our first polygon with the Grab tool (*G*).

2. We will then begin to form the first face loop around the eyes. We will select the edge on the right-hand side of the plane and pressing *Ctrl* and a left-click, we will create new polygons in sequence on the surface of the sculpted mesh. There is no need to be very accurate while tracing the first face loop. We will be able to reposition the vertices and adjust the number of polygons thereafter. So, we will make the first face loop, which passes through the eyebrow, the cheek, and joins the symmetry axis right at the nose. At the corner of the eye, we need to be careful while placing an edge that extends the diagonal direction of the eye (refer step **2** in the following screenshot). This face loop is called the **mask**.

Pair number of polygons

Be careful to always have a pair number of polygons whenever you form a face loop. This will allow you to connect the polygons more easily. If in some cases you only have an odd number, you can try to delete an edge loop and replace the polygons around (with **G**) it.

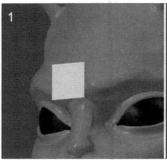
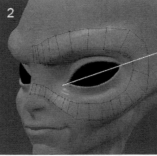
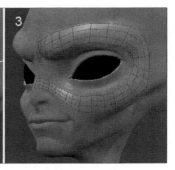

3. We will then add two edge loops (*Ctrl + R*). Try to equalize as much as possible the size and the distribution of the polygons. We will reposition the vertices to have a rounded shape (refer to step **3** in the preceding screenshot). For our selected components snap on to the sculpture, we have to move them with the Grab tool (*G*). Remember to do this often, but only with the components that directly face your point of view.

4. We will add an edge loop to the nose in order to have enough polygons to better define the outline shape. We will have a 28-face face loop.

5. We will join the nose with the new polygons (refer to step **4** in the following screenshot).

6. To save time, you can start making a shape with a few big polygons to cover a large area that you want to work on. You can then define the number of cuts that you need and snap the topology, rather than make many little polygons one after the other.

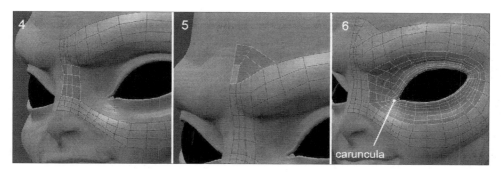

Try to follow the shape of the sculpted mesh as much as possible.

F2 add-on

We mentioned this while preparing the environment. *F2* is an essential add-on in Blender that allows us to quickly create faces.

Between the two rows of the edges, the *F2* add-on can generate the missing faces. You can also generate a face by selecting one vertex on the intersection of two faces by pressing *F*. Repeat the process to quickly make a face loop, and remember to weld them (select the polygons, and then press *W* and select **Remove doubles**).

You can also generate the face loops in the edge mode. You need to select a starting edge (the one to the left and perpendicular to the *x* axis according to the following screenshot) by pressing *F*. The sense of creation of a face can be determined by the placement of the mouse if the starting edge is at the center of the face loop that is to be created.

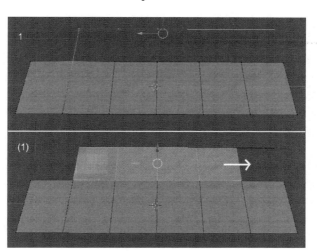

[97]

7. We can see that we have a pole. We will avoid making it too visible, so we will place it under the eyebrow.

8. We complete the topology of the upper nose with a polygon reduction on the forehead (refer to step **5** in the preceding screenshot).

9. Now, we will select the edge loop that bypasses the eye, and we do an extrusion by changing the scale (*E* and *S*). We will then place the vertices on the outline of the eye (*G*). We will have a 24-face face loop (refer to step **6** of the preceding screenshot).

10. We will add two edge loops (*Ctrl + R*) around the eye that we will reposition correctly (*G*). A first edge loop takes the shape of the eye, marking the fold with the eyebrow. A second edge loop makes the link between the two shapes.

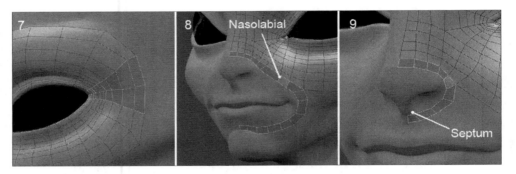

11. At the left outer corner of the eye, we will tighten the vertices. We will take care to have a conical shape that spreads outwards (refer to step **7** in the preceding screenshot).

12. Now, we create a face loop from the nose to the chin. It is called the nasolabial loop. We will add the polygons using *F2* (by selecting a corner vertex and pressing *F*). Just like the eye, we extrude an edge and form a face loop from it that follows the circular shape of the mouth. We will have a 16-face face-loop (refer to step **8** of the preceding screenshot).

13. We will add a face loop that comes around the nose. This allows us to define the nose. Remember to slightly bring the edges at the bottom to the septum of the nose. We will have a 9-face face loop (refer to step **9** of the preceding screenshot).

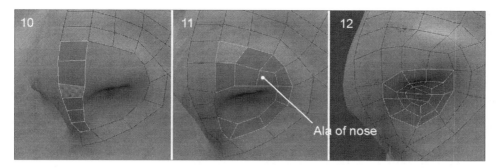

Ala of nose

14. We will create the topology that forms the top and bottom of the nose. We will have a 6-face face loop (refer to step **10** of the preceding screenshot).

15. Once the nose shape is outlined, we will begin the ala of the nose. We will extrude a face loop that starts from the top of the nose down to the bottom of the nose, avoiding the nostril. This arrangement allows us to better create the shape of the nostril loop (refer to step **11** of the preceding screenshot).

16. We will extrude the edge loop of the nostril with a scale transformation (*E* and *S*). We will then close the hole by connecting the edges (refer to step **12** of the preceding screenshot). If you don't have enough edges to make four-sided polygons, you can use a triangle. It must be as hidden as possible.

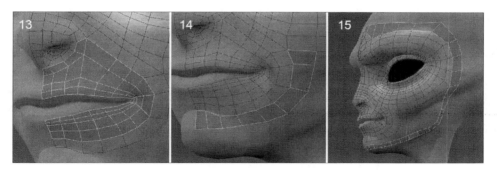

17. We will start from the corner of the nose to make a face loop that goes under the mouth.

18. We will then close this part by following the shape of the lips. Take care to slightly pinch the corner of the mouth. The topology must be as symmetrical as possible between the top and bottom of the mouth in order to connect them later. We will have a 14-face mirrored face loop (refer to step **13** of the preceding screenshot).

19. We will continue around the mouth by adding a polygon strip above the chin (see **14** and **15** in the preceding screenshot).

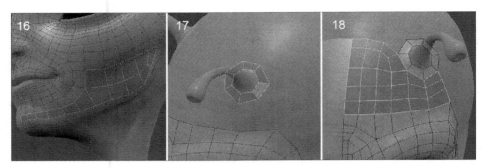

20. Now, we will make the face loop of the jaw, which ascends to make the contour of the face. We have a 22-face mirrored face loop (refer to step 15 of the preceding screenshot). We need to align the faces correctly for an easy connection and close the area of the jaw (refer to step **16** of the preceding screenshot).

21. We will make the contour of the antennas with an extruded vertex on the top of the forehead in a circular manner (refer to step **17** of the preceding screenshot).

22. We will then continue to form the polygons of the forehead, in line with what was done, by making a reduction in the number of faces, avoiding the antennas (refer to step **18** of the preceding screenshot).

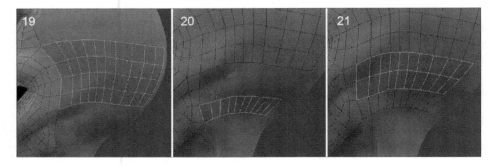

23. We will select three edges on the temples and create a polygon strip that follows the back of the head. We need enough faces to have a nice rounded.

24. We will then select the edge located at the jaw, and we will continue to make the topology of the back of the head (refer to step **20** of the preceding screenshot).

25. Now that the face strips are facing each other, we can fill the missing topology with the Fill and Loop Cut tools. (Refer to step **21** of the preceding screenshot.)

26. We will continue to make the faces on the back of the head in the same way. We will form an angle to close the top of the head later more easily. (Refer to step **22** of the following screenshot.)

The Smooth option

In order to have a topology as homogeneous as possible, we can use the **Smooth** option of the **Specials** menu (**W**). This allows us to relax the polygons. We first need to select the faces we want to modify (**C**). Be careful as you have to snap them after the process (**G**), so select only the visible faces in the view.

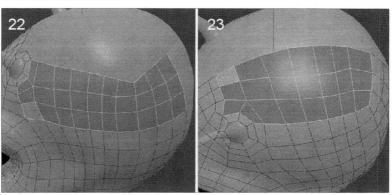

We now need to close the topology of the top of the head. We must pay attention to respect the number of edge loops created previously. You can apply the smooth option to quickly relax some misaligned faces.

Now we are going to make the antennas that require another technique:

1. We will duplicate the edge loop situated at the base of the antenna already created to make a new object (by pressing *P* and select **Selection**).

2. We need to deactivate the **Snap** option and the **Project Individual Elements** option.

3. We can extrude this new object following the shape of the antenna. The polygons must completely cover the surface of the sculpted mesh. You can set **Wireframe Shading Mode** in order to view your geometry better.

4. Once we get the desired topology, we add **Shrinkwrap** modifier and select the sculpted mesh in the **Target** parameter, called **Body**. This modifier allows us to snap a mesh on another.

5. We must apply the modifier by clicking on **Apply** button, and then we will join it back to our other piece of geometry. For this, we select the mesh of the antenna, then the mesh of the head, and we press *Ctrl + J*.

6. As we want to snap our components on the sculpture again, we will restore the **Snap** and **Project Individual Elements** options.

7. We can add a few edge loops to the antenna in order to get a good enough shape.

8. We will connect the faces in the back of the head in continuity with the topology already done.

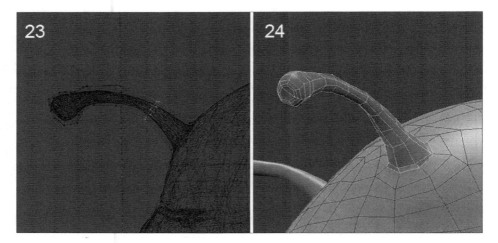

9. From the angle of the jaw, we will create a face loop that ends at the symmetry axis on same level of the glottis (refer to step **25** of the following image).

10. We will then connect the face loop to the chin by adding enough edges. We need to connect the entire underside of the jaw. We have a 10-face face strip (refer to step **26** of the following screenshot).

11. This area forms a triangular shape. We need to make loops to reduce the number of polygons around the chin. We can easily reduce the polygon flow by redirecting the loops on the axis of the symmetry (refer to step **27** of the following screenshot).

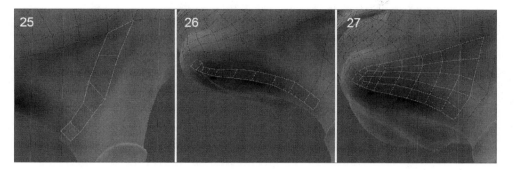

12. To better visualize your polygons, you can hide the ones that you do not want to see. You can use the *H* shortcut. Press *Alt + H* to make them reappear.

The neck and the torso

We will continue this retopology with the neck.

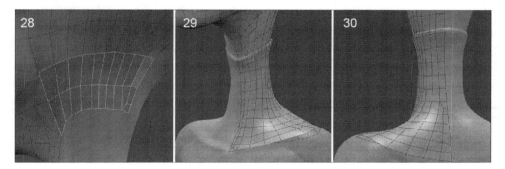

1. We will make a small polygon reduction at the back of the neck in order to lighten the density a little bit. We only need to progressively extrude the polygons along the neck. We will then align the polygons on the collar. We slightly pinch the edges to restore the volume of the collar outline.

The challenge is to properly harmonize the polygon flow along the front and the rear.

2. We will continue to extrude to the clavicles. Using loops, we will add a polygon row in the middle of the nape, and we will reduce one on the sternum (refer step **28** of the preceding screenshot).

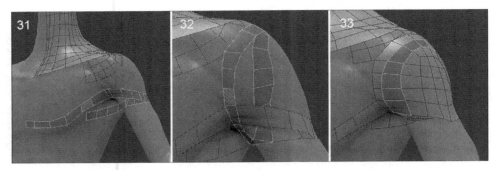

3. There is an important face loop to place in case we want to animate the arms later. It follows the lower pectorals and shoulders muscles. We will have a 20-face mirrored face loop (refer to step 31 of the preceding screenshot).

4. We will make another important face loop that goes vertically around the shoulder and passes under the arm. We will have a 16-face mirrored face loop (refer to step 32 of the preceding screenshot).

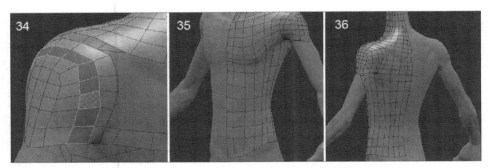

5. Therefore, we will connect the polygons to form the chest and the upper back. On the shoulder, a new face loop links the polygons that intersect vertically and horizontally (refer to step **33** of the preceding screenshot).

6. We will extend the topology straight to the pelvis in a cylindrical manner. There is no particular difficulty on this part (refer to steps **35** and **36** of the preceding screenshot).

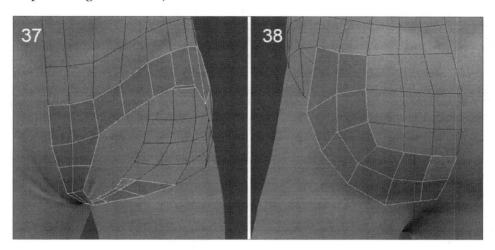

7. We end the hip with a strip of polygon that joins the axis of symmetry and we will create the crotch by connecting the buttocks polygons. Don't add too many edge loops, just what is needed. We will have a 6-face strip to make the connection (refer to step **37** of the preceding screenshot).

8. Now, we will make a face loop that follows the shape of the buttocks. This face loop allows us to have a good deformation when animating the legs. To connect the vertical polygons that come from the back, we will make a second face loop right in this area (refer to step **38** of the preceding screenshot).

The arms and the hands

It is time to make the topology of the arms. Considering they are quite thin and not very muscular, we are going to use the same technique that we used for the antennas.

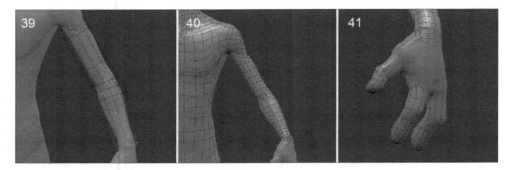

1. This time we will add a 10-face cylinder (*Shift + A*) positioned around the arm. Be careful to match the number of faces on the shoulder (refer to step **39** of the preceding screenshot).

2. To facilitate the visualization of two meshes, we will parent our semitransparent material by first selecting our retopology, and then selecting our new cylinder by pressing *Ctrl + L* and selecting **Materials**.

3. We will add a **Shrinkwrap** modifier with the sculpted mesh as a target.

4. We need enough polygons to get a sufficiently smooth shape. We will bring, little more loops on the elbow in case we need to animate the arm later so that it will bend appropriately.

5. As for the antennas, we will apply the **Shrinkwrap** modifier in order to freeze the new shape. We will then join the arm to the rest of the body (*Ctrl + J*).

6. Now that we have only one mesh, let's connect the arm to the shoulder by selecting the two opening loops and by bridging them together (by pressing *W* and selecting **Bridge Edge Loop**). Since we have the same number of vertices on the two sides, Bridge must work fine. We will then need to adjust the topology by adding some edge loops here and there. Don't forget to snap back the vertices on the sculpture (refer to step **40** in the preceding screenshot).

Let's start the hand. It is a particularly delicate part of the anatomy to do:

1. We will start by doing the fingers using an extruded circle again and the **Shrinkwrap** modifier for each finger. This is the same technique used for the antennas and the arm. This time, we need to extrude a 10-edge circle for each finger. This number is important because we need to have enough polygons for the hand. Pay attention to the orientation of the thumb (refer to step 41 in the preceding screenshot).

2. Once this is done, each finger is closed by joining six four-sided polygons. Our character has only two phalanges by the finger, so be sure to place three cuts around each of them if you want to properly animate the fingers later.

3. Then, we will make some of the important face loops of the palm. There is a 10-face face loop that passes around the thumb (the thenar muscles). There is a 14-face face-loop on the opposite side of the hand near the little finger (the hypothenar eminence) (refer to step 42 in the following screenshot).

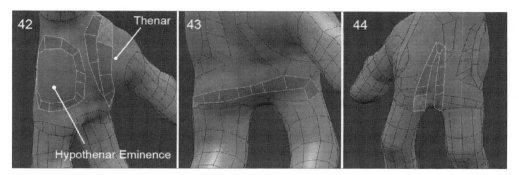

4. We will create a face strip in order to accentuate the basis of the fingers. It is also important to leave a space between each finger (refer to step **43** in the preceding screenshot).

5. Now, all the face loops have to be connected. We have the needed density to only use four-sided polygons without too much difficulty. Train yourself to fill holes with the number of polygons that you have. In this case, we can't change the number of polygons that wraps around each finger (ten in our case) (refer to step **44** in the preceding screenshot).

6. We will add a few more horizontal edge loops around the phalanges in order to have a smooth shape.

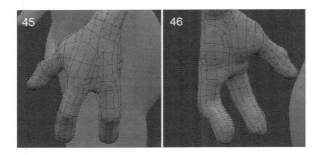

The legs

We are going to finish this retopology with the legs. Let's begin with the thigh:

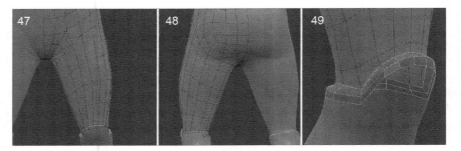

1. We will select the edge that makes the outline of the leg and extrude it to the knee (*E*). As before, we will add a few edge loops (*Ctrl + R*), and then adjust and snap the topology on the surface of the sculpted mesh. We could have used the technique used for the antennas and arms with a cylinder but the thigh is wide enough and less complex (refer to steps **47** and **48** in the preceding screenshots).

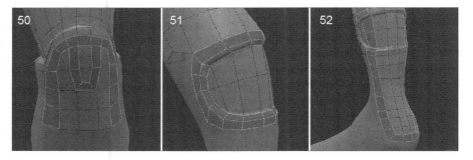

2. We will add an edge loop a little tighter near the knee.

3. We can see that the boots are just above the knees, so we will make two edge loops that stick to the relief (refer to step **49** in the preceding screenshot).

4. On the front of the knee, there is a loop that will reduce the number of polygons on the shin. It goes up and down along the thigh (refer to step **50** in the preceding screenshot).

5. There is another face loop to be created that will follow the rounded shape of the boot at the knee. It goes up toward the thigh (refer to step **51** in the preceding screenshot).

6. We must create the missing polygons on the top of the boot in line with what was done until the opening of the calf.

7. This opening of the boot requires two face loops that allow us to maintain the hole. We must pay attention that it is easily connectable between the top and bottom. This looks like the circular topology case that we had analyzed before. We have two 18-face mirrored face loops.

8. We will continue the retopology by creating a loop that goes under the heel and connects with the upper leg (refer to step **52** in the preceding screenshot).

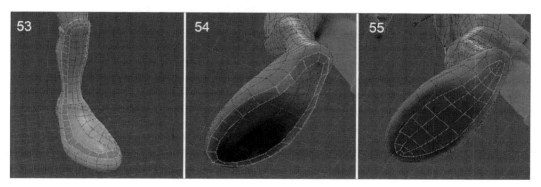

9. Let's go back to the front of the thigh and continue to form a strip of polygon that goes around the foot and forms a long face loop. It goes through the knee. This allows us to control the polygon flow by adapting it to the shape. We just need to keep the same number of polygons on both sides of that face loop in order to connect them properly (refer to step **53** in the preceding screenshot).

10. A final important loop remains to be made. This is located under the foot. It follows the outline of the plantar arch with a 20-face face loop aligned so that we can easily connect it to the rest of the foot (refer to step **54** of the preceding screenshot).

11. We still have to connect the inside of this underfoot face loop. To move from one row to three rows of polygons along the length of the foot, we must create a face loop by cutting the faces at the ends of the feet (refer to step **55** of the preceding screenshot).

The retopology of this little character is now over. We complete a mesh that offers many possibilities, such as creating textures or doing animations. All of this couldn't be envisaged with a very high polygon density and sculpted 3D model. Having a few polygons will facilitate the process. The important thing now is to get the small details that we had sculpted back on our mesh that we can describe as a **low poly mesh**. For this, we must discover a process called UV's unwrapping.

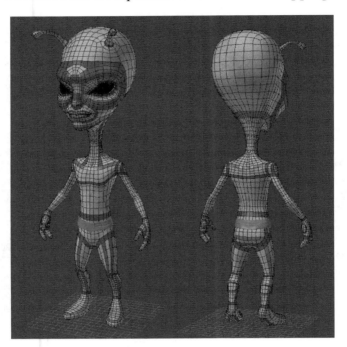

A presentation of each important face-loops of the alien

Unwrapping UVs

Now that we have a clean topology, we can learn more about the UV unwrapping process that we introduced in the first chapter. We have to do this in order to project the sculpted details on our clean mesh. Before starting, let's see what UVs are.

Understanding UVs

The goal of the UV unwrapping process is to flatten the 3D mesh in a 2D space in order to project textures (2D images) on it. To understand the process better, imagine that we are going to remove the skin of our alien in order to flatten it (I know that the metaphor is a little gory, but stay with us, there won't be any blood). If we have to do this, we would need to detach the skin by cutting along the imaginary seams and then flattening it down.

Another way to better understand UV unwrapping is to think about how clothes are made and take the steps in the reverse order. For instance, at the beginning, a shirt is a flat piece of tissue where all the seams are marked down. Then, the different cut pieces are attached together in order to form the volume of the shirt, like the sleeves. So, if we were unfolding a cloth along its seams, we will tell Blender where the seams are placed on our 3D mesh. After this, the ones that have been marked and the model that has been flattened down will correspond to each vertex, edge, or face between the 3D model and the flattened version of it; this is actually a 2D representation of the geometry.

In general, we call the coordinate axes of a 2D space the x and y axes, but in this case they are named as U and V. Hence, the name **UV unwrapping process**. Another really important thing to note is that we often want to avoid any overlap of geometry in the UV space. This is because when we use UVs of an object in order to project 2D textures on it, we seldom want to have the same texture information twice on the 3D model. We will also need to optimize the UVs so that they don't generate strange distortions.

Lastly, similar to the shirt example, our UVs will be usually separated in different parts called islands. For instance, we will disconnect the head of our alien from its hands or other limbs. These islands need to have a proportional scale to the geometry data they represent (that is, the head is bigger than the hands, so it needs to be bigger in the UV space).

The placement of the seams

It's now time to unwrap the UVs of our alien character. So, as we stated before, we first need to tell Blender where the seams are going to be:

1. We will first select all the edges that start from the lower back of the neck to the middle of the forehead (the ones that are on the symmetry axis). We can also select four perpendicular connected edges together at the end of the previous group of edges selected. It will look like an inverted T shape from the front view.

2. Now, in order to mark our selection as seams, we will go to the **Edges** menu (*Ctrl + E*) and select the **Mark seam** option.

3. Always try to think as if you were using a cutter, so the mesh will be disconnected in the UV space along the marked edges. Also, note that the seams are in red.

4. Now, we will select the top collar edge loop (press *Alt* and the RMB) where it meets the previously marked edge and mark it as a new seam again. This will completely separate the head and neck portion into a new island.

5. In order to have less deformation under the chin, we will select edges starting from the top of the collar (where we placed the seam) to the chin along the axis of symmetry. We will add five perpendicular edges to our selections and mark our selection as new seams. We've done this in the same way as the forehead.

6. In order to separate the antenna in its own island, we will select the circle loop of its base and mark it as a seam. We will also have to mark a vertical line of edges that start from the previously marked seam and end at the top of the antenna.

7. Then, we will end this seam by following the circular cap of the top of the antenna without closing it completely, leaving an edge unmarked. When you are marking the seams, try to think of an approximation of the shape that you know in the real life. For instance, in this case, the antenna looks like a candy wrapper.

8. To end with the head, we will select an edge loop around the eye and mark it as a seam. If you want to remove a seam, you can simply select a seam, and in the **Edges** menu (*Ctrl + E*), you can select the **Clear Seam** option. We've now completed the UVs of the head, but we will finish the body before looking at them unwrapped.

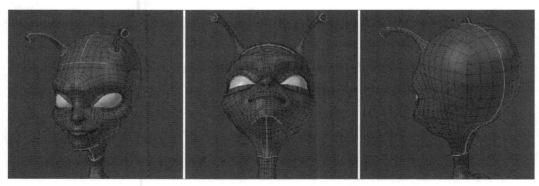

The head seams

9. Now, we will select a vertical edge loop around the shoulder and mark it as a seam. This is going to represent the separation between the arm UVs and the torso UVs.

10. In order to clearly see that the arm UVs are disconnected from the rest of the body, you can go in the **Face** mode, hover your mouse on the arm and press the *L* key (selection of the linked parts).

11. We will then separate the torso UVs from the legs by marking an edge loop situated under the belt.

12. It's best to consider the torso UVs as two separate islands, the front and the back. So, we will split this by marking the edges that connect the shoulder's vertical seam to the seam of the collar. These edges follow the angle created by the neck and the shoulder.

13. After this, we will mark a line of edges that start under the arm and go right to the belt seam. As you can see, using the linked parts method presented before, the torso is now in two parts that are delimited by the collar, belt, and shoulder seams (of course, we always have the mirror modifier turned on, so we can only see half of the torso's linked parts)

14. We will then mark an edge loop that follows the top boot outline.

15. As we did with the torso, we will split the legs UVs into two islands. To do this, we simply mark the edges that start from the belt seam (following the same direction of the seam on the side of the torso) and end at the boot seam.

16. For now, the legs are still in one part, so we will add a new seam starting from the boot seam and ending below the pelvis bone. Now, our legs UVs are split into two islands.

17. It's now time to mark the seams of the boots. To do this, we will to the bottom view (*Ctrl + 7* numpad key) and mark a loop that follows the footprint of the boot. We will also mark the loop that follows the hole of the boot on the calf muscles.

18. We will then mark the vertical edges of the back that connect the footprint seam to the hole seam and the ones that connect the hole seam to the top boot outline.

19. Lastly, we will mark the seams of the hand and the arm. We will mark the wrist edge loop in order to disconnect its UVs from the arm. Now, we will mark a continuous line of edges that start from the tip of the thumb and follow the silhouette of the hand by connecting to the wrist seam. As you can see, we didn't split the top of the thumb so that the interior palm and the back of the hand share the same UV Island. Then, we will mark a continuous line of edges from the wrist to the shoulder in order to do the UVs of the arm.

Congratulations! You've finished marking all the seams, and we are now ready to unwrap the alien. In order to do this, we must first apply our **Mirror** modifier. As you can see, all the seams are now mirrored to the other side; what a time saver!

1. Now it's time to unwrap the alien. Let's see how this is done. We will first select all its geometry by pressing *A*.

2. Now, we will press the *U* key to get the **UV Mapping** menu and select the **Unwrap** option. Unwrap is now done!

3. To see the UVs, we will open a new **UV/Image Editor** by splitting our 3D view into two and changing the new window to the appropriate editor.

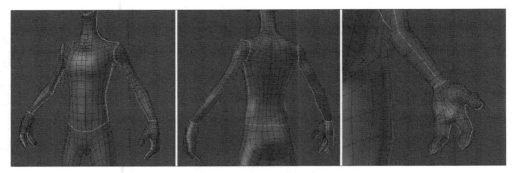

The upper body seams

The seams follow the volume of the each part of the character.

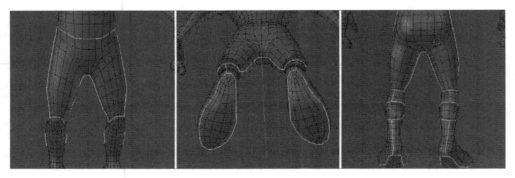

The lower body seams

As you can see, in the **Edit Mode**, all our 3D geometry is being flattened down in the UV space. We are now ready to reorganize each island. Note that if you still have problems while understanding the relation between the 3D space and the UV space (don't be disappointed if this is the case, UVs are hard to understand in the beginning), you can use the linked method presented before to see how each part is represented in the UV space.

The placement and adjustment of the islands

We are now going to adjust each island in the UV space. As you can see, all our islands are bounded to a square. Everything that is on the outside won't be used, so all the islands need to be tightly packed in it. Moreover, we'll have to check whether there are any important deformations on our 3D mesh. If this is the case, it means that each texture will be stretched whether we want it or not.

1. In order to adjust the different island placements, in the **UV/Image Editor**, we will first need to enter the **Island UV selecting** mode.

   This allows us to select every island and place it with the grab (*G*) tool, scale (*S*) or rotate it (*R*) in the **UV/Image Editor**.

2. When we try to place the islands correctly on the UV space, we need to be sure that they don't go out of the square bounds (represented by a grid).

3. You can also use the **Pack Islands** tool located under the **UVs** menu, in order to have this automatically done. But it's always best to do it by hand.

4. Another thing to remember is to have the island proportional in scale to what they represent on the mesh. This was automatically done when you first unwrapped your mesh, but if you scale the islands by hand, be aware of this. However, you can sometimes counter this rule when you need more texture details on a specific location. For instance, the head is one of the most important part of the alien, so we can scale its island a little bit more.

5. Once you've packed all your islands, you can add a checker texture to check whether there are any important stretches with your UVs. We will add a predefined texture by first entering into the **Edit Mode** of the alien.

6. We will click on the **+ New** button in the header of the **UV/Image Editor**, and select a **UV Grid** image under the **Generated Type** drop-down menu. We can then validate it with **OK**.

7. In order to see the test grid on our alien in the viewport, we will need to enter the **Texture shading** mode located under the **Viewport shading** drop-down menu in the 3D viewport header. We can also toggle it on or off by pressing *Alt + Z*.

Now that we see our test grid on our alien, how can we interpret it? If all the squares are still approximate squares, then it means we don't have any important deformation. Their orientations don't matter too much here.

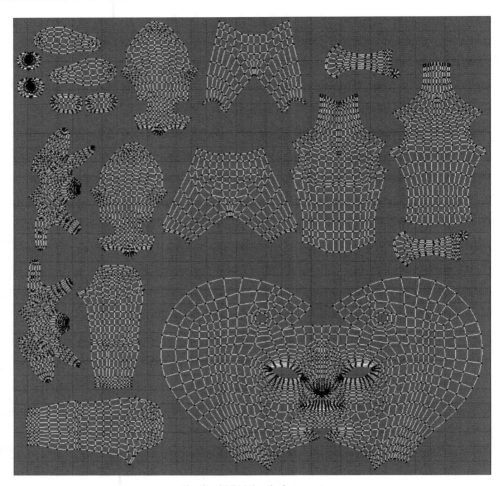

The final UV Island placement

The baking of textures

Now that we have UVs on our little alien, we can take a look at how we can transfer all the details from our sculpture to the new **retopologized** mesh. The details in the sculpture are simply there because of the amount of geometry it is composed of, but in the retopology, we have kept the amount of details to about 5000 polygons, in order to have a manageable mesh.

The baking of a normal map

The best solution that we have in order to transfer the details is to bake a normal map that will act with lights to give the impression of detail.

What is a normal map?

At its lower state, a normal map is an image or a texture that will be projected on the mesh through the UVs. This' is why it's important to UV unwrap the object. Note that if the UVs are stretching at some place, the details that are in the normal map will then be stretched too. As mentioned before, a normal map will do its magic with the lighting. It is composed of red, green, and blue pixels that respectively represent the X, Y, and Z orientations of the normal of a face. So, we will need to create a normal map that will contain all the normal information of the high poly sculpture. The higher the definition of the normal map texture will be, the most precise the details will be.

Making of the bake

In order to create a normal map from our sculpture, we will need to use the bake tools of Blender.

1. We only need to see the sculpture and the retopology in the 3D view. To hide the rest, we will select them both and press *Shift + H*.

2. We can now deselect all our objects by pressing *A*.

3. In order to do the bake, we will have to first select the alien sculpture and then the retopology (this becomes the active object).

4. Now, in the Properties editor, under the **Render** section, we will expand the **Bake** subpanel.

5. The first option to choose is what type of map (or texture) we want to bake. So, under the **Bake Mode** drop-down menu, we will select **Normal Map**.

6. The next thing we'll have to check is the **Selected to Active** option that tells Blender to bake from the sculpture to the active object (our retopology).

7. We will then need to add a blank texture to bake our normal map on. So, we enter the **Edit Mode** of the retopology and click on the **+ New** button (or the + icon on the right-hand side of the texture list), and instead of selecting a UV grid, we choose a **Blank** texture with a width and height of 4096 pixels.

8. Before baking our map, we need to click on the **Smooth Shading** button; otherwise, we will see the polygons on our bake.

9. Last but not least, we will come back to the **Bake** panel and click on the **Bake** button. Don't forget to save your map (**Image | Save As Image** or simply press *F3*) or it will be lost!

At this point, you should see that the normal map has started to appear. If you get an error message, it may be because you didn't add the texture on the low poly while you were in **Edit Mode**, or that you've selected the retopology before the sculpture. If you want to have your normal map packed into the `.blend` file, you can go to the **File** menu and select the **Pack All into blend file** in the **External Data** subpanel.

About the size of the textures

Usually, textures aren't rectangle. They are set with the power of two of the width and the height. The common sizes are 256 x 256, 1024 x 1024, 2048 x 2048, and 4096 x 4096.

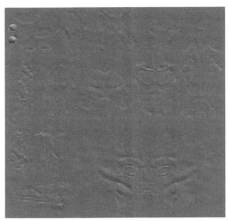

The baked normal map of our alien

Displaying the normal map in the viewport

Now that we have a nice normal map baked, we will show to you how to display it in the viewport:

1. We first need to be in the **GLSL** mode (press *N* and select **Shading Subpanel | Material mode** dropdown).

2. We also need to add a new material on our low poly. To do this, we can click on the **New** material button under the **Material** tab of the Properties editor.

3. We will then go to the **Texture** tab of the Properties editor and click on the **New texture** button.

4. Under the **Image** subpanel, we can choose our normal map with the left-hand side drop-down menu.

5. Then, we will check the **Normal Map** check box under the **Image Sampling** subpanel.

6. For now, Blender will only interpret the map as a diffuse map. We want to tell Blender to use the normal information of the map. So, under the **Influence** subpanel, we uncheck **Color slider** and check **Normal slider**.

7. Now, we will need to add a light in the 3D viewport (press *Shift + A* and navigate to **Lamp | Hemi**) and orient it correctly.

8. Lastly, we need to enter the **Texture shading** mode. We can now appreciate the comeback of our sculpture details. If you want, you can move the light around to feel the relief of the normal map.

The baking of an ambient occlusion

Now that we have the normal map set, we will improve our alien with another map called an ambient occlusion.

Understanding the ambient occlusion map

An ambient occlusion is a black and white texture that represents the contact shadows of a mesh. The contact shadows are the shadows produced by the small proximity of objects. In order to have a nice ambient occlusion, we need to increase a sampling parameter that corresponds to the "noisiness" of the shadows. The more samples you have, the smoother the shadows will be. This map will then be multiplied on top of our diffuse material color.

Multiplying colors

In computer graphics, black is represented by a value of 0 and white by a value of 1. So, when we multiply a color with black, its result is 0, and when we multiply a color with white, its result is the color. For instance, we will take two colors, J and K, a pure blue that is represented by R(J): 0, G(J): 0, and B(J):1 (**RGB** means **Red Green Blue**), and white, R(K): 1, G(K):1, and B(K):1. When we multiply both, we will have $R(J)*R(K) = 0 * 1 = 0$, $G(J)*G(K) = 0 * 1 = 0$, and $B(J)*B(K) = 1 * 1 = 1$, so the resultant color is R:0, G: 0, and B:1. It is the original blue.

Creation of the bake

We will now follow the same principle as the normal map, but we will change the sampling value:

1. The sampling slider is situated under the world tab of the Properties editor in the **Gather** subpanel. Even if it's grayed out, it will work for the bake. We will set it to **10** in our case. Don't go too high with this as it will increase your baking time.

2. Now, refer to the normal map baking process, but instead of choosing a normal map in step 5, choose an ambient occlusion. Again, don't forget to add the blank texture in **Edit Mode**, and save it after the bake. You can also name your textures in the **UV/Image Editor** in the header with the corresponding text field.

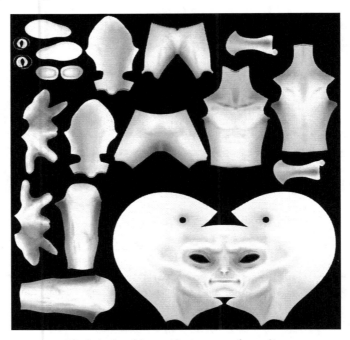

The baked ambient occlusion map of our alien

Displaying the ambient occlusion in the viewport

In order to see the ambient occlusion applied to our mesh, we will have to add a new texture to our material. This is done as follows:

1. First, we will select our alien, and then we will select the material that has the normal map on it in the **Material** tab of the Properties editor.

2. We will, then, go to the **Texture** tab of the Properties editor and add a new texture below the normal map. In order to do this, we select the second slot and click on the big **New** button.

3. We can now choose our ambient occlusion under the **Image** subpanel.

4. Under the **Influence** subpanel, we turn the color slider on but we change the **Blend Mode** from **mix** to **multiply**, as we had previously explained. As you can see, this perfectly works in the viewport when the **Texture** shading mode is turned on. We can clearly see the contact shadows of our mesh around his eyes, for instance.

The alien with a proper topology (shown on the left-hand side) and with its normal map
and ambient occlusion (on the right-hand side)

Summary

In this chapter, we saw how to create a proper retopology based on the sculpture made in the previous chapter and retrieve its details with a normal and ambient occlusion map. There are other maps that you may want to create, such as a diffuse, displace, or lighting map. Now let's go to another project, the Haunted House!

Haunted House – Modeling of the Scene

5

Welcome to the scary project!

In this chapter, we will model a haunted house that we will texture and render in the future chapters. You will use the modeling techniques that we have already seen in the previous chapters and learn some new techniques using some useful modifiers and time-saving tools. Moreover, you will learn how to correctly organize your scenes by grouping objects and placing elements in layers. Now that you have more experience with Blender, we aren't going to show you all the steps in detail but rather describe the key points of the process. If you have any difficulties, you can always go back to *Chapter 2, Robot Toy – Modeling of an Object*, and *Chapter 4, Alien Character – Creating a Proper Topology and Transferring the Sculpt Details*, in order to review some of the modeling techniques. Let's start our scene! In this chapter, the following topics will be covered:

- Modeling on scale
- Blocking the house
- Advance modeling tools
- Modeling with curves
- Organizing the scene

The final haunted house should look like the following screenshot:

Blocking the house

Before going into detail, we will start by testing different shapes in order to create the concept of our house. It is like a 3D sketch.

Working with a scale

In order to create our haunted house and its environment, we need to work with a real world scale. Indeed, when you are working on objects, such as buildings, where the scale matters, it is important to remember to adjust the units of measurement of Blender.

Blender uses, basically, its own unit of measure: the **Blender units** that correspond to a fictitious unit of measure. You aren't going to encounter Blender units in the real world.

There are two other unit systems of measurement in Blender that you can use: the metric system and the imperial system. We prefer the **metric system**. For this, go to the Properties panel on the right-hand side of the user interface under **Outliner** (in the default layout). In the **Scene** tab, you will find the **Units** tab. Choose **Metric** and **Degrees**.

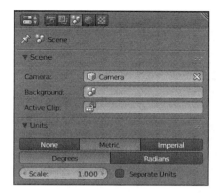

The metric system allows us to work in kilometers (km), meters (m), centimeters (cm), millimeters (mm), and micrometers (µm). Let's choose meters in our case. For this, we set the **Scale** value to **1.000**. A value of **0.1** would make us work in centimeters.

To know the size of your 3D models, in the **Object Mode**, you can look at their size in the **Transform** tab on the right-hand side panel of the 3D viewport (*N*). This information is also given in the **Dimensions** section for the x, y, and z axes.

You can then display the size of the selected edges. In the **Edit Mode**, under the **Transform** tab, go to the **Mesh Display** tab, and check the **Edge Info | Length option**. If you want to measure something, Blender gives you a ruler under the **Grease Pencil** tab in the left 3D view panel (*T*). To use this, simply click on the **Rule/Protractor** button and drag it in the 3D view.

Be careful to always apply your scale and move or rotate the transformation of your objects when you manipulate them in the **Object Mode**. To do this, we open the **Apply** menu (*Ctrl + A*) and select **Rotation and scale**. It is important to avoid involuntary deformations after this.

Blocking the bases of the house

To make this house, we don't start from concept art but from an idea and a few references found on the internet.

It is very important during any creation to spend a little time documenting to confront the different possibilities of shapes and styles. We need to see what has been done previously and be informed enough to be precise in our work.

As we are not completely sure of the form as a whole, we will adopt a method that involves testing and quickly developing ideas with simple forms. This method is called **Blocking**. This is done as follows:

1. We will begin the modeling by adding a cube at the center of a new scene (*Shift + A* and select **Mesh | Cube**), which will represent the central part of the house.

2. In the **Object Mode**, we will adjust the size in the **Transform** tab to have something realistic. It is an imposing house, so we will set 7 m on the *z* axis, 7 m on the x axis, and 8.5 m on the *y* axis.

3. In the **Object Mode**, let's duplicate our cube (*Shift + D*) in order to make the terrace. So we will scale it to a height of 1.26 m, then we will place it at the base of our haunted house under the main block previously created.

4. The terrace is not completely cubic. We will add two edge loops and an extrusion to the front, which is less wide (on the *x* axis) than the main block.

   It is necessary that this terrace is large enough to be credible, so we will create a passage of at least two meters wide. It is not necessary to be very accurate for the moment, but be aware of your measures, and remember to apply the transformations when you switch back to the **Object Mode** (refer to step **1** in the following screenshot).

5. To improve the general shape of our house a little, we will add a new cube that fits in the front of the central part of the house, centered on the *x* axis.

   The height of this cube exceeds the height of the other cube by one third. The rest is hidden in the central block. It has a square base, and it is higher than the main block by about 45 cm (refer to step **2** of the following screenshot).

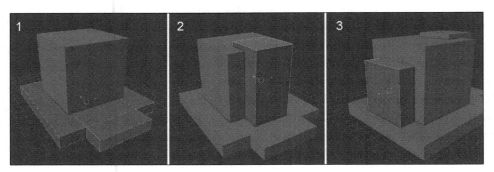

6. Likewise, on the rear part, we will duplicate our front block (*Shift* + *D*) and move it to the other side on the *y* axis. This block is lower than the main block. Its size is 4.7 m on the x axis, 1.67 m on the *y* axis, and 5.3 m on the *z* axis.

Now we have our basic volumes. We can now make the roof that is composed of several parts; one for each block. This is done as follows:

1. We will begin with the roof of the front block by adding a new cube (press *Shift* + *A*, and select **Mesh | Cube**). We need to adjust its size to be larger on the *x* and *y* axis.

2. We will move down the top face to flatten it. It is the bottom part of this section of the roof.

3. Then we will do an inset (*I*) and an extrude (*E*) to the top. We will adjust the scale of the top, and then we will add two extrusions (*E*) to make the top thicker and finish the shape (refer to step **4** of the following screenshot).

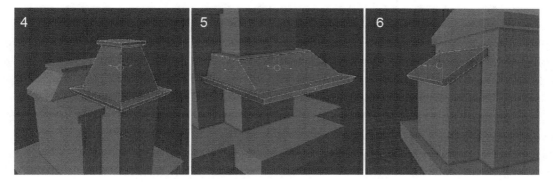

4. We will duplicate this part of the roof (*Shift* + *D*), and we will place it on the rear half of the central block. We will scale it on the *x* axis (press *S* + *X*) in order to have the same width as the central block. This is also lower than the roof of the front part, so we will also scale it on the *z* axis (*S* + *Z*) (refer to step **4** of the following screenshot).

5. In the same way, we will make another roof that covers the front portion of the terrace. It will be supported by pillars. We will again duplicate our roof that is cut in half, and we will adjust it according to the dimensions of the front of the terrace. We will remove the top part to form a small balcony (refer to step **5** of the preceding screenshot).

6. For the roof of the rear block, we will slightly change the style with a simple tilted platform. We will change the rear block to bevel it. We will duplicate the top face (*Shift + D*) and make a new object with it (press *P* and select **Selection**). We will need to make an extrusion on the z axis to add a thickness, then we will adjust the size and the position of the wireframe in the **Shading Mode** (refer to step **6** in the preceding screenshot).

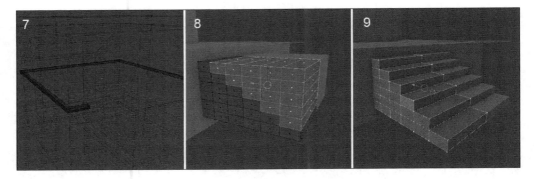

7. We will now mark a boundary of two floors with a concrete ledge. For this, we will need to add a new cube (press *Shift + A* and select **Mesh | Cube**) scaled on the y and x axes (*S + Shift + Z*) to be around the main block. We will give it a height of 15 cm and make it exceed the block by about 20 cm (refer to step **7** in the preceding screenshot). We will do an inset (*I*) on the top and bottom faces, then we will delete the nonvisible faces.

8. Let's form the stairs. We will add another cube, then we will resize it to be 84 cm on the z axis and 1.5 m on the y axis. We will need to divide it into six equal parts horizontally and vertically. In order to gain time, we will add a **Mirror modifier** (refer to step **8** in the preceding screenshot). We will remove the unwanted faces, and then extrude the contour of the top towards the symmetry axis to create the missing faces (refer to step **9** in the preceding screenshot). We will place our stairs in the middle of the front part of the terrace.

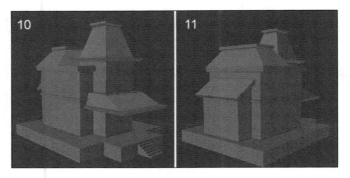

These few simple 3D models done in a short time gives us an idea of what our haunted house will look like with further modeling.

Refining the blocking

Now that we have the foundations of our model, we will go into the details by adding more defined objects.

Adding instantiated objects

If we analyze the majority of the houses, we can see that they are mainly composed of repetitive shapes such as windows and doors.

So we will use the techniques that allow us to duplicate objects by instance. This means that if we change the geometry of the source object, all the duplicates will change too. As you may have understood, this is really useful in order to save time: for instance, with UVs. Now, perform the following set of steps:

1. Let's start with the low wall around the steps. We will add a cube that we will orient with the slope of the stairs.

2. We will add an edge loop in order to break the slope. Then we will add a thinner piece that recovers the slope. To do this, we will extrude the top faces and scale them appropriately on the same level, and we can redo an extrusion.

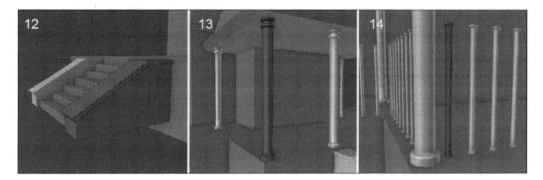

3. In order to mirror the other side of the low wall, we will center the pivot point of the stair object at its center (*Ctrl + Alt + Shift + C* and select **Origin to Geometry**). Now we can safely add a mirror modifier with the stairs as the mirror object (refer to step **12** of the preceding screenshot).

4. Next, we will do the columns that will support the roof that covers the front of the terrace. We will need a 16-face cylinder that is 18 cm wide with a height of 2.8 m. In the last tool options in the left 3D view panel, we will choose the **Nothing** option under **Cap Fill Type**. We will then position it on the left-hand side of the stairs, and we will duplicate it as instances with the **Duplicate Linked** (*Alt* + *D*) function.

5. In the **Object Mode**, we will place our columns at the four corners of the terrace roof. In order to add some details to the columns, we will add some loop cuts (*Ctrl* + *R*) on the top of the roof and extrude the face loops along the normals (*E* + *Alt* + *S*) (refer to step **13** of the preceding screenshot).

Duplicate Linked

This tool allows you to duplicate your 3D model as instances. This means that when you do a modification in the **Edit Mode** on the source object, the transformations are applied to the other duplicated objects in real time. The UVs are also instantiated. However, when you manipulate the object in the **Object Mode**, the changes are not reflected in the other instances.

In order to break the instantiation link, we can use the **Make Single User** menu (**Call Menu** (press *U*) | **Object and Data**).

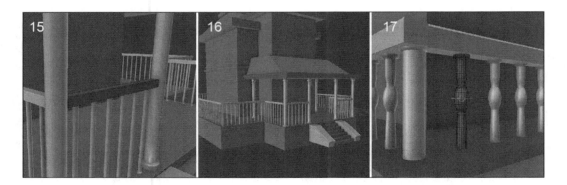

6. We will now work on the bars that delimit the terrace. We will take a new cylinder, this time thinner with a radius of 5 cm and a height of 1.2 m. We will again remove the caps that are pointless here.

7. In order to duplicate our 3D object, we are going to use the Array modifier. We will use a relative offset of 3.100 on the *x* axis. We will take advantage of the replication of the array in order to improve the shape of the bars a little bit with some loop cuts and extrusions (refer to step **14** of the previous screenshot).

8. Since the bars are along a straight line, we will duplicate them with a normal duplicate (*Shift + D*) to place them on each side of the terrace. We will also need to adjust the number of bars to match the surface of the terrace.

The Array modifier

This modifier allows you to duplicate your 3D models with a customizable offset. You only need to choose the number of repeated objects that you need with the **Count** parameter and the distance of the offset (constant or relative) on any axis. You can also automatically merge your duplicated polygons with the **Merge** option.

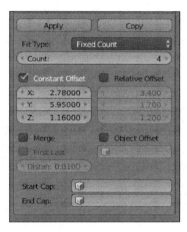

If you want to modify the geometry of a mesh, the array takes the object volume into account, so be careful. A transformation in the **Edit Mode** can change the offset.

9. We will complete this with ramps. The ramp is a simple cube scaled on the *x* axis to make it longer. We will duplicate the ramp as an instance (*Alt + D*) wherever needed, but remember that you need to duplicate with *Shift + D* if you want to do some changes in the geometry (refer to steps **15** and **16** in the previous screenshot).

The Duplicate Linked tool is very useful, but it is not very flexible when we only want to do a transform on certain objects.

1. Let's repeat the same technique to make a balcony railing on the top of the roof that covers the front of the terrace. We are going to change the shape of bars a little (refer to step **17** of the preceding screenshot).

2. We will also use an **Array modifier** to make the wall brackets that will support the different parts of the roof. We will use one Array modifier to make a pair and another to duplicate it with a good offset (refer to steps **18** and **19**).

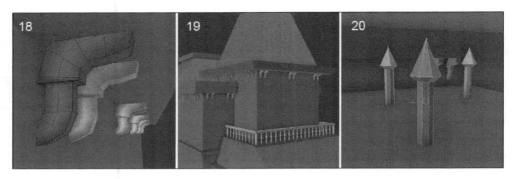

3. The same thing is done for the pikes on the roof that give a threatening look (refer to step **20** in the preceding screenshot).

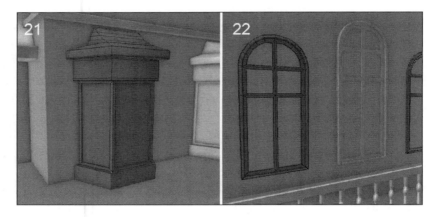

4. The walls are a bit flat at the moment, so we are going to model a bay window with a particular shape (refer to step **21** in the preceding screenshot). We will start with a new cube (press *Shift + A* and select **Mesh | Cube**), and we will resize it on the *x* axis to form the base.

5. We duplicate it to make the top part and add an inset for the frames of the windows. When this is done, we will duplicate it as a new instance (*Alt + D*), and we will place it on both sides of the main block of the house.

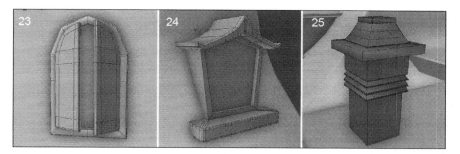

It is also time to make a few conventional old-style windows. We will start with the windows on the front of the house (refer to step **22** in the previous screenshot). Let's start again from a cube:

1. We will delete the left side to use a **Mirror** modifier. From the front view, we will make the shape of the window with a few edge loops (*Ctrl + R*) and add an inset. From this model we will can make the frame and extract the shutters (refer to step **23** in the preceding screenshot).

2. We will create another window model for the roof. We will start its base with a flattened (*S + Z*) and beveled (*B*) cube. The central part is an extruded edge with an inset, and there is a little roof with a curved slope (refer to step **24** in the preceding screenshot).

3. Let's add a fireplace (refer to step **25** in the preceding screenshot). This is also fairly simple to model, starting from a cube that is extruded and scaled. It uses the same basic modeling techniques that we have previously covered.

Reworking the blocking objects

Until now, we had quickly added a series of 3D objects to form a fairly rudimentary house and have a general idea of the entire model of the house. Now we will finish the modeling and review the topology of our models in order to make them more presentable.

There is still a final important object to be made: the front door. It is composed of several 3D objects. There is the frame, door, lock, handle, and there is the top frame with a decorative pattern. The frame and the door are quite similar to the windows. The door will be created as follows:

1. We will use a mirror modifier each time. The lock is quite simple, just an extruded cube with a few **insets** (*I*) (refer to step **23** in the preceding screenshot). For the decorative pattern, we will use a circle in order to get a better round shape.

The rays are extruded and moved by hand. Don't forget to add a few edge loops when you add the **Subsurface** modifier (refer to steps **24** and **25** in the preceding screenshot).

2. We will place the address number of the house. For this, we will use the **Text tool** (*Shift + A* and select **Text**). We will use the basic **Bfont** font of Blender, but you can download and use any font instead. We will use the **Extrude: 2.3 cm** and **Depth: 1.2 cm** parameters to make a small bevel. We will make two small nails to hold them.

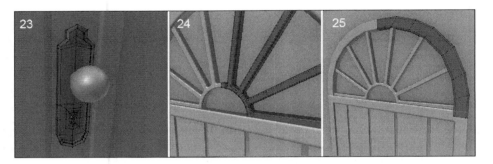

3. We will now review every asset and remove the nonvisible polygons that are useless in our case. Instantiating many of our objects has greatly facilitated the work.

4. We will also often add a **Subdivision Surface** modifier when it's needed.

   But sometimes, this is not the case, as a simple bevel will do the job as well. As always, you need to maintain your geometry with loop cuts or bevels. In both cases, we want to activate the **Smooth Shading** (in the left panel of the 3D viewport).

5. We will also detach some parts of the geometry from other objects. To do this, we will go in the **Edit Mode** and we will select the faces that we want to detach by pressing *P* and selecting **Selection**.

   This will allow us to rework certain objects and add the **Subdivision Surface** modifier with ease. For instance, for the roof, we will detach the center part and add tight edges near the four corners with the **Bevel** tool. We can also increase the windows' resolution by adding and placing some edge loops to form a nice round shape in the corners.

All the improvements that we've done here are, in our case, pretty easy because we don't have to get a realistic result. We are taking a more "cartoony" path, and in the next chapter, we will paint textures by hand in order to add more details.

Breaking and ageing the elements

It's now time to refine some elements in order to give them an old/destroyed look. This will mainly come from the texturing work that we will do later, but we can still work on the geometry a little bit:

1. We will begin by working on the stairs. We will delete the side faces that are invisible. (Refer to step **1** in the following screenshot.)

2. Let's add loop cuts below the angle of each stair. This will allow us to extrude a face in the front direction of the top of each stair. (Refer to step **2** of the following screenshot.)

3. We will then add two edge loops at the center to add more resolution.

4. Now with **Proportional Editing** turned on (*O*), we can select some vertices on the stairs and move them to break the shape a little bit. (Refer to step **3** of the following screenshot.)

5. We will now enter the stair ramps object and delete the one on the left. We will have to delete the invisible faces, those that are in the ground and in the house.

6. After this, we can move the origin back to its center (*Ctrl* + *Alt* + *Shift* + *C*) and duplicate the object (in the **Object Mode**) with *Shift* + *D* in order to move it back to the left-hand side.

7. We can then add definition to the object on the right-hand side with the Loop Cut tool.

8. At the top of the ramp, we will use the **Knife** tool and cut around a loop cut that we had made before. We will then push this hole inwards. (Refer to step **4** in the following screenshot.)

9. We can then repeat this process elsewhere on the other object. (Refer to step **5** in the following screenshot.)

10. The stairs are now finished. (Refer to step **6** in the following screenshot.)

11. We can also add a cut in the back wall of the house and move the vertices a little bit to add some sag.

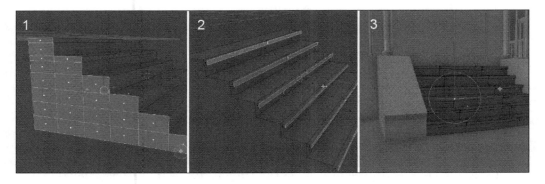

We now encourage you to go over each object and slightly move the geometry, with the **Proportional Editing** tool turned on (*O*), in a random manner in order to break each object's silhouette. You can also rotate the objects, such as the curtains. This is a house that is not new, plus it's probably abandoned!

Simulate a stack of wooden planks with physics

We are now going to add little bit more details by adding a stack simulation of wooden planks in the front of the house. But instead of placing each plank by hand, we will take advantage of the physics engine of Blender that will do the job for us. In order to keep our stack simple and manageable, we will use the instancing principle that we've seen before. Let's start with the modeling of the plank:

1. The plank will be very easy to model by starting with a cube primitive.

2. We will then rescale this cube to make it thinner and larger. Note that if you do this in the **Object Mode**, you will have to apply the scale with *Ctrl + A*.

3. In order that the plank catches the light on its edges better, we will add a small bevel to it. There are two ways of adding bevels in Blender. The first one is the one that we've already used before with *Ctrl + B*. The other method is by adding a **Bevel** modifier. That's what we've done here. Note that if you want, you can apply the modifier too.

4. We will now duplicate the planks by instancing them (*Alt + D*). You need to place them one on top of the other. In order to add a little bit of randomness, we will rotate them slightly in an unordered way.

About the Bevel modifier

The **Bevel** modifier is nice because it is applied on the whole object, so we don't have to manage a lot of geometry while we are in the **Edit Mode**. We can adjust the **Width** slider to tighten or enlarge the effect of the bevel. The **Segments** option allows us to choose the number of cuts the bevel will be made of. The **Profile** of the bevel corresponds to the direction of the bevel; if it's negative, it will go inwards.

Creation of the simulation of a stack of planks

We will now create our simulation. In any rigid body simulation, the objects have some properties that define them. For instance, you can set their mass, velocity, or simply let gravity act on them as the sole force. In any decent physics engine, you can have static and dynamic objects. A static object is an object that, as its name implies, can't move at all but will be considered in the simulation when collisions occur.

A dynamic object is an object that can receive forces. In Blender, static objects are defined as **Passive** and dynamic objects as **Active**.

1. We will select all our planks, and in the **Physics** tab, in the left 3D view panel (*T*), we will press the **Add Active** button. They will have a green outline.

2. Now we will set the ground object as passive by pressing the **Add Passive** button so that the planks don't pass through the house.

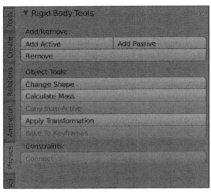

The Physics tab

3. In order to simulate our stack, we will launch the animation. To do this, we will use the *Alt + A* shortcut or press the **Play** button of the **Timeline** editor. Note that if the simulation doesn't seem to launch, you can replace the Timeline bar on the first key frame.

The final stack of wooden planks

4. As you may have seen, there is an orange line on the Timeline that tells us that a simulation has been cached, but as soon as you go backwards in time, the simulation will be removed. So after the simulation has been completed, we will have to apply the placement of each of the planks. In order to do this, we will select them and click on **Apply Transformation** in the **Physics** tab. We can now safely replace the Timeline bar at the first frame, and our stack will rest still.

Modeling the environment (8 pages)

Now that we've finished the house modeling, we will improve our scene with an environment composed of a cliff, a barrier, a cart, and some rocks.

Modeling the cliff

Let's now model the cliff:

1. We will start by modeling its ground part. In order to do this, we add a plane and scale it.
2. We will then move the ground, so the house is placed above it.
3. We will use the scale tool in order to make the ground wider.
4. In the side view, we will enter the **Edit Mode** and activate the wireframe (*Z*). We will select the two vertices in the front of the plane, and by pressing *Ctrl* and the LMB, we will extrude the cliff profile to the left.
5. We will then reshape the geometry from a top view by moving the vertices with the Grab (*G*) tool. The cliff should be narrower where the house is.
6. The whole geometry will then be extruded down to form the height of the cliff.

[Note that you may have the normals of the face pointing inwards causing lighting mistakes. In order to recalculate them, use the *Ctrl + N* shortcut.]

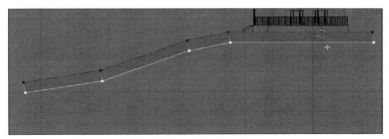

Starting the cliff modeling

7. At this point, we can add some new horizontal loop cuts (*Ctrl + R*) in order to add definition to our model.

Now our goal is to give the impression of a rock with the few polygons that we have. To get the shape, we will go in the top view, and with the wireframe turned on, we will select the edges of the contour of the cliff and move them to form ridges and a valley. This will give an angular look. Remember that all the details will come with the texturing process in the next chapter, so we only have to give the overall shape here.

1. We can improve the model with some randomness. To do this, we go in the **Tool** tab of the left 3D view panel, and under the **Deform** section of the **Mesh Tools** subpanel, we click on **Randomize**. The effect of the tool can be tweaked with the **Amount** slider in the last tool option panel. This tool will simply push all the individual selected components in a random direction.

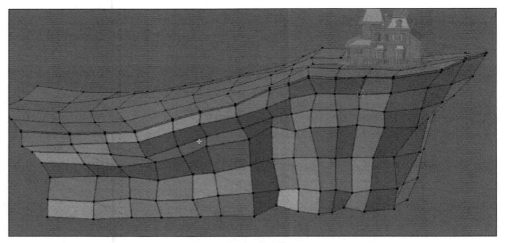

The final cliff

2. Lastly, we can arrange the global shape of our object with **Proportional Editing**. For instance, we can scale the tip of the cliff with it.

Modeling a tree with curves

We are now going to learn a new way of modeling certain objects with curves. Curves are entities that can be useful to model ornaments, shoelaces, ropes, tree branches, and so on. In our case, we will model an entire tree with them.

A word about curves

A curve is defined by control points that are connected together. Each point has a handle type. This can be changed by first selecting the control point that you want and by pressing the *V* key. By choosing the **Vector** type, the point will be angular. We are choosing **Automatic** or **Aligned**, so you will have Bezier handles that define the smoothness of the point. Handles always work in pairs. You can break their link by selecting the handle that you want to disconnect and by pressing *V* and select **Free**. In the beginning, you will find that curves are hard to manipulate, but with a little bit of practice, it will become as easy as pie. But, of course, there is lot more to discover about them!

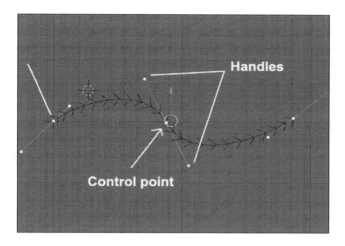

3. We will add a new curve of the Bezier type (press *Shift + A* and select **Curve | Bezier**). Then we will enter in the **Edit Mode**.

4. We will then turn off the handles and the normals of the curve. To do this, we will uncheck the **Handles** and **Normals** check boxes under the **Curve Display** subpanel in the right 3D view panel (*N*).

The Curve display options in the N panel.

5. When you start working on a shape that uses curves, it's easier to set all the control points as **Vector** (press *V* and select **Vector**).

6. Now we will leave the **Edit Mode** and add a new curve object of the bezier circle type (press *Shift + A* and select **Curve | Circle**). This circle will define the volume of our bezier curves.

7. We will select the bezier curve, and in the Properties editor, we will click on the object data icon. Under the **Shape** subpanel, we will then select the circle as the **Bevel Object**. As you can see, the curve is now getting a volume defined by the circle. If you change the circle, its scale, for instance, will change the curve volume.

8. We will then close the holes on each side of the curve by checking the **Fill caps** option under the **Bevel Object** one.

9. We can now modify our curve to form the trunk of the tree. To do this, we can simply vertically rotate the two points that we already have and extrude the tip several times with *E* or press *Ctrl* and LMB. You can also subdivide the curve by selecting at least two consecutive points and pressing *W* and select **Subdivide**.

10. Now we can change the radius of each point by changing its value in the **Transform** subpanel in the left 3D view panel. This is how we will taper the trunk.

11. We can now add new branches to our tree by simply adding a new point by pressing *Ctrl* and LMB without anything else selected. This point could then be extruded.

    We can also change the radius of the branch. If you want to quickly select a branch, you can either select one of its points and press *Ctrl + L*, or select one of its points and press *Ctrl* and the + numpad key several times.

12. We will now add more branches by duplicating the first one that we've created. The process simply involves the duplication and placement of a lot of branches that differ in size and radius.

13. Next, we can convert our curves to a mesh object. In order to do this, we will have to first decrease the subdivision of our branches and our circle profile object by going to their **Object data** tab in the Properties editor and by changing the **Preview U** (for the viewport) and **Render U** (for the final render) sliders. We can now select our curve object and press *Alt + C* and select **Mesh from Curve/Meta/Surf/Text** to convert our curve object into polygonal geometry.

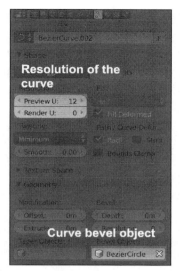

The curves option in the Properties editor

We will now show you how to deform the tree with a special type of object called a lattice. This will serve us to change the overall shape of it.

What exactly is a lattice?

A lattice is a very useful object that is bound to another object. It is a cube that can be subdivided along three axes: U, V, and W. This needs to encapsulate the object to which it is bound. Then, when we move its control points, it performs a sort of a projection that allows us to deform the bound mesh.

The **Lattice** options in the Properties editor.

1. We will add a new lattice by pressing *Shift + A* as usual.

2. Now that we have a new lattice, we can place it around our tree. No geometry should be outside the lattice or it will cause problems.

3. We will now increase the subdivisions of the lattice in U, V, and W to **4**. This will gives us enough control points in order to tweak our tree.

4. Now it's time to bind our lattice to our tree by simply selecting our tree and adding a new **Lattice** modifier. We will now have to specify to Blender the lattice object that we want to bind to our mesh in the **Object** parameter. In our case, we only have one lattice so it's easy to find it in the list, but if you have many lattices, don't forget to name them.

5. We can now enter **Lattice Edit Mode** and move the control points as if they were vertices.

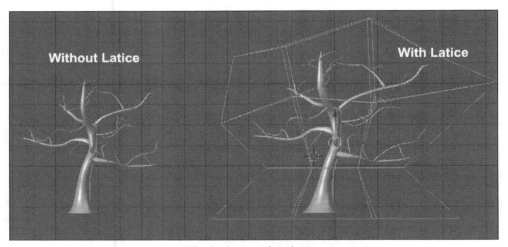

The final tree with its lattice

Enhancing the scene with a barrier, rocks, and a cart

We will now enhance our scene by adding some cool assets using the techniques that we've seen in this chapter:

1. Let's start with the easiest asset, the rock. We will start this element with a cube.

2. Now in **Edit Mode**, we will use the **Subdivide smooth** option (press *W* and select **Subdivide smooth**).

3. In the last tool subpanel of the left 3D view panel, we can tweak the **Fractal** slider in order to add some randomness to the subdivision.

4. We can now repeat steps **2** and **3** several times.

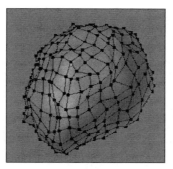

A single rock

5. Now that we have a pretty spherical rock, we will use a **Lattice** modifier to shape it more like a rock. In our case, we will set our lattice with three subdivisions in U, V, and W, and after we've done the job, we will apply the modifier on the rock.

6. We can now use the instance duplication (*Alt* + *D*) tool in order to populate our terrain with rocks. This is a little bit of cheating, but we don't have to do any other objects in order to give the impression that there are many different rocks. Indeed, we can simply rotate and scale the rocks in a random manner! In this case, the Free Rotation tool (press *R* key twice) is quite useful.

The rocks are now placed all around the house.

We will now create a barrier in front of the house with a very nice modifier.

1. We will first add a new cube that we will scale on the *x* and *y* axes to make it thinner.

2. Next, we can select the top face in the **Edit Mode** and move it to change the height of the plank.

3. With the top face selected, we will extrude the top part of the plank and scale it on X.

4. We can then select all the objects (*A*) and use the **Bevel** tool (*Ctrl + B*) to smooth their edges.

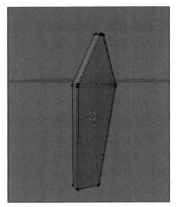

The barrier plank

5. We can now place it on the far left of the cliff in front of the house.

6. The next thing is to use the **Array** modifier in order to do a line of planks to the middle of the house.

7. We can duplicate this barrier piece on the other side.

8. In order to break the boring alignment of these objects a little bit, we will use a path curve (*Shift + A* and select **Curve | Path**) that will guide the planks.

9. The path object looks like a curve. We can select each control point, extrude them, and subdivide them. We will extend the path object from the far left to the far right of the cliff and subdivide it several times (*W* and select **Subdivide**).

10. We can now break the path by moving each control point in a random way.

11. On the barriers, we will add **Curve** modifiers and select our path as the object. In our case, the deformation axis is *x*. Be careful that curve modifier is placed above the array of the stack. Indeed, we want to deform only one plank. As you can see, we now have our barrier following the path.

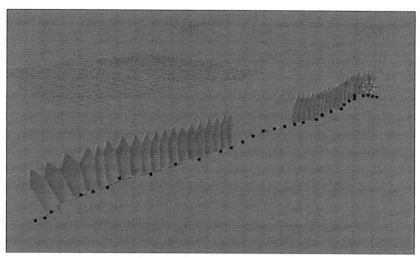

The final barriers with their curve

The following screenshot shows the barrier modifiers:

The barrier modifiers

It's now time to model the cart, which is a more complex object, but still simple to do with all the tools you've learned until now:

1. Let's start by duplicating one of the planks that we used in our physics simulation. This time we want to modify it without breaking the ones that are part of our simulation, so we press the *U* key and select **Object & Data** to make it a single user.

2. We can now use an **Array** modifier to make the bottom part of our cart. We can specify a little margin between each of them.

3. Now we will apply the modifier and tweak each plank so that they don't look the same.

4. We will now add a small cube and change its height. We can break its silhouette a little bit with **Loop Cut** (*Ctrl + R*) that we will move, and finally, add a bevel.

5. Now we can duplicate this object (*Shift + D*) at each corner of the cart.

6. We can now add a small plane that we will extrude by following the outline of the cart. We will add a **Solidify** modifier and apply it.

7. We can now add a new cube that we will shape into handles. As always, it's a matter of loop cuts, bevel, and placement.

8. Now, the last thing we need is two big wheels. To do this, we will add a circle, and in the **Edit Mode**, we will extrude it along the normals (press *E + Alt + S*). We can also extrude the wheel to give it a thickness. Remember to check your normals' orientations and clean them with *Ctrl + N* if needed.

9. Now we will add some radius. To do so, we first select one of the inner faces of the wheel, duplicate it and extrude it. We can select the whole radius and press *P* for **Separate selection**. We will also need to change its pivot point at the center of the wheel (press *Ctrl + Alt + Shift + C* and select **At center**).

10. We then duplicate the wheel with *Alt + D*, and without validating the action, we will press *R* to rotate it. This is because now we can press *Ctrl + R* to repeat the duplication and rotation process. What a time saver!

11. In order to cap the wheel, we will add a cylinder that will be extruded several times.

12. Finally, we can duplicate the wheel on the other side with *Alt + D* and add a cylinder that will connect both wheels. Remember to delete the unneeded faces on each side.

The final cart

As you can see, the items that we created are quite simple, so we encourage you to add more of them, such as a dead trunk or a scarecrow. Be creative, you have all the tools needed to do that yourself.

Organizing the scene

This is maybe the largest scene you have ever made, in terms of details and number of objects. So we will take some time to learn how to organize ourselves in order to have a more manageable scene.

Grouping objects

One interesting thing that Blender has to offer is the grouping tool. Let's see how it is working:

1. We will group objects that have a logical relationship between them. So we first select every part of the house, such as the foundations, the walls, the curtains, and the fireplace, and we will place them in a group by pressing *Ctrl + G*.

2. If we look at the last tool options in the left 3D view panel, we can enter a name for our newly created group.

3. Now we can select barriers and create a new group with them.

4. We'll leave the cliff alone, so we don't have to put it in a group.

5. The rocks will also be part of a group.

6. We will also group all the cart pieces.

Using groups

Groups are very useful as they allow you to organize a scene better. You can see all the groups that are in a scene in the outline by changing the **All Scenes** drop-down menu to **Groups**. Here you can select them, disable their render, and hide them. You can also select one object that is part of a group in 3D view and press *Shift + G* and select **Group** to select all the other objects of the same group. You can add or remove an object from a specific group in the **Object** tab of the Properties editor under the **Groups** subpanel.

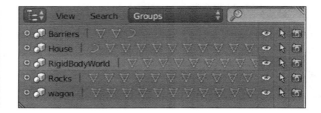

Working with layers

Another thing that can help your scene organization are the layers. They are located in the 3D View header. You can move objects on specific layers with the *M* key. A popup will show you all the layers. You can move an object on multiple layers by pressing shift and selecting the layers that you want. The layers that have objects are marked with a little circle. You can display multiple layers at a time by pressing the *Shift* key and clicking on them in the header bar. Note that you can also see the layers in **Scene** tab of the Properties editor. In our case, the house is on layer one and the other elements on layer two.

Layer one is selected, but we can see that there are objects on layer two

Summary

You have completed the first part of the Haunted House project! You have learned some tricks to save time, such as how to instantiate objects or how to use the array modifier. You have also learned another modeling method with curves. You will clearly see the purpose of duplicating objects by instance in the next chapter where we will UV unwrap the objects. But don't think that it's over with the modeling process here. We can later change our objects after the texturing part in order to break the likeness between each instantiated object. Let's texture our scene!

6
Haunted House – Putting Colors on It

This chapter will be devoted to the texture creation pipeline. We will explain new ways to you for the UV unwrapping processes, such as the **Project From View** or the **Smart UV** method. Then we will cover the basis of the powerful Texture Paint tool in order to create hand-painted textures for our house and environment. You will also learn about the tiling method in order to save time. In order to enhance the final set, we will show you how to create transparent textures, such as grass or grunge to age the house. In this chapter, you will not learn how each object is unwrapped and painted step by step, but you will gain a thorough understanding of the process. Finally, you will learn how to produce a test render with Blender Internal. This will be a good transition to the next chapter. So let's dive into the texture creation process with Blender!

In this chapter, we will cover the following topics:

- Learning the different ways to project UVs on an object
- Painting your model with the Texture Paint tool
- Creating hand-painted and tile-able textures
- Baking diffused textures on proper UVs
- Making transparent textures
- Creating a draft render in Blender Internal

Unwrapping UVs

We will now cover the UV unwrapping process that will later allow us to add textures to our objects.

Using Project From View

In order to quickly unwrap the UVs of the walls of the house, the shape and size of the wall still being accurate, we can use the **Project From View** method.

For this to work, we need to align the walls on the axis of the world coordinates (X, Y, Z). Indeed, we are going to make use of the angle of the 3D View of Blender to project the UVs. So, for each wall, we are going to rotate our view so that the wall that we are going to project is flat. This method only works for objects that are flat and aligned, so don't use it for organic shapes:

1. We will enter the Orthographic mode (5) and then enter the view that corresponds to the face that we want to unwrap. For instance, in order to unwrap the UV of the front wall we go into the front view (1).

2. In the **Edit Mode** and in the **Face Mode**, we will select all the polygons of the 3D model that we want to unwrap and be careful with the beveled parts.

3. In the **UV Mapping** menu (*U*), we will select the **Project From View** option.

    We will obtain a perfect UV Island that is well proportioned according to the mesh. Usually, we don't need to tweak UVs with this method, except when we are willing to scale them. To check the size of our UVs, we will use a UV grid texture.

4. We will create a new editor by selecting **Split Area**, then we will go to **UV/Image Editor**.

5. We will need to create a new image. So we will chose **Image | New Image** and **Generated Type | UV Grid**.

This UV grid allows us to adjust the island's size at the uniform scale for all walls of the house.

We will use **Project From View** for all the walls as well as the big flattened surface such as the platform of the terrace. For the later one, we will avoid having seams that are too visible:

1. We will select all the top faces with the bevel part. We will then go into the top view (*7*), and we will do a **Project From View** unwrap.

2. Still being in the **Project From View**, we will select and unwrap the polygons of the sides, one after the other.

3. To make some seams invisible, we need to weld the vertices of some of the side islands of the platform with the central island. In order to weld the vertices in the **UV/Image Editor**, we will select them and press *W* | **Weld**. This acts like the merge tool in the 3D Viewport but in the UV space.

Unwrapping the rest of the house

For the other parts of the house — that is, the front door, windows, fireplaces, roofs, staircase, columns, bars, railing, and other little objects that form the house — we will place the seams to demarcate the UV islands like we did before with the Alien Character – Creating a Proper Topology and Transferring the Sculpt Details in *Chapter 4, Alien Character – Creating a Proper Topology and Transferring the Sculpt Details*. We keep using the UV Grid to check the scale.

We will start with a pretty simple object, that is, the roof of the front block of the house:

1. We will place the seams to delimit the four sides evenly. We will select the desired edges with a right-click, and then we select **Mark Seam** in the **Edges Menu** (*Ctrl + E*).

2. We will make an automatic unwrap (press *U* and select **Unwrap**) that allows us to reveal the UV without any deformation, but to check this we will use the **Stretch** option in the right panel (press *N* and select **Display | UVs | Stretch**). You will recall that blue means there are no noteworthy deformations.

3. We must keep a little space between the different UV islands. Indeed, we will have a small gap that exceeds the islands later with the baking process. We will need to provide sufficient space in order to not see the seams on the 3D mesh displaying the textures.

4. We will reduce our UV islands and try to keep the same scale for the walls and the platform of the terrace. The position is not important for the moment.

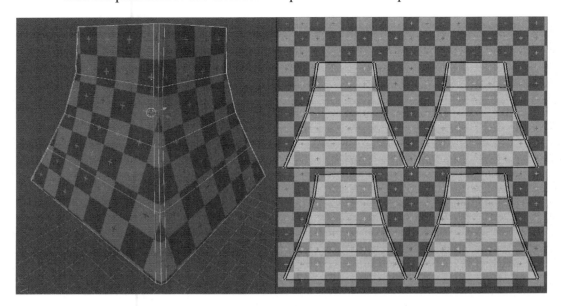

We will continue with a slightly more complex object: the bay window.

You may have observed that the object has formed recurrences. It is angular. So we will avoid laying the seams directly on steep angles and take advantage of the beveled geometry if possible. We will also try to get a UV continuity on the window frame, the lower part and the upper part of the window frame. We must, therefore, make some adjustments after the UV unwrap.

The goal by doing the UV is to try to reproduce a flattened shape of the 3D mesh with the least distortion possible. This is done as follows:

1. We must place the seams at the roof level of the bay window. We will only use seams on this part of the object. We will cut the roof into three parts and three others for the bottom part.

2. As we have detached the other parts of the bay window before, we don't need to place the seams. If, in your case, all the faces are welded, take the time to place the seams.

3. We will select the entire object, and we will perform an **Unwrap** operation (press *U* and select **Unwrap**). This gives us seven UV islands that we can place in a corner for the moment.

We don't have to select all the faces of an object to unwrap the UVs; we can select and unwrap only a few selected faces, but we will lose the scale based on the other faces. This forces us to make some adjustments.

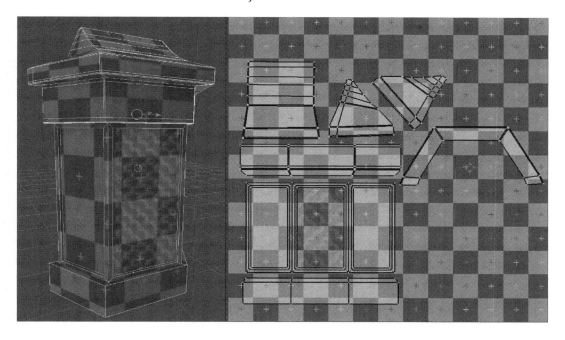

1. We will check whether there are deformations with the **Stretch** option (press *N* and under **Display** select **UVs** and **Stretch**).

2. Now we will align the edges that need to be like the window frame. We will select the edges that must be vertically aligned, and we will scale them on the *x* axis (use the *S*, *X*, and *0* shortcuts).

3. Similarly for the edges that need to be horizontally aligned, we will select them and we will scale them on the *y* axis (use the *S*, *Y*, and *0* shortcuts).

4. Once the object is aligned, we will place a UV Grid texture to check the scale.

Aligning the edges is a process that can be long but it is important to do this for objects such as pipes or angular structures. There are add-ons that can save us some time, such as **Quad Unwrap**.

In this way, we will continue unwrapping the UVs of other objects that compose the house.

The tree with the Smart UV Project

We will now learn a new unwrapping technique with the tree. The tree will be quite far in the scene, so we don't need to have perfect UVs on it. This is why we are going to use an automatic method that Blender provides called the **Smart UV Project**. This is done as follows:

1. In order to unwrap an object with the **Smart UV Project** method, we don't have to put seams on it. So, in order to UV unwrap our tree, we will need to select it entirely in the **Edit Mode**, press *U*, and select **Smart UV Project**.

2. As you can see, we now have the ability to tweak some options. The most useful is **Island Margin**, which allows us to choose how much space there is between each UV Island.

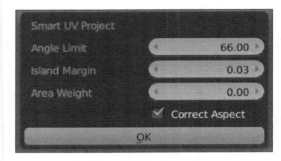

The Smart UV Project options

3. Now we can see our new UVs in the **UV/Image Editor**.

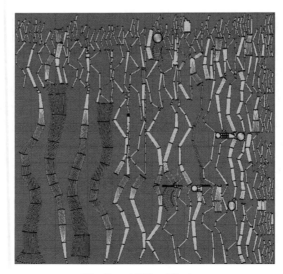

The Smart UVs of the tree

This method is quite useful but not very accurate. It generates a lot of seams that can cause visual artifacts. This is why it is only interesting for objects that are far away, small, blurred (in the depth of field), or with a small number of polygons. In the case of our tree, the wood texture will also be quite repetitive, so this will do the trick!

Unwrapping the rest of the environment

There are other methods to unwrap objects such as cube, sphere, or cylinder projections, but in our case, they won't be very useful. In order to unwrap the rest of the environment, we will use techniques that we have already seen in the Alien project. If you don't remember how to put seams on an object, we encourage you to read *Chapter 4, Alien Character – Creating a Proper Topology and Transferring the Sculpt Details*, again. To refresh our mind, we will just do the cliff together as follows:

1. The cliff will be separated into three islands. The first seam separates the top where the ground will be from the lower section. We simply select a horizontal edge loop near the top and mark it as a seam (*Ctrl + E* and select **Mark seam**).

2. We will now separate the sides into two islands by placing a vertical seam from the front tip to the bottom of the cliff.

3. We will then select our whole object, press *U*, and select **Unwrap**.

4. Lastly, we can rearrange our islands in the **UV/Image Editor** in order to align them vertically.

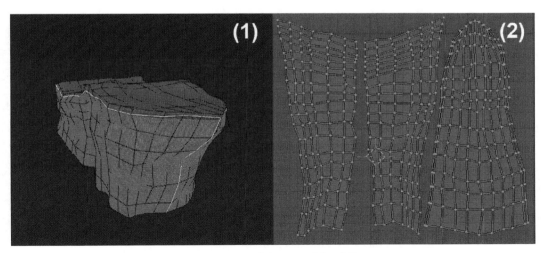

The seams and the UVs of the cliff

Now that you are nearly a pro, you can unwrap the rock and the barrier alone by following the same method.

Tiling UVs

Now comes the interesting part! We will show you a very useful technique in order to save time with the texturing process, so we won't have to paint our objects entirely. So let's learn a little bit more about tiling.

What is tiling for?

The main goal of tiling is to allow a texture to repeat itself on the mesh. For instance, in the case of a very large wall, it would be very tedious to paint each brick one by one over the entire wall. So what is preferable to do is to use a "tile-able" texture and scale the UV islands. Scaling the islands will simply repeat the texture. Later, we will show you how to paint a tile-able texture within Blender. If you remember the UV unwrapping part of the alien project, we had mentioned that all the islands will be placed in the UV finite space. This was because we didn't want repeated textures. But in this project, we can use this to our advantage. But it doesn't mean that we won't keep our UV islands in the finite UV space too. This is why we are going to need different UV coordinates on each object.

The UV layers

As we said before, we need to find a way to keep our proper UV (in the UV "square") and create a new set of UVs. Blender allows us to use multiple UV layers on each object. We can use a layer when we want to have another UV layout while maintaining the UV that we've already done before. It is similar to storing different UVs on the same object. We will show you how to create a new layer that will contain the scaled islands for tiling. As this will be the same for many objects, we will just show you the method for the wall of the house, and let you repeat the process for the rest of the objects:

1. We will select the wall and enter **Edit Mode**.

2. We will then click on the **Object Data** icon in the **Properties** editor, and under the **UV Maps** subpanel, we will click on the + (plus) icon. This will create a copy of the current UV set of our object.

3. We will now need to change the UVs on this particular layer. Be sure that it is selected, and in the **UV/Image Editor**, scale the current UVs with the *S* key. You can always check the tiling effect with a checker. Our wall has now two sets of UVs.

The UV layers options

There are very few options to manage our different sets of UVs. The first one is the little camera icon that tells Blender which UV set should be used at render time and the second one is the ability to rename a set by double clicking on its name. The only thing that you need to think about is which set to select.

Now that you know the technique, you can add a **Tiling** UV set for each object.

Adding colors

Now that we have the proper UVs on our objects, let's dive into the fun part, that is, the texturing. It is the more artistic part of the process, so let's start by discovering the Texture Paint tool of Blender.

Basics of the Texture Paint tool

The **Texture Paint** tool is a mode that allows you to paint directly on a 3D object in the 3D Viewport while applying color to the texture. This requires having textures with a sufficiently high resolution. One of the interesting points is to paint on a 3D polygonal mesh with a low density.

To observe the paint of our textures in 2D, we need to split the 3D Viewport in two and switch the second type editor to **UV/Image Editor**.

To activate this, we first select an object, click on the **Mode** drop-down menu in the **Header**, and switch to the **Texture Paint** mode.

If you don't have any UVs, a message will warn you in the left panel (*T*) of the 3D Viewport. You can generate UVs automatically with the **Add Simple UVs** option, but it is much better to unwrap them yourself as we saw earlier.

In the **Slots** tab, there is an important parameter, that is, the **Painting Mode**. It gives a choice between two options. The **Material** option allows us to paint automatically linked textures to a material in Blender Internal. The **Image** option allows us to paint the texture without necessarily having a material linked to the object. For this first approach of the Texture Paint tool, we will be especially interested in the **Material** option.

If in **Texture viewport** Shading Mode (Z) your object displays a pink color and you see the message **Missing Data** in the left panel (T). Select **Tools**, to correct this; you will need to click on the **Add Paint Slot** option. Here, several texture types are available. This will automatically create a texture corresponding to a slot of the material with the required settings during the painting phase.

We can start testing a **Diffuse Color** map. Several options are proposed. They are the same as when we create a new texture. You can rename the texture and choose the height, the width, and the color with an alpha value. You can also choose whether you want an alpha layer (it is the opacity), the type of texture to generate, and finally, the 32-bit float option. Press **OK** to create this texture. A new material is then automatically created if there are none of them. You can visualize it in the **Material** editor on the right-hand side of the work space.

To modify this, you can change the name with a double left-click on the name.

It is possible to create several stacked textures one above the other like layers in the material. You must select the one that you want to paint in the **Slots** tab of the left panel. The bottom slot is the one that is first visible. You can also choose the Blend Type to mix pixels. There are the usual Blend Types (add, subtract, multiply, and so on.) that we can find in every decent image editing software. The **Slots** tab allows us to also change the UV layers, which can be very useful.

Now that you know the basics to generate and manage a texture for painting, we will look at the brushes.

Discovering the brushes

As in the **Sculpt Mode** that we saw previously, we have multiple brushes in order to paint our texture. They all have some specific purpose that we will test on a simple sphere object in a new scene file. Be aware that the goal here is not to do something beautiful but to test our brushes.

The TexDraw brush

This is the brush that allows us to paint the desired color in a localized manner.

You can use the blender mode in order to create effects. For instance, the **Add** mode is very useful for lighting texturing effect (refer to **1** on the following screenshot).

The Smear brush

The Smear brush allows us to move the color while blurring it. It is very useful to create some blown or flame painting effects. If you change the strength parameter to a higher value, you can stretch your paint to a higher distance (refer to **2** on the following screenshot).

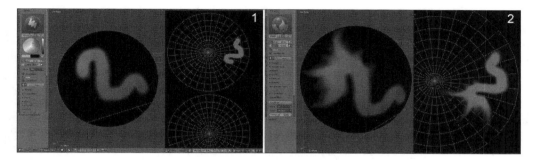

The Soften brush

This brush allows us to blur the painting. It is useful to mix the colors and create gradients (refer to **3** in the following screenshot).

The Clone brush

This brush allows you to copy a specific zone on another place. This is very useful when you need to fill some untextured space or when you want to correct the seams. You select the zone that you want to copy by placing the 3D cursor on it with *Ctrl* and LMB (refer to **4** in the following screenshot).

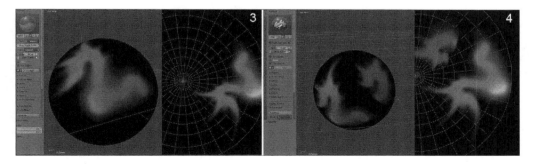

The Fill brush

This is a new brush that Blender has had since version 2.72. This brush allows us to fill the whole object with the selected color. With the **Use Gradient** option, you can do a gradient that stretches over the whole object. Remember to set the strength parameter to **1** to have a sufficient opacity. A line under the mouse cursor will inform you where the start and the end of the gradient will be. You can also use the **Multiply Blend** mode while using it (refer to **5** in the following screenshot).

The Mask brush

As with the **Sculpt Mode**, it is possible to mark a zone that you want to avoid painting. To do this, you will create a stencil image. Don't worry, Blender will ask you to create the image as soon as you create a mask, if it can't find one. You only need to click on the **New** button or select a preexisting image in the .blend file and validate the image settings like we are used to. To clear a masked part, press *Ctrl* and LMB. To remove your mask, you can remove the mask option in the **Slot** tab. Be aware that the masks are not visible in **Material Viewport Shading Mode** (refer to **6** in the following screenshot).

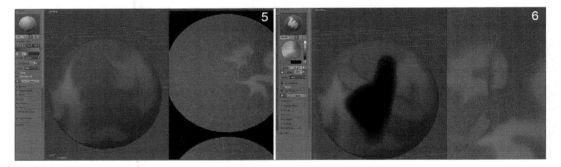

If you have a pen tablet, you can check out the small button on the right of the radius and strength parameters (an icon with a hand). This allows you to vary the amplitude of the parameter according to the pressure sensitivity of your stylus.

The Stroke option

The **Stroke** option allows us to completely modify the brushes' behavior. It is, therefore, important to focus on this for a little while.

First of all, there is the **Stroke Method** option that allows us to choose among several methods for applying the colors:

- **Space**: This is the basic method with a variable dot space.

- **Curve**: This is a new method since Blender 2.72 that allows us to paint in a well-defined curve with controllable points. Press *Ctrl* and left-click to create the points defining the curve. Each point can be controlled with the transform tools: Grab (*G*), Scale (*S*), and Rotate (*R*). In order to apply your painting, you need to press *Return*.

- **Line**: This method simply allows you to draw lines. You must do a pushed left-click to draw the line from one point to another. The paint is then projected onto the 3D mesh.

- **Anchored**: This allows you to drag your stroke. You first need to select the placement of the stroke or the texture you want to paint, and then, without releasing the mouse, you will be able to control its scale. This method is especially interesting when projecting a texture.

- **Airbrush**: This method could be used to project a multitude of little spots, for instance, you can change the radius so that it is smaller with **Rate** of **0.10** and **Jitter** of **2**. It is useful to create skin textures, for example.

- **Drag Dots**: This allows you to paint points or spots by placing them one by one.

- **Dots**: With a **Jitter** parameter at **0**, you get a textured line to paint. With a **Jitter** parameter at **1**, you will get a multitude of spots.

There is another key element that will determine the settings of your brush. It is the curve located just below the **Stroke** tab. It works exactly in the same manner as the **Sculpt** mode that we saw previously. Depending on whether you want a hard or thin brush to paint the details, remember to use and test several curve profiles. There are already several predefined shapes that can meet your needs.

Delimiting the zones of painting according to the geometry

So that we paint in a precise manner, it is possible to limit the zone that we want to paint by selecting polygons.

After you have selected the desired faces in the **Edit Mode**, you can go to **Texture Paint** and check the **Face Selection Masking for Painting** button on the left-hand side of the layers in the 3D View header. The icon shows a small cube with a checker pattern on a side.

You can now paint without fear of overflow.

Painting directly on the texture

If for any reason you have difficulties when painting directly on the mesh in the 3D View, you can also paint on the texture.

You simply need to select your texture in the **UV/Image Editor**, click on the **Mode** drop-down menu, and choose **Paint**. The **View Mode** is the one by default.

You have all the painting tools that you already know in the left panel (*N*). For your comfort, you can always set your view in full screen with *Shift + Space*.

Painting the scene

We are now ready to apply what we've learned previously about the **Texture Paint** tool on our haunted house. Let's start!

Laying down the colors

For any image that uses colors, it is necessary to lay down a color palette. This means that we will need to find the colors that will make up our image. In our case, for the house, we have chosen the following color codes:

- R: 0.259 – G: 0.208 – B:0.149
- R: 0.180 – G: 0.141 – B: 0.102

- R: 0.149 – G: 0.102 – B: 0.082
- R: 0.337 – G: 0.318 – B: 0.310
- R: 0.188 – G: 0.145 – B: 0.055
- R: 0.251 – G: 0.192 – B: 0.075
- R: 0.780 – G: 0.596 – B: 0.231
- R: 0.212 – G: 0.267 – B: 0.373
- R: 0.176 – G: 0.063 – B: 0.067

We have the ability to create a color palette by clicking on the + (plus) button near the color wheel. However, in order to have an idea of the whole color scheme, we will start by fulfilling the 3D mesh that we had unwrapped object with the colors. This is done as follows:

1. We will select one of our objects.
2. We will split our screen into two, and we will open **UV/Image Editor**, if it's not already the case.
3. In the **Edit Mode**, we will move the UV in a corner. We will keep a space for a margin, and we will not place our UVs too close to the border.
4. We will create a new diffuse map with a resolution of 4096x4096.
5. With the Fill brush, we will apply the corresponding base color for the object.
6. We will select another 3D mesh.
7. In the **Edit Mode**, we will select **Diffuse Map** for this mesh, and we will move the UV near the UVs of the previous mesh. This will be easy as you will see the previous fill.
8. Again, with the fill brush, we will apply our color for this new object.

We redo these steps for all the objects. Since our objects' UVs are proportionally scaled, their size should be sufficient in order to place the maximum number of objects on the same diffuse map.

Be careful to not select the tiling layer for the UVs while filling your objects.

Tiled textures

It's now time to take advantage of our tiled UVs by painting our own tiled textures by hand! In this section we are going to show you how to create the roof texture step by step, and as the process will be very similar for the wood plank, ground, brick wall, and rock texture, we will only give you some advice in order to get a nice result. So let's get started by setting up our painting environment.

The settings of our workspace

One of the strengths of the Blender painting tool is to be able to paint in the **UV/Image Editor** in such a way that the strokes that you paint repeat themselves on the borders.

1. We will first open the **UV/Image Editor**, and make it full screen by pressing *Ctrl + Space* while hovering over it. After that we will create a new 1024 x 1024 Texture with a greyish dark blue color (**Image | New Image**).

2. We now need to enter the **Paint** mode by choosing it in the header drop-down menu. By default the mode is set to **View**.

3. Now we will activate the **Wrap** option in the **Option** tab of the **UV/Image Editor** (*T*). This allows our stroke to repeat to the other side while painting on an edge.

4. Another nice feature is to check the **Repeat** option located in the Right panel (**N**) under the **Display** subpanel. It allows us to see the tiling effect.

5. Let's try this by painting on our texture with the basic brush and a different color. As you can see our strokes are repeated and we can see the tiling effect! Press *Ctrl + Z* to undo your testing strokes.

The **Wrap** option in the **Options** tab

Advice for a good tiled texture

Before starting the painting of our roof texture, we will give you some good advice that can lead you with a nice tiled texture. We first need to remember that the goal of a tiled texture is to give the impression of a pattern that repeats on a surface but in real life, even with a perfect wall pattern for instance, we can see differences between each brick. That's why we need to have a pretty homogenous texture.

We will need to balance the contrast of our tints so they don't disturb our eyes after the tiling. Another important thing to remember is that the pattern should be repetitive in some way. We cannot paint a computer keyboard texture in a tileable manner for instance, because the keys are not the same size and don't contain the same letters. But it can work with a lot of things such as a brick wall, concrete, wood, and so on. We also need to think about the scale of the elements that compose the pattern. For instance, in the case of our roof tiles, we don't want to have one that is very small compared to the others; it will break the illusion of repetition. So now that we know the pitfalls of the tiled texture art we can start working on our roof-tiled texture.

Painting the roof-tile texture

Let's start our roof tile texture from the texture that we've created in the **UV/Image Editor** in the previous section.

1. Before starting to paint our texture we will change our curve to be a little bit pointier. We can easily select a curve preset in the **Curve** subpanel.

2. The first thing that we need to lay down is the tile pattern. In order to trace that we will use the same tint as the background color that we chose when creating the texture but darker. We then re-size our brush size (*F*) and start to paint a row of 'U' shapes for the first top tiles. We need to space them proportionally according to the size of our texture. For the next rows we will do the same thing with a little offset. The top-left part of the 'U' shape needs to touch the middle of the above ones. Note that if you are lost while having the repeat option activated, you can always help yourself with small helping markers that you can erase later (refer to **1** in the following screenshot).

3. Now that we have the basic pattern drawn, we can start to add a little bit more detail with the shadows. For this we are going to select a darker color, but still in the blue shades. Because shadows will be faded, we are going to decrease our strength a little bit (*Shift + F*). Here, the shadows that we are going to paint are projected because of the tiles that are placed above. This will act like contact shadows (refer to **2** in the following screenshot).

4. Now that we have our shadows we can start to add some scratches on the tip of each tile. You need to remember the fact that it needs to be as homogeneous as possible, so don't paint big scratches or it will break the tiling effect (refer to **2** in the following screenshot).

5. The last thing that we are lacking here is some highlights. When painting highlights we use a white color and decrease our strength and size. We then slightly paint the highlights where we think we have hard edges. For instance we can emphasize the scratches (refer to **2** in the following screenshot).

6. That's all, you've now completed your first hand-painted texture (refer to **3** in the following screenshot).

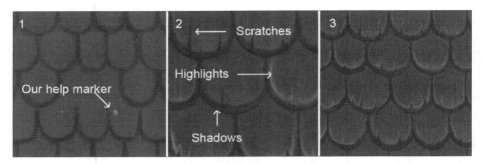

Steps for the roof tile texture creation

Quick tips for other kinds of hand-painted tiled textures

We aren't going to show you step by step how to do each tiled texture as it would require a lot of space and it would be a very repetitive task. Indeed when we are doing such a texture we first always create a texture with a flat color, and then lay down the pattern with a darker color. Once we are satisfied with the pattern and the way it tiles, we add the shadows, more details, and finally the highlights (the specularity).

As you can see on the wood texture, it is quite difficult to add the ribs and having a good tiling, so later we will need to take this problem into account on the objects that will receive the texture. But we can't add ribs on wood or it will look strange. For the ground we can add a little bit more detail, such as small rocks and crackles. The bricks are quite easy to do, but if you feel you can add more detail, you can easily paint moss between each brick.

Examples of other tiled textures painted in the **UV/Image Editor**

Baking our tiled textures

We are now going to project our tiled textures on other textures that correspond to the UVs of our different objects.

Why bake?

As we saw it with the Alien character, texture baking is very useful in order to capture relief, shadow, or color information. In the case of our haunted house, we are going to capture the color information of the tiled textures in order to have them on a large texture with the proper UVs. This lets us achieve our tiled patterns on one big map in order to add all the tweaks that we want later on. We could for instance paint the window contact shadows, add some grunge, and age our objects.

In our scene we aren't going to bake everything. So some objects are still going to use their tiling UV layer. It will simplify our work and still leave us with a nice result.

How to do it?

To obtain a successful bake, the manipulations will be quite similar to what we've done with the normal and ambient occlusion map of the alien. We will start by doing the baking of the walls.

1. We select our walls joined as one object and we go into **Edit Mode**.

2. In the UV Map subpanel under the **Data** tab we click on the camera icon on the right of the Tiling layer. This will tell Blender to use this layer for the render and baking process. We then select the first layer in order to project the details on it with the proper UVs that are normalized.

3. Still being in **Edit Mode**, we create a new map that we call **Color_walls_01** with a 4096 x 4096 resolution. We also un-check the **Alpha** checkbox. This image will contain the result of our bake.

4. We now go to the **Bake** tab from the **Render** tab.

5. Under the **Bake** button we select **Texture** as the **Bake Mode.**

6. In the **Margin** option we choose **10px.**

7. Repeat those steps with the objects that share the same UV space.

8. We can now click on **Bake** in order to start the process. Voilà! Your baked texture is now ready to be placed as a diffuse color texture on a material.

Creating transparent textures

One thing we haven't learnt until now is how we can produce texture with an alpha channel. Indeed this could be very useful in order to add some details on the previously baked texture (grunge or leaks, for instance) or even grass.

The grass texture

Usually, when doing grass, fur, or hair, we use the integrated particle hair system of Blender, but in our case we will show you a technique that can do the job as well and can save us render time. It will also accommodate very well with the style of our scene. This technique will simply consists of a plane mesh on which some grass strands will be projected; using the alpha we will be able to just render the strands. Note that this is a very common technique in the video game industry. So let's start our grass texture by first setting up our transparent texture!

1. We will first go in the **UV/Image Editor** and create a new texture. In the color setting of the texture, we will change the alpha channel to **0** in order to have a full transparent image. We then leave the 1024 x 1024 resolution and validate our settings.

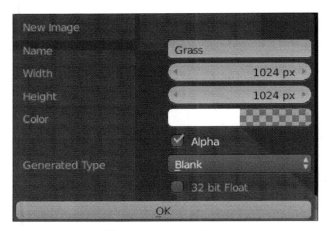

The grass texture settings

2. We can now use a pointy curve and start to paint some strands starting from the bottom of the texture to the top with a de-saturated green. We really need to think about painting a dense grass mound.

3. In order to add more realism to our grass texture, we can add some touch of yellow. We also need to add some white on the tip of each strand. It is quite important to use a reference when painting some textures; it helps to develop our sense of perspective and come with more believable results.

4. Remember to save your texture on your hard drive or you will lose it (**Image | Save as image**)!

5. We can now place our texture on a new plane (*Shift + A*). We do a quick UV on it by simply pressing *U* and selecting **Unwrap** in the **Edit Mode**.

6. We will now create a new material that will use our texture. To do that, go to the **Material** icon in the **Properties** editor and press the plus icon. If you already have a default material, you can delete it with the minus icon.

7. So our material can understand the alpha channel, we will have to activate the check box of the **Transparency** subpanel and select the **Z-Transparency** mode with its Alpha value set to **0**.

8. Now we will tell our material to use our grass texture. To do this we click on the texture icon of the **Properties** editor and click on the first available texture slot. Under the **Image** subpanel we click on the far left drop-down menu and select our grass texture. The last thing we need to do is to activate and set the **Alpha** slider under the **Influence** subpanel to **1.0**.

9. We can have a preview of our texture in the 3D Viewport by activating the GLSL mode in the right panel of the 3D View (*N*) under **Shading**. Note that you will need to be in the **Texture** Shading mode (located under the **Viewport shading** drop-down menu in the 3D View header) and you also need to have lights.

10. We can now duplicate the plane object as an instance to have more grass. Note that you can also add a subdivision to the plane and in the last tool options you can change the **Fractal** slider in order to add a little bit of randomness. Remember that the render in the viewport is a preview, not the final render.

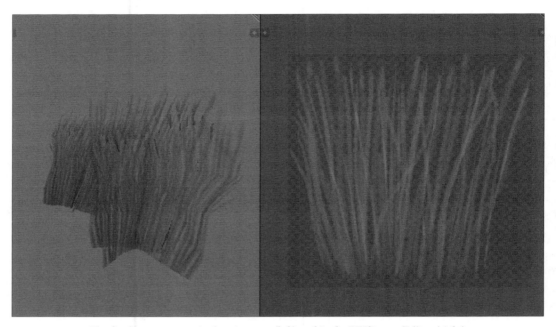

The final grass texture in the viewport (left) and in the **UV/Image Editor** (right)

More about the color wheel window

When selecting a color in Blender we have many options. You can of course select the color that you want with the color circle or by changing the slider's values. In **RGB Mode** we can act on each red, green, and blue component plus on the Alpha channel. In **HSV Mode** we can change the hue (the tint), the saturation, and the value of the color. If you put the saturation down to **0** the color will be on a gray scale. The **Hex Mode** allows you to type a hexadecimal value such as FFFFFF (white) or FF0000 (red). Hexadecimal simply means that instead of counting from 0 to 9 we count from 0 to F. It represents 16 possible values. The easy thing to remember when dealing with hexadecimal colors is that the first two digits represent the Red value, the next two digits represent the green, and the last two represent the Blue: RR GG BB. FF is the full color, 00 means no color. For instance 00FF00 is full green.

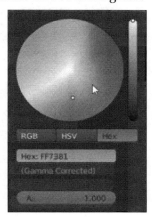

The grunge texture

The grunge texture will be useful in order to add details on the wall texture of the house. The technical process is the same as the grass texture. For the painting we simply use a dark brown color and paint some vertical leaks from the top to the middle of the texture.

Now we can stamp this texture on our wall.

1. We select the wall and ensure that its baked texture is selected in the **UV/ Image Editor** while being in **Edit Mode**. Another thing you may want to do if you are still in **GLSL** mode is to create a new material with the baked texture set.

2. In order to paint our leaks we will use the **Anchored** stroke method located in the **Stroke** subpanel. It allows us to precisely place our leaks near the top and the bottom of the wall.

The grunge placed on the house in the viewport (on the left) and the grunge in the **UV/Image Editor** (on the right)

Doing a quick render with Blender Internal

Welcome to the bonus section! Here we are going to do a quick render with the Blender Internal render engine to get an idea of what the whole scene will look like. Note that this is totally optional as we are going to create a render with cycles later. In order to do our render, we will need to add a material for each object in the scene like we did for the walls but with their corresponding textures.

Setting lights

Now that we have all our materials created we will need to turn up the lights! Of course if you don't have light you won't see anything like in the real world.

1. We add a sun lamp (press *Shift + A* and select **Lamp | Sun**) and change its color to a grayish yellow in the light settings situated in the **Properties** editor. We leave its energy to a value of **1**. We place it behind the house and rotate it so it hits the back of the house.

2. The next light we will add is point light. This one is going to be much more intense so we bump up the energy value to **20** and also change its color to a light yellow. This one will fill the scene a little bit more.

3. Now we need to add lights behind the house to fake the lighting of the windows. In total we added three yellowish point lights with a value of **10** for their energy.

4. The last point light we can add will be near the camera, so we would have to place it correctly after choosing our point of view. This light allows us to see a little bit more of the close environment.

5. If you want to see the lighting effect in the viewport, it is best to turn off the **Texture Shading** mode and the **GLSL** option.

The final light placement

Placing the camera

We can now choose our point of view, by moving our camera. If you don't have a camera, you can add one (press *Shift + A* and select **Camera**). You can also add many cameras and switch between them by selecting the one you want to look through and pressing *Ctrl + P*. In order to look through your camera in the viewport you can press the *0* numpad key. Usually it's a good habit to change the focal length of your camera in the Camera setting tab in the **Properties** editor (click on the Camera icon). In our case we wanted a fleeting camera so we set a focal length of 20mm.

Setting the environment (sky and mist)

Now in order to improve our render we will change the sky color and add a mist.

1. To do that we go into the world settings in the **Properties** editor (click on the earth icon).

2. Under the World subpanel we check the **Paper sky** and **Blend sky** option; we change the **Horizon color** to a dark brown color and the **Zenith color** to an even darker color. It's not realistic, but this image is not intended to be realistic.

3. We can now check the **Ambient Occlusion** checkbox and set it in the **Multiply** mode.

4. The **Environment Lighting** option will serves to light the scene with the **Sky Color** option (and not **White**, the default option).

5. Lastly we can activate the **Mist** subpanel and change the **Depth** parameter to **30m**. We also set the start option to **0**. You may have to tweak those values in order to match your own scene.

6. Now you can press the **Render** button in the **Render** tab of the Properties editor or press *F12*. Note that if you want to improve your render with some automatic compositing you can go to the **Scene** tab of the **Properties** editor and under **Color Management** you can use a look preset; you won't have to re-render your scene! You can also tweak **Exposure**, **Gamma** and change the **CRGB** (Contrast, Red, Green and Blue) curve by clicking on the **Curve** checkbox. As you can see, you render is displayed in a **UV/Image Editor**, so you can save your image (**Image | Save Image as**). Congratulations, you've done your first render of the haunted house!

The world settings

The final haunted house after the Blender Internal render will look like the following screenshot:

Summary

In this chapter you completed the UVs and the textures of the scene. You have learned a technique to paint textures by hand with the Texture Paint tool of Blender and how to create and use tileable textures. You also learned more about baking. Now that we have introduced the rendering process with the Blender Internal render engine, we can start to learn more about the other render engine called Cycles, which has different approach. So let's dive into Cycles!

7
Haunted House – Adding Materials and Lights in Cycles

This chapter will be devoted to the Cycles render engine. You will learn how to achieve a convincing render of the haunted house by understanding the different types of light work and by creating complex materials using the previously made textures. You will learn some nice tricks such as how to produce normal maps of our hand-painted textures without leaving Blender or how to create realistic-looking grass. You will also discover how to use the Cycles baking tool. In order to conclude our project, we will show you how to integrate a mist effect in the final composition.

In this chapter, we will cover the following topics:

- Understanding the essential settings of Cycles
- Using lights
- Painting and using an Image Base Lighting
- Creating basic materials with nodes
- Using procedural textures
- Baking textures in Cycles for real-time rendering

Understanding the basic settings of Cycles

To switch to the Cycles render engine, you must select it in the list of proposed engines that Blender offers in the menu bar. We will see in the first part of this chapter some of the very useful settings that should be known while using Cycles.

The sampling

If you directly try to make a render with Cycles without changing the parameters of Blender, you will certainly see some noise in the image. To make this less visible, one of the first things to do is change the sampling settings. Unlike Blender Internal, Cycles is a Raytracer Engine. While rendering, Cycles will send rays from the camera in order to generate pixels. The noise is due to a small amount of the samples. Cycles, therefore, needs more samples; the more sampling, the more accurate the final render.

The following sampling settings are in Properties editor. Just select
Render | Sampling:

- **Render samples**: This is the number of samples for your renders. The more samples you add, the longer the rendering time will be.

- **Preview samples**: This is the number of samples Blender will calculate to preview your scene in the 3D viewport in Rendered Viewport Shading. A value between 20 and 50 samples is correct. This value depends on the performance of your computer.

The Render sample must be higher than the Preview sample.

The GPU device

If you have a fairly recent CUDA®-compatible graphic card, you can opt for GPU rendering. This allows you to make renders very quickly and visualize your scene in the 3D viewport nearly in real time.

For this, go to **User Preferences | System | Computer Device** and select **CUDA**. Then, in **Properties**, go to **Render | Device** and select **GPU**.

Note that the most recent AMD GPU has been supported since Blender 2.75.

Clamp direct and indirect

This allows us to clamp the intensity of the rays of light launched from the camera. This can also help to reduce the noise effect, but it blurs the pixels together.

Light path settings

You will find the following light path settings in the menu:

- **Max and Min Bounces**: This is the number of minimum and maximum bounces a ray of light can do in the scene to render a pixel. This mimics the way photons bounce from objects in real life. The higher the value of the maximum bounce, the greater the precision will be, and the quality of the rendering will increase. A high value of minimum bounce will also improve the quality but may considerably increase the rendering time. It is advisable to set the same minimum and maximum value.

- **Filter Glossy**: This will blur glossy reflections and reduce the noise effect. You can put a 1.0 value.

- **Reflective and refractive caustics**: Caustics are light effects related to transparent and reflexive materials. We can observe this light effect with diamonds, for instance. This uses a lot of resources and generates some noise. By unchecking these two options, you can completely turn off these effects during rendering. In the case of our haunted house scene, we are going to disable them.

Performances

You will find the following performance settings in the menu:

- **Viewport BVH Type**: There are two types of this: **Dynamic** and **Static**. This is a way to let Cycles remember some of its rendering calculations for the next render. The **Static** option is highly recommended to optimize the rendering time, if you have no more polygonal modifications in your scene. Otherwise, you can use the **Dynamic** mode.

- **The Tiles**: This helps to manage the pixel groups that are to be rendered. So you can control their size along the x and y axes and also control the method to render the image (if you prefer to start rendering through the center of the image, or from left to right, and so on). The size of the pixel group to be rendered should be chosen according to your machine settings. If you are rendering with your CPU, you can choose a smaller tile size than if you were rendering with your GPU.

For more information, you can have a look at the official Blender manual at these addresses:

```
http://www.blender.org/manual/render/cycles/settings/
integrator.html
```

```
http://wiki.blender.org/index.php/Dev:2.6/Source/Render
```

Lighting

We are now going to look at a very important aspect of the rendering process: the lighting. Without lights, you won't see any objects, as in the real world. Good lighting can be hard to achieve, but it can give a nice atmosphere to the scene. One of the things that is true with a scene with good light is that you won't even notice the lights as they look like natural lighting. In order to get our lighting job done correctly, we are going to add a basic shader to every object in our scene.

Creating a testing material

Let's add a very basic material with Cycles in order to see the effects of the lights. In order to better understand the lights in the next section, we are going to create a blank scene and test our lights on a cube that is laid on a plane:

1. Let's start by creating a new scene and by adding a plane scaled ten times (**S > 10**) under the default cube.

2. We also want to delete the default light and turn the Cycles render engine on.

3. We aren't going to explore material creation in depth for now, so we advise you to follow these steps in order; later you will have more information about this process. We need to select the cube and open the **Material** tab of the **Properties** editor.

4. Now we will create a new material slot by clicking on the **New** button.

5. Under the **Surface** subpanel, we will click on the color and change its value to **1.0** in order to have a full white color. That's all for the material. It will be a handy material to test the different types of light.

6. The last thing we need to do is to add the same shader to the plane. To do this, we can copy the material of the cube. We will first select the object (or objects) to which we want to copy the material, in our case, the plane, and then we will select the object that owns the material that we want to copy. Then we will press *Ctrl + L* and select **Material**. The plane should now have the same white material.

Understanding the different types of light

The goal of this section is to understand how each type of light can affect our objects in a scene. We will give you a brief explanation and a short preview of what effects they can provide you with:

1. Before our tests, we will need to change the world shader that contributes to the lighting of the scene. If you press *Shift + Z* or change the **Viewport** Shading mode to **Rendered** in the 3D View header, you can see what the scene will look like, but you will see it in real-time in the viewport. Here you can clearly see the objects even if we don't have any lights. That's because the background color acts as if there was an ambient lighting.

2. If we go into the world settings of the Properties editor and change the Surface color to black, we will not see anything.

3. We can now add a light and have a better understanding of its effect without being disturbed by the world shader.

The settings of the lights can be found under the **Object Data** tab of the Properties editor (a yellow dot with a ray icon) while the light is selected. There are five types of lights (but four work in Cycles) that have many options in common: **Size** influences the hardness of the shadows they produce on objects and **Max Bounces** tells Blender the maximum number of bounces the light rays can travel. They also have the ability to cast shadows with the **Cast Shadow** checkbox turned on. Of course, they also have a strength that you can tweak in the **Nodes** subpanel. Note that, if you can't see the strength option, you need to click the **Use Node** button.

The shared light options

The different types of light are as follows:

- **Point**: As its name implies, it emits lights according to its position. It emits light rays in all directions, but these rays are limited to a certain distance from the center of the light. We often call it a spherical lamp.

A point light with a strength of 500 and a size of 0.1

- **Sun**: As you can imagine, this type of light represents the way the sun works. As the sun is very far away from earth, we can admit the way we perceive its rays as parallel. So in Blender, the sun produces parallel rays, and we also don't care about its location, but only its orientation matters. With a small size, you can quickly represent the lighting of a bright day. You will mostly use it as a global light as it lights the entire scene. Also, notice that its strength should be less than the point light that we saw previously.

A 45-degree angle on Y and Z sun light with a strength of 2 and a size of 0.05

- **Spot**: The spot light is a conic light. It looks like the lamps used on stage in order to light the show presenter. The lighting that it will produce depends on its location, direction, and the spot shape. You can change its shape in the **Spot Shape** subpanel, and **size** will determine the size of the circle of light influence. The **blend** will define the hardness of the circle shadow. The circle size and the strength of the spot light will depend on its distance from the objects.

A 45-degree angle on a Y spot light with a strength of 5000, a size of 0.5, a shape size of 30 degree, and a blend of 0.8

- **Hemi**: For now, the Hemi type of light is not supported in Cycles. If you use it, it should react like a sun lamp.

- **Area**: This is one of the more common lights. It emits light rays from a plane according to a direction represented by a dotted line. It could be squared or rectangular. Its size, like for the other types, will affect the hardness of the shadows. The strength of the light will also depend on its distance from the objects. With this light, you can achieve a very precise lighting, so we strongly advise you to test this in order to be familiar with the way it reacts.

An area light with a strength of 500 and a square size of 5

Another option that many Blender users appreciate is using an emission shader to act as a light on an object (a plane, for instance). The emission shader is, in fact, the base shader of the other types of lights.

1. First let's add a plane.
2. Then, under the **Material** tab of the **Properties** editor, we will add a new material slot.
3. Change the diffuse surface shader from **Diffuse BSDF** to **Emission**.
4. As you may notice, if the plane is in the camera field, you can see it. We don't want this, so go into the **Object** tab of the **Properties** editor, and under the **Ray visibility** subpanel, uncheck **Camera**.

You may find this easier, but, in fact, with this method we lose a lot of control. The main problem we've found with this method is that we can't control the way the rays are emitted, for instance, with the area light. This can be useful when you want visible objects to emit light, but this is not very good for precise lighting.

The cube with an emission shader

Lighting our scene

As you can see from the previous part, there are many types of light that we can manipulate in order to achieve a nice lighting effect. But in the case of our haunted house, we are only going to use area and sun lights because the other types of light are often used in specific situations.

1. We will start by opening our haunted house scene and saving it in another name (`HauntedHouseCyles.blend`, for instance).

2. Now we can delete all the lights that we used in the Blender Internal render.

3. While doing a lighting effect, it's a good to have an idea of the volume of your objects with a neutral material. So we will select one of the objects in the scene, remove its existing material, and create a new material in the **Material** tab of the Properties editor. As we did for our testing scene, we will change the color value to **1.0**.

4. Rename the material as `Clay`.

5. Now we will select all the objects in scene (*A*), and reselect the object that is the clay material while pressing *Shift* in order to make it the active object.

6. Press *Ctrl* + *L* and select **Material**. All objects will now share the same material.

7. We can now split our interface in two. One of the 3D views will display the camera point of the view (the *0* numpad key) and will be rendered in real time (*Shift* + *Z*) with a preview sampling of 50 (decrease it if you don't have a powerful computer).

8. The first light to be added is the sun. We will orient it, so it lights the right-hand side of the house. It will be nearly horizontal. Our goal here is to have a dawn lighting. The sun has a size of 5 mm in order to have harsh shadows and a strength of 1.0.

9. The next light that we will add will fill up the front of the house a little bit. It will be an area light that is a slightly tilted down and located on the front left side of the house. We want smooth shadows, so we will change its size to 5 m. Its intensity will be around 400. We can also change its color to be a little bit yellowish.

10. The last light will act as rim light. It will be an area light that comes from the back of the house on the left-hand side. Its size will be 10 m and its strength around 700. We have also tinted it a little bit towards blue.

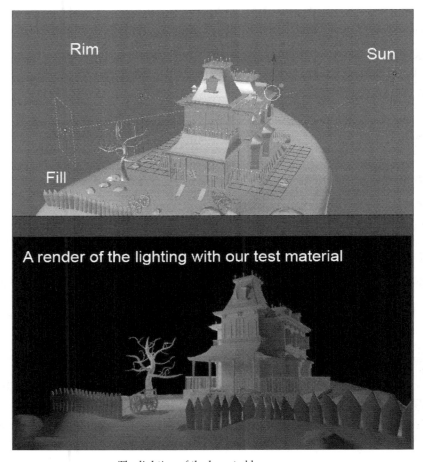

The lighting of the haunted house scene

11. That's all for the basic lights. The light settings are in constant evolution during the whole image creation pipeline, so don't be afraid to change them according to your needs later. Note that we are missing an environment lighting that we are going to set up in the next part of the chapter.

Painting and using an Image Base Lighting

An **Image Base Lighting** (IBL) is a very convenient technique that allows us to use the hue and the light intensity of an image to lighten up a 3D scene. This can be a picture of a real place taken with a camera. HDR images provide very realistic results and may be enough to light a 3D scene, but for our haunted house scene, we will paint it directly in Blender with Texture Paint. This technique allows us to do complex lighting in less time and will enrich the lighting that we have prepared previously. We will start by seeing how to prepare the painting phase of a customized IBL:

1. We will open a new scene in Blender.

2. We will split the working environment in half with a **UV/Image Editor** on the right-hand side and a 3D View on the left-hand side.

3. We will add a UV Sphere at the center of the world (*Shift + A* and select **Mesh | UV Sphere**) on which we will paint the sky.

4. We will delete the vertices at the two poles of the sphere. We will make a scale extrusion (*E* and *S*) of the edges and slightly reposition them again for a well-rounded look. We will obtain a sphere pierced on both ends. It is important to have these holes for the UV projection.

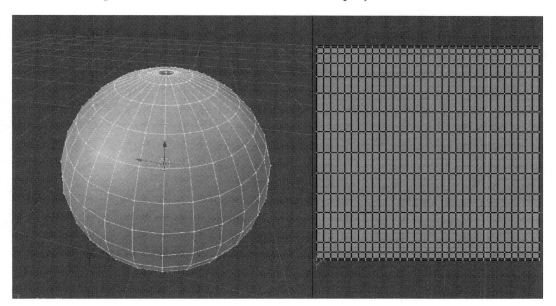

5. We will select all the polygons of the sphere (*A*), then we will apply **Unwrap Cylinder Projection** (*U*). In the **Cylinder Projection** options on the left panel (*T*) of the 3D Viewport, we will change the **Direction** parameter by selecting the **Align to Object** option. This allows us to get straight UVs that occupy the most space on the entire UV Square.

6. Once the UVs are created, we will select the edge loops that form the holes at the poles of the sphere, and we will merge them each in turn to form a complete sphere. This will form triangles in the UV, but it does not matter.

7. We will again select all the polygons of our sphere, and we will then add a new texture by clicking on the **+ New** button in the **UV Image** Editor.

8. In Blender Internal Renderer mode, we will create a new material on which we will place our IBL texture. To better visualize the texture, we will check the **Shadeless** option (**Material | Shading | Shadeless**).

9. In **Texture Paint,** we can start to paint.

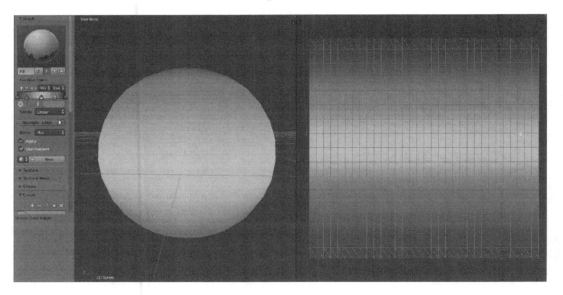

10. We will use Fill Brush with the **Use Gradient** option in order to prepare the gradients of the sky. We will use the following Gradient Colors from left to right. The color marker number **1** on the far left is **R: 0.173, G: 0.030, and B: 0.003**. The color marker number **2** is located at **0.18**, and its color is **R to 0.481, G to 0.101, and B to 0.048**. The color marker number **3** is at position **0.5**, and its color is **R to 0.903, G to 0.456, and B to 0.375**. The color marker number **4** is located at **0.78**, and its color is **R to 0.232, G to 0.254, and B to 0.411,** and the last marker at the far right is the color **R: 0.027, G: 0.032, and B: 0.085**. We will then apply the gradient upwards on the sphere.

11. On the texture in the **UV/Image** Editor, we can see some black near the poles, which may interfere with the lighting calculation. Thus, in the **Paint Mode**, we will take the nearest color of the black triangles by pressing the *S* shortcut (without clicking), and we will fill the black triangles with **Fill Brush** (without Gradient).

12. When this is finished, we can save this image as **IBL_Sky**.

13. In the **Texture Paint** mode, in the **Slots** tab, we will add a **Diffuse Color** texture that will be transparent this time. For this, we will check the **Alpha** box, and we will change the alpha value of the **default fill color** to 1 in the **Texture Creation** menu. This will allow us to create clouds on another texture while keeping our sky visible.

14. With the **TexDraw** brush and the **R: 0.644, G: 0.271, B: 0,420** color, we will draw a few clouds. We must think that there will be only the upper half that will be displayed on the framing of the haunted house. This part will have the greatest importance for the lighting. So we must focus on the upper half of the texture.

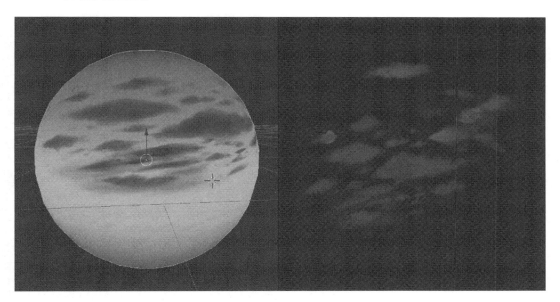

15. We will save the image as **IBL_Cloud**.

16. From this cloud texture, we will make a mask that allows us to properly mix the sky and the clouds. For this, we must save our image, with the **BW** (Black and White) option and not in RGBA, by naming it as **IBL_Mask**.

17. We will then return to the haunted house scene, and in the **Node Editor**, we will click on the **World** icon that is represented by an earth, and we will check the **Use Node** option.

18. We have two nodes that appear: **Background** and **World Output**. We will add an Environment Texture node (press *Shift + A* and select **Texture | Environment Texture**).

19. We will duplicate the **Environment Texture** node twice (*Shift + D*). We will place them one above the other and to the left.

20. In each **Environment Texture** node, we will open the IBL textures created previously.

21. We will add a **Mix RGB** node (press *Shift + A* and select **Color | Mix RGB**) that will allow us to mix our textures. We will connect the **IBL_Sky** Color Texture Image Output socket to the **Color1** input socket of **Mix Shader**, the **IBL_Cloud** Texture Image Color Output socket to the **Color2** input socket of **Mix Shader**, and the **IBL_Mask** Color Output Socket to the **Fac** input socket. We will keep **Mix** as the Blending mode.

22. We will add a **Mapping** node (press *Shift + A* and select **Vector | Mapping**) that we will duplicate once, and we will position them one above the other on the left-hand side of the **Environment Textures** node. We will rename them as **Mapping_1** and **Mapping_2**. We will connect **Mapping_1** to the **IBL_Sky** Texture Image node and **Mapping_2** to the two other **Environment Textures**.

23. We will add a **Texture Coordinate** node (press *Shift + A* and navigate to **Input | Texture Coordinate**) that we will position at the left. We will connect the **Generated** socket of the **Texture Coordinate** node to the **Vector Input** socket of the two **Mapping** nodes

24. To get a better contrast for the **IBL_Mask**, we will place a **RGB Curves** node (*Shift + A* and select **Color | RGB Curves**) between the **Environment Texture** node and **Mix RGB**. We will set the following two points: the first point at the **X= 0.24** and **Y= 0.65** position, and the second point at the **X= 0.65** and **Y= 0.58** position.

25. We have all the necessary nodes. To finish, we will need to modify the mapping of the **IBL_Sky** texture. Therefore, we will modify the **X= 6°**, **Y= 23.9°**, and **Z= 0°** rotation parameters. These values vary according to the painted texture, so adjust them accordingly.

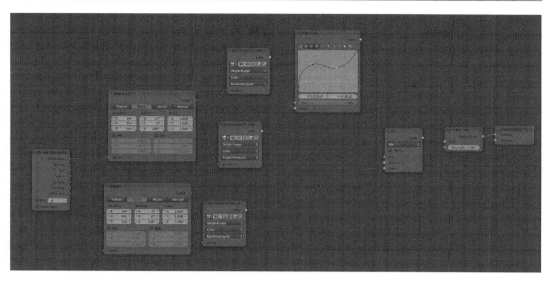

To visualize your **Image Base Lighting** (IBL) better, you can display it in the viewport. In the **Solid** mode, in the right panel of the 3D Viewport, check the **World Background** option (**Display | World Background**).

Creating materials with nodes

It's now time to discover the material creation process with Cycles. In this section, we are going to create the basic shaders that are composed of our previously painted textures. The shaders won't be at their final stage here. Later, we are going to improve them with normal maps.

Creating the materials of the house, the rocks, and the tree

Let's start with the wall shader of the house:

1. We will first select the corresponding object.

2. We are going to duplicate the clay shader that we had added in order to test our lighting in the previous section. As you can see, it is used by 68 objects in the scene. If you click on the 68 button on the right-hand side of the material name in the material tab of the Properties editor, you will duplicate the shader and make it unique. At this time, we can now rename it as HouseWall.

3. We are now going to switch to the **Node Editor** in order to have more control on our shader. In fact, we can do everything in the Properties editor, but it will be quite hard to manage with a complex shader. So open a new editor and change it to a **Node Editor**.

4. As you can see, we already have **Diffuse BSDF** plugged into the **Surface** input of the **Material Output** node.

5. A diffuse shader has no shine on it. It looks flat. In real life, every surface is at least a little specular, so we are going to mix our diffuse shader with another shader that will bring us the shiny effect. To do this, we will first add a **Glossy BSDF** shader (press *Shift + A* and select **Shader | Glossy BSDF**) and place it under the diffuse shader. Don't connect it for the moment.

6. In order to mix the two shaders together, we will use a **Mix Shader** node (*Shift + A* and select **Shader | Mix Shader**). As you can see, this node has two shader inputs. Plug the BSDF output (green dot) of the diffuse shader to the first shader input of the **Mix** shader, and the BSDF output of the Glossy shader to the second shader input of the **Mix** shader. Now plug the **Mix** shader output to the surface input of the **Material Output** node. As you can see, both shaders have been mixed together. You can now use the **Factor** slider in order to choose which one is predominating. If you put a value of **0**, you will only use the shader connected to the first input (the diffuse), and if you put a value of 1, you will only use the shader connected to the second input (the glossy one).

7. The blend between these shaders is not going to look right with any value, so we are going to connect a **Fresnel** node to the **fac** input (press *Shift + A* and select **Input | Fresnel**).

About the Fac input

The role of the fac input is to control how both shaders will be mixed. Usually, the **Fac** input needs to be fed with black and white information where the amount of black tells us how much the first shader will be used, and the amount of white tells us how much the second shader will be used for the final output.

8. We can now change the value of the Fresnel to **1.4**.

About the Fresnel

The Fresnel node will produce a black and white texture according to the volume of the geometry. It will be calculated according to the light ray's incidence. We usually use a Fresnel node in order to catch the highlights better. You can use a pretty interesting add-on called node wrangler that allows you to quickly see the result of each node without shadows. In order to use it, right-click on the node you want to see while pressing *Ctrl* and *Shift*.

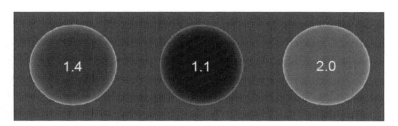

9. We will now change the glossy color to a yellowish tint. Don't forget to turn on real-time shading in order to have a preview of what this will look like in the render. You can also drag a rectangle to the zone you want to preview with the *Shift + B* shortcut while being in camera view. If you want to remove the rectangle zone, drag a new zone to the outer zone of the camera in the camera view.

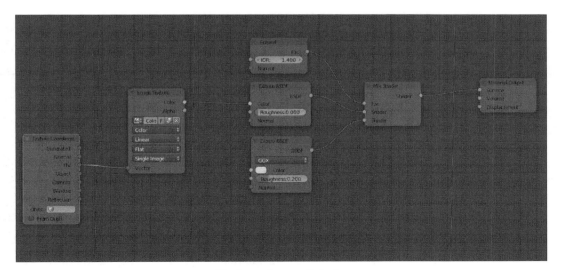

The base of our wall shader

The last thing we will do with this material for now is plug it into our texture:

1. We will add a new Image Texture node (press *Shift + A* and select **Texture | Image Texture**).

2. We will need to connect the **Color** output of this node to the **Diffuse BSDF** color input.

3. It's also a good idea to add a **Texture Coordinate** (press *Shift + A* and select **Input | Texture Coordinate**) node and plug the UV slot to the **Vector** input of the **Image Texture** node.

By default, the Vector inputs are set to be UV, but with this node, we can clearly see the mapping method used for the textures.

1. We can now select one of the roofs and change its clay shader to the one we created because the roof shader will be nearly the same. Now, in order to break the link between the roof and the wall shader, we can press the button with the number of objects that share the same material in order to copy the material.

2. We will rename this shader to `HouseRoof1`.

3. The only thing we need to do for now is to change the texture of the Image Texture node to the corresponding roof texture.

4. We can now select all the objects that need to share the same material (the other blue roofs), and finally, we select the roof that has the shader that we want to share, press *Ctrl + L*, and select **Material**.

5. We will now repeat the process of creating a new material by copying it from the previous one, changing its name and texture information, and linking it to its corresponding objects.

We will now have a shader on the rocks, the tree, and all the different objects that make up the house. The only shader that will be different is the one on the top window. It needs to emit light. In order to do this, we will copy the previous material, delete the diffuse, glossy, and mix shader (*X* or *Delete*), replace them with an **Emission** shader (press *Shift + A* and select **Shader | Emission**), and plug the window texture to this. Now the top light is going to emit light! You can tweak the emission value if you want more light. As you can see, we need to do this for the other windows as well, but in the case of the other windows, we can't do this simply because they are not planes and their color information is located on the wall texture. That's why we need to paint a mask.

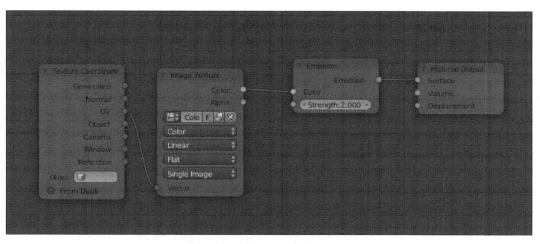

The top window shader

Adding a mask for the windows

We are now going to improve our wall material by creating a mask that will separate the windows that are shining from the rest. These windows are going to be painted white and the rest will be black. So when we plug the mask in the **Fac** input of a Mix material node, we will be able to choose an emission shader for the white parts.

1. We are going to paint our map in the **Blender Internal** context. Note that we can actually use the **Texture Paint** mode while being in Cycles, but this implies that we add and select a texture node that uses the texture that we want to paint.

2. So we will select the wall object, and in the **UV Image** editor, we will create a new 1024 x 1014 black texture. Usually, masks don't need large resolutions.

3. Now in pure white paint the windows that shine (the light yellow ones on the color map).

4. Let's go back to our wall material and add a mix shader just before the output node. If you want to save time, you can drag the node on the connection line of the previous **Mix** shader and the **Output** node. This will automatically do the connections for you.

5. The first shader input is already used by our old **Mix** shader. Now we are going to add a new **Texture** node with our mask and plug its output to the **Fac** input of our new **Mix** shader.

6. The second shader input will be fed with an **Emission** shader (press *Shift + A* and select **Shader | Emission**). In the **Color** input of this node, we will plug our color map (the same as in **Diffuse** shader).

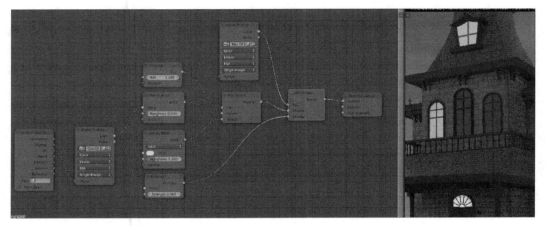

The wall material with the mask on the left-hand side and the result in the real-time rendered 3D view.

7. Now we can increase the strength of the Emission shader to 2.0. As you can see, now our shining windows (and only them) emit light!

Using procedural textures

One thing that could be very interesting when creating materials is generating their textures procedurally. In this render, we are going to replace the hand-painted ground by a procedural material. This is done as follows:

1. We will select the cliff and create a new material for it.

2. The next thing is to add a **Diffuse BSDF** node. The color input of this diffuse material will be fed with a mix of procedural textures.

3. Let's add a Noise texture node (*Shift + A* and select **Textures | Noise**) and duplicate it (*Shift + D*). The first one will have a scale of 2.0, and the second one will have a scale of 10.0. Our goal is to have a mix of both levels of noise. Both of them will use the Tiled UV layer, so add a **UV Map** node (press *Shift + A* and select **Input | UV Map**), select the correct map, and feed the **Vector** input of the noise textures with the **UV Map** node output.

4. As these nodes are textures and not shaders, we aren't going to use the **Mix Shader** node but the **MixRGB** node instead. So we will add one of these nodes (press *Shift + A* and select **Color | MixRGB**), and feed the inputs with their noise **Fac** output. Don't use the color output as we want a black and white mix here. Remember that you can always test your results with the Node Wrangler add-on (press *Shift + Ctrl* and right-click on any node).

5. We are now going to mix this result with a **Musgrave** node (press *Shift + A* and select **Texture | Musgrave**). We also need the Tiled UV for the vector input. We will set the **Scale** to **20.0**, the **Detail** to **3.5**, and the **Dimension** to **1.7**. Its effect will be pronounced in the final result, so we are going to mix it with white. To do this, we will add the **MixRGB** node and plug the first **color** input with the **Fac** output of the **Musgrave** Texture. The second color slot can be changed to white. We are going to change the **Fac** slider of the **MixRBG** node to 0.98; this will make Musgrave very subtle.

6. We can now mix our noises and the **Musgrave** results together with one more **MixRGB** node.

7. If we plug this directly to the color input of the diffuse, we will get a black and white result. In order to introduce color, we will need another **MixRGB** node, but instead of feeding the color inputs we are going to plug our texture in the **Fac** input and choose two brownish colors. Now we can plug the result to the color input of the Diffuse shader.

8. Lastly, we can plug the black and white texture to the displacement input of the Material output node. In order to raise the displacement effect, we can place a **Math** node in-between (press *Shift + A* and select **Converter | Math**). We can change its operation to **Multiply** and use a **3.5** value.

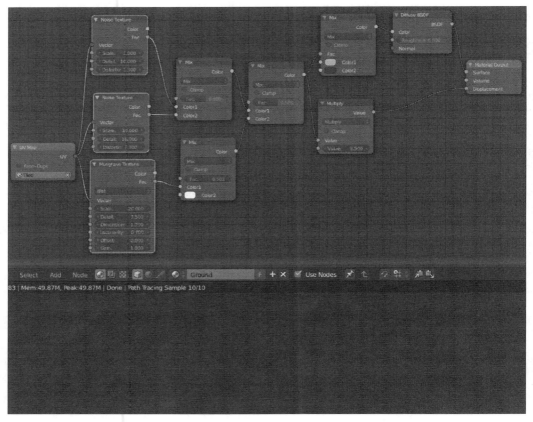

The ground material with the procedural texture made with a noise and Musgrave combination on the left-hand side and, the result in the real time rendered 3D view.

Making and applying normal maps in Cycles

As we saw it previously with the alien character, normal map allows us to simulate a relief on a 3D mesh very efficiently. It would be good to generate a few of them in order to add some relief to our scene. We will explore a method to easily generate normal maps from tiled, hand-painted textures:

1. We will open a new Blender scene.

2. We will delete the cube (*X*) and then we will add a plane in the middle of the scene (press *Shift + A* and select **Mesh | Plane**) that we name as **Plane-1**.

3. We will split the screen in two parts to open the **UV/Image Editor** at the right-hand side.

4. We will add a **Multires** modifier to our plane and a **Displace** modifier. We will place the Multires modifier above the Displace modifier.

5. In the Texture tab, we will create a new texture by pressing **New,** and then we will load the tiled texture of wood, that is, **WoodTilePlank.png.**

6. We will check that the texture is loaded in the **Displace** modifier.

7. In the **Multires** modifier, we will check the **Simple** mode, and we will click on **subdivide** until we get to **level 8**. The more the mesh is subdivided, the more the Displace effect is accurate, but we must pay attention to the RAM of the computer.

8. We will modify **Strength** to **0.25**. This can vary depending on the texture. We must avoid important deformations on the mesh.

9. We will duplicate the plane (*Shift* + *D*), and then we will delete the modifiers of this new plane that we name as **Plane-2.**

10. We will select all the faces (**A**) of **Plane-2** in the **Edit Mode**, and we will do an unwrap (**U | Unwrap**) with a square shape taking all the UV surfaces. Then, we will add a new image. In the **UVMap Editor**, we will click on **New Image** (**Image | New Image**). We will name it as **WoodTilePlank_NM.png.**

11. We will move **Plane-2** to the same height as **Plane-1.**

12. Enter the top view (the *7* numpad key) for a better view of the mesh.

If the Displace doesn't give exactly the effect we want, we can make a few modifications with the **Sculpt** mode after applying the displace modifier by pushing on **Apply**. This is what we will do with the rock and the tile roof textures.

We can now bake a normal map as follows:

1. We will need to click on the **Smooth Shading** button, otherwise we will see the polygons on our bake.

2. Then, we will have to first select **Plane-1 (RMB)** and then **Plane-2** (press *Shift* and the RMB). This becomes the active object.

3. Now, in the **Properties** editor, under the **Render** section, we will expand the **Bake** subpanel.

4. The first option to choose is what type of map (or texture) we want to bake. So, in the **Bake Mode** drop-down menu, we will select **Normal Map.**

5. The next thing we'll have to check is the **Selected to Active** option that tells Blender to bake from the sculpture to the active object (our low poly plane).

6. Now you can click the **Bake** button. Don't forget to save your map (select **Image | Save As Image** or press *F3*), or it will be lost!

We will use the same process of Normal Map creation for every tiled texture. Once this is done, we can return to our shaders and apply our normal maps.

We will start with the House-Rock shader, which is very simple for the moment:

1. We will add a **Glossy** node (*Shift + A*) and navigate to **Shader | Glossy BSDF**, which we will mix with **diffuse** using a **Mix Shader** (*Shift + A* and select **Shader | Mix Shader**). To better visualize the normal maps, we will need glossiness.

2. We will add **Fresnel** (*Shift + A* and navigate to **Input | Fresnel**) that we will position in the **FAC** input socket of the **Mix Shader** node. We will put a **IOR** value of **1.4**.

3. We will add a **Normal Map** node (*Shift + A* and select **Vector | Normal Map**) with a **Strength** value of **1.0** and connect its output to the Normal input socket of the Diffuse and Glossy shaders.

4. We will duplicate an Image Texture node (*Shift + D*), and we will open the normal map texture named Roch-Tilling-NM.png file. We must switch the **Color Data** option of this second Image Texture to **Non-Color Data**. The data should not be interpreted as color data but as normal direction data.

5. We will add a UV Map node (*Shift + A*) and navigate to **Input | Glossy UV Map**. Then we will change the UVLayer to **Tiled**. You will recall that the rocks have two UV layers, so we must select one.

We can apply this process for almost every shader using hand-painted tiled textures, except the brick walls in our case. It is a special case that requires that we bake the normal map on a larger map with a little modification of painting in order to hide the bricks behind the windows.

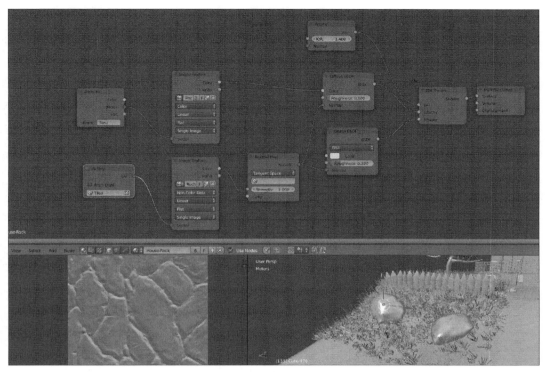

The normal map of the rock (low left corner) and its material in the nodal editor (top)

Creating realistic grass

In this section, you will see how we can create realistic grass in place of the actual grass planes. In order to create our realistic grass, we are going to use a hair particle system.

Generating the grass with particles

A particle system will be used here in order to generate the grass strand without modeling and placing them by hand:

1. We will first select the cliff and isolate it (**/ Numpad**). Then, we can go into the **Particle** tab of the **Properties** editor and add a new particle system. This will add a new modifier in the stack, but we can only control it here.

2. We will now have to change the type from **Emitter** to **Hair**. We can activate the **Advance** tab.

3. In the **Emission** subpanel, we can change the **Number** value to **10000**, which corresponds to the number of grass strands that we will have. We will also emit the particle from the faces in a **Random** manner. We can also change the **Hair Length** to **0.26**.

4. In the **Physics** subpanel, we can change the **Brownian** value to 0.120 in order to add more randomness to the grass.

5. In the **Children** subpanel, we can set the amount of strands we want to spawn around the main guides. In our case, we will activate the Simple mode and set **10** children for the **preview** (in the viewport) and **100** for the **render**. In the effect section, we can change the **Clump** value to **-0.831** so that the children start near the base of the guide strand and are sprayed out near the tip. We can also change the **Shape** value to **-0.124** to shrink the children in the middle a little. We will also change the **Endpoint** value to 0.018 to add more randomness.

6. We will now paint a vertex group with the **Weight paint** tool in order to choose where we want grass on the cliff. For instance, we don't want strands under the house. To do this, we will switch from **Object mode** to **Weight Paint** mode while the cliff is selected. As you can see, you have brushes as in the **Sculpt** mode. We can use the **Add** brush to add weight and the **Subtract** brush to remove weight. **Red** means that it will be full of grass, **Blue** means you won't have grass. Now, we can choose the vertex group that we have painted in the **Density** field of the **Vertex Groups** subpanel in the Particle System settings.

7. Now we can add a new particle system in order to add long grass. To do this, we will add a new slot in the particle settings. We will also copy the settings from the previous particle system but unlink them (the button with the number on the right-hand side of the name). We can lower the number of particles to **1000** and change the **Hair Length** to **1.120**. The number of children will be **5** in the **Simple** mode.

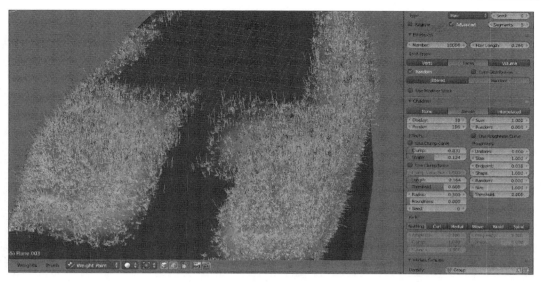

The settings of the grass

Creating the grass shader

Now the last thing that we will create is the grass material:

1. The first thing we will need to do is change the **Cycles Hair Settings** in the **Particle Systems** tab. We will change **Root** of the strand to **0.20** and set **Tip** to **0.0**.

2. We can now add a new material slot for the cliff and rename it as Grass. In the particle settings, we will change the material to **Grass** under the **Render** subpanel.

3. We will now select the grass shader and open the **Node** editor. The first node that we will add is the **Hair BSDF** shader (press *Shift + A* and select **Shader | Hair BSDF**) and change it from **Reflection** to **Transmission**. We will mix it using **Mix Shader** with a **Glossy BSDF** shader. We will change **Glossy Roughness** to **0.352** so that the glossiness is more diffuse.

4. Next, we will have to plug a **Fresnel** node to the **Fac** input of **Mix Shader**.

5. For the color of **Hair BSDF**, we will add a **Color Ramp** node (press *Shift + A* and select **Converter | Color Ramp**). For its **Fac** input, we will add a **Hair Info** node (press *Shift + A* and select **Input | Hair Info**) and choose the **Intercept** output. This will enable us to set the different colors along the strand. We will do a gradient that starts from a brownish color (to the left) to a desaturated green (to the right). Usually, the tip of the grass strand is white, so we will add a small amount of white on the far right of the color ramp.

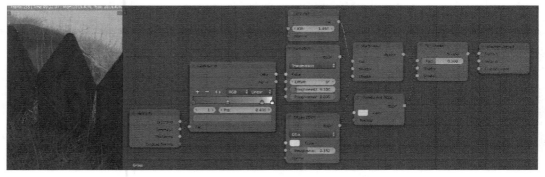

The grass shader (to the right) and the result (to the left)

6. We will also mix the result of our Mix shader with a **Translucent BSDF** shader (press *Shift + A* and select **Shader Translucent**). Indeed, the grass is very translucent. We will change its color to a desaturated yellow and change the **Fac** value of the shader to **0.3**. We can finally plug our latest **Mix** shader to the surface input of the **Material** output node.

Baking textures in Cycles

Cycles allow us to bake textures as does Blender Internal, but there are some differences between the two render engines.

Cycles versus Blender Internal

As we have seen previously, texture baking in Blender Internal can be very efficient to produce normal maps, ambient occlusion, color textures, and many other kinds of maps that we won't cover here. All of this in a very short time. So you might wonder why it is interesting to bake in Cycles.

Cycles is a ray tracer render engine based on physical parameters with global illumination. It is then possible to get some very realistic renders in a much more efficient manner. Baking in Cycles allows us, for example, to calculate a few heavy special effects only once, such as caustics. When a render is baked on a texture, you can visualize the effect in real time. This can be very useful if you want to change the frame and make several renders. In this way, it is possible to create a realistic environment in real time.

However, in the context of a video game, if you have many dynamic assets you must pay attention. You could be limited by fixed lighting. Even though baking in Cycles can be very interesting, it has some faults. Doing a good baking without noise requires the same settings as a normal render, so you do need a high sampling value, which greatly increases rendering time compared to Blender Internal.

 For more information, you can have a look at the official Blender Reference manual at this address:
`http://www.blender.org/manual/render/cycles/baking.html`

Baking the tree

We won't bake the maps of every objects in our scene with Cycles; however, we will see how to proceed with the 3D mesh of the tree as an example.

In order to optimize the render time, we will import our 3D mesh to another Blender window:

1. We will launch Blender a second time.
2. We will select the tree in the scene of the haunted house, and we will press *Ctrl + C* to copy it. You will see the **Copied selected object to buffer** message in the header of the work space.
3. In the other Blender window, we will press *Ctrl +V* to paste the tree. We will see the **Objects pasted from buffer** message.
4. In the same way, we will also import all the lights, and we must recreate the shader of the Image Base Lighting (we can append it from the main file). We don't modify the location of the tree and the lights in order to keep the same light configuration. But this wont be exactly the same lighting effect as we don't have the house here.
5. We will need a second UVs layer with UVs that are restrained in the UV square this time. We will use the *Ctrl + P* shortcut to automatically replace the UVs. Then we will adjust the margin in the options of the left panel of the 3D viewport.

6. We will start with color baking using the new UVs. For this, we will add an **Image Texture** node (*Shift* + *A* and select **Texture | Image Texture**) to the shader of the tree.

7. We will select all the polygons of the tree in the **Edit Mode** (*Tab* and *A*), and then we will create a new image named **Tree_Color**. A size of 2048 x 2048 is enough.

8. In the **Image texture** node that we have just created, we will select the **Tree_Color** texture. This node must stay u.nconnected.

9. Now we will need to go into the **Bake** tab in the **Render** options. Here, we will change the type to **Diffuse Color**. We will set the **Margin** value to **5**, and then we will press **Bake**.

10. When we have our color map, we must adjust the seams with Texture Paint. We will use the **Soften Brush** in order to blur the problems of the too visible seams.

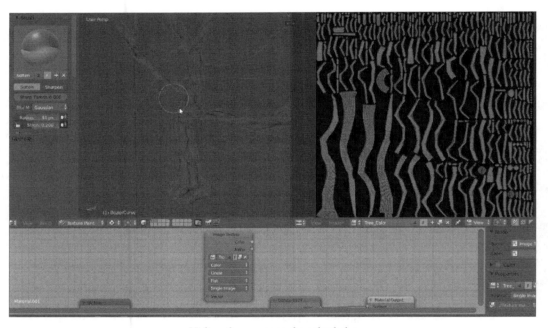

Hiding the seams on the color bake

11. When the color texture is fine, we will again select the polygons of the tree in the **Edit Mode**, and we will create a new image (the same size) and rename it as **Tree_Combined**.

12. Now we can make another combined baking following the same process, which this time allows us to get all the lighting information on the texture. Make sure you open the good image in the **Image Texture** node with a high enough sample value. In our case, we have 500 samples to obviate the noise.

13. We can now go back to our haunted house scene and replace the tree with the one with new UVs (*Ctrl + C* and *Ctrl + V*); then we can replace the old texture with the **Tree Combined** texture in our shader.

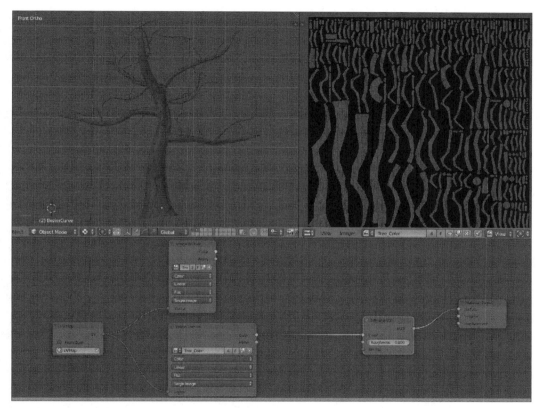

The combined bake of the tree

Compositing a mist pass

As a bonus, we are going to learn how we can create and composite a mist pass with Cycles. But to do this, we will need to do a render. So let's do a render with 500 samples:

1. We will first have to activate the mist pass in the **Render Layer** tab of the Properties editor. Now we can access the mist settings in the World setting panel. We will set **Start** to **0 m** and Depth to **37 m**.

2. In order to see the mist, we will need to composite it over the render. We will learn more about compositing in further chapters, so don't worry if we don't go deep into the subject right now. In the Node Editor, we will have to switch to the Compositing Node mode (the second button after the material in the header). We will need to check **Use Nodes** and **Backdrop** in order to see our changes in real time. As you can see, we already have a RenderLayers node plug in the **Composite** node (the final output of the image).

3. In between, we can add a **Mix** node (press *Shift + A* and select **Color | Mix**) and feed the first color input with the Image output of the **RenderLayers** node. The **Fac** input of the **Mix** node will receive a **Map Value** node (press *Shift + A* and select **Vector | Map Value**) with **Offset** of **0.105** and **Size** of **0.06**. For the input of Map Value, we will simply plug our **Mist** pass (the fourth output of the **RenderLayers** node). The **Map Value** will control the amount of mist we see.

4. In order to view the result in the **Node Editor** in real time, you will have to add a **Viewer** Node. To do this, we will simply press *Ctrl + Shift* and right-click on any node.

The final Cycles render of the Haunted House project

5. We now have a nice mist! In order to change the aspect of the final render, we can tweak the **Color Management** options as we did in the previous chapter. Congratulations, you've completed the Haunted House project.

Summary

This chapter was really robust, but you now understand how to create nice materials with the Cycles Render engine and how to light a scene properly. You also learned how to produce normal maps and how to bake your objects. This last technique would be very interesting for video games. We also covered Blender's Compositing tool to a slight extent by mixing a mist pass. Now let's create a new project!

8
Rat Cowboy – Learning To Rig a Character for Animation

This chapter will cover the rigging and the skinning of a character. This character will be a Rat Cowboy that has been already modeled for you. Here, you will understand what the rigging process involves. We will start by placing deforming bones. After this, we will learn how to rig these bones with controllers and constraints such as IK or Copy. Then, we will skin our character so that the mesh follows the deforming bones. As a bonus, you will learn how to use shape keys in order to add some basic facial controls that will be controlled by drivers. The rig, which is covered here, will be basic, but you will have all the necessary knowledge to go further. We are going to use this rig to animate our character in the next chapter. Enjoy!

In this chapter, we will cover the following topics:

- Making a symmetric skeleton
- Using the basic bones constraints
- Rigging the eyes
- Correcting the deformation of the meshes with weight painting
- Improving the accessibility of the rig with custom shapes
- Using shape keys

An introduction to the rigging process

We are now going to discover the process of character rigging. The point of this is to prepare objects or characters for animation in order to pose them in a simple way. For instance, when rigging a biped character, we will place virtual bones that mimic the character's real skeleton. Those bones are going to have relationships between them. In the case of a finger, for instance, we will usually add three bones that follow the phalanges. The tip bone will be the child of the mid bone, which in turn will be the child of the top bone. So when we rotate the top bone, it will automatically rotate its children. On the top of the network of the bones, we will need to add some constraints that define automation so that it is easier for the animator to pose the character. The next step is to specify to the geometry to follow the bones in some way. For instance, in the case of a character, we will tell Blender to deform the mesh according to the deformable bones. This stage is called **Weight Painting** in Blender and **Skinning** is a common term, too. However, we will not always face a case where skinning is necessary. For instance, if you have to rig a car, you will not want to deform the wheels, so you will create a bone hierarchy or constraints in order to follow the rig. The entire process could be tricky at some point, but mastering the rigging process allows you to better understand the animation process and is the reason why having a good topology is so important.

Anatomy of a bone in Blender

A bone has a root and a tip. The root corresponds to the pivot point of the bone, and the tip defines the length of the bone. Bones can have a parent-child relationship in two ways. The first method is by connecting them, so the root of the child is merged with the tip of its parent. The other method is by telling Blender that they are visually disconnected while still having a parent/child relationship. Each bone has a roll that corresponds to its orientation on itself. When manipulating an **Armature** object, you can be in the **Edit Mode** to create the network of the bones and set their relationships, or you can be in the **Pose Mode** where you can pose the rig as if you were posing a marionette.

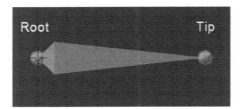

Rigging the Rat Cowboy

Let's do the rig of the Rat Cowboy. We are not going to show the modeling process here as you already know how to model proper characters from the Alien project.

Placing the deforming bones

The first thing that we will need to do for our rig is place the bones that will directly deform our mesh. These are the main bones. In Blender, a rig is contained in an **Armature** object, so let's go!

Let's begin with the process:

1. We will first be sure that our character is placed at the center of the scene with his feet on the *x* axis.

2. Now we can add a new bone that will be placed in an **Armature** object (press *Shift + A* and select **Armature | Bone**).

3. Next, we will enter the **Edit Mode** of our new **Armature** object, and we will place the bone in the hip location and rename it as hips. You can rename a bone in the right panel of the 3D view in the **Item** subpanel. Be careful to rename just the bone and not the **Armature** object.

4. We can now start to extrude the bones of the spine. To do this, we will select the tip of the hips and extrude it (*E*) twice as far as the base of the neck. It's very important that you don't move these bones on the X axis. We will rename the bones as **Spine01** and **Spine02** respectively. From the side view, be sure that these bones are slightly bent.

5. We will now extrude the left clavicle according to the Rat Cowboy's structure and rename it as **Clavicle.L**. The **.L** part is really important here because Blender will understand that this is on the left-hand side and will manage the right-hand side automatically later when mirroring the rig.

6. Now, from the tip of the clavicle, we will extrude the bones of the arm. Rename the two bones as **TopArm.L** and **Forearm.L**.

7. Now it's time to extrude the bone of the hand, starting from the tip of the forearm. Name this as **Hand.L**.

Please note that if you want to follow the process step by step, you can download the starting file for this chapter on the Packt Publishing website.

8. In order to create the finger bones, we will start from a new chain and parent it back to the hand. This will allow us to have bones that are visually disconnected from their parents. To do this, we will place the 3D cursor near the base of the first finger and press *Shift + A*. Since you can only add bones when you are in the **Edit Mode** of the **Armature**, this will automatically create a new bone. We will orient it correctly and move its tip to the first phalange. We will extrude its tip to form the next two bones. It's important to place the bones right in the middle of the finger and on the phalanges so that the finger bends properly. Analyze the topology of the mesh to do this precisely. If you want, you can activate the Snap option (the magnet in the 3D view header) and change its mode from **Increment** to **Volume** to automatically place the bones according to the volume of the finger.

9. Then we will create the chains for the other fingers and the thumb and rename them as **Finger[Which finger]Top.L**, **Finger[Which finger]Mid.L**, and **Finger[Which finger]Tip.L**.

10. We will now need to re-parent them to the hand so, when the hand moves, the fingers follow. To do this, we will select the top bone of each finger (the root of each finger chain) and then select the hand bone (so that it is the active selection) while holding *Shift*, pressing *Ctrl + P*, and selecting **Keep Offset**. Keep Offset means that the bones are going to be parented but they will keeping their original positions (that is, they are not connected to their parent).

11. We will now change our cursor location to the left thigh of our character and press *Shift + A*. We can then place the tip of this bone to the knee location. Also, check the side view and put this tip a little bit forward. We can then extrude a new bone from the knee to the ankle. Rename these bones as **Thigh.L** and **Bottom Leg.L**.

12. We can then extrude the foot and the toes. Name them as **Foot.L** and **Toes.L**.

13. The leg chain needs to be parented to the hips. This can be done with *Ctrl + P* and selecting **Keep Offset**. Remember to first select the child and then the parent while doing your selection for parenting.

14. Now we can add the bones of the tail. We will create a chain of bones starting from the back of the Rat Cowboy to the tip of the tail where the tips and roots of each bone are placed according to the topology of the mesh. Remember to rename the bones properly from **Tail01** to **Tail07**.

15. Then we will parent **Tail01** to **Hips** by pressing *Ctrl + P* and selecting **Keep Offset** so that the whole tail is attached to the rest of the body.

16. The last bones that we will need to extrude are the neck and the head. The neck starts from the tip of the **Spine01** bone and goes straight up along the Z axis. Then we will extrude the head bone from the neck tip. We will rename them as **Neck** and **Head**.

Now we will have to verify on which axis the bone will rotate. You can display the axes of the bones in the **Armature** tab of the **Properties** editor under the **Display** subpanel. We will need to adjust the roll of each bone (*Ctrl + R* in the **Edit Mode**) to align them along the x axis. You can test the rotations by going to the **Pose Mode** (*Ctrl + Tab*) and rotating the bones around their x local axis by pressing *R* and then pressing *X* twice. Beware, rolls are very important!

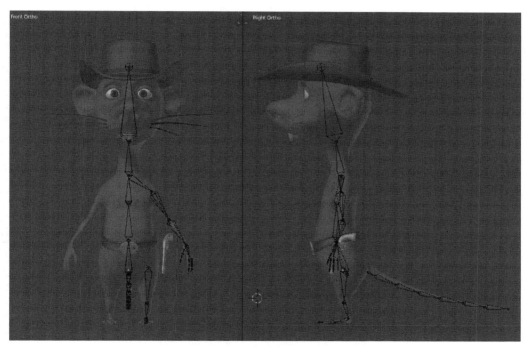

Placement of the deforming bones

The Display options

You can find different display options for your bones in the **Display** subpanel in the **Object Data** tab of the **Properties** editor. A nice way to display the bones is to activate the **X-Ray** display mode, which allows us to see the bones through the mesh even in **Solid** shading mode. We can also display the axes of orientation and the name of each bone and change its shape.

For instance, we can use the B-Bone mode that changes the bones to boxes that we can rescale with *Ctrl + Alt + S*. This is a nice way to display bones that are on top of each other. You can also use the **Maximum Draw Type** drop-down menu in order to change the shading of your selected object in the **Display** subpanel in the **Object** tab of the **Properties** editor.

The following image will show the placement of the deforming bones of the hand:

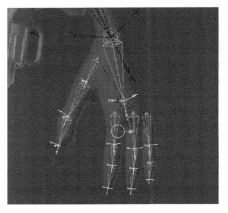

Placement of the deforming bones of the hand with a correct roll

The leg and the foot

Now that we have all the deforming bones that are needed, we are going to add some bones that will help us to control the leg and the foot in a better way.

1. We will now add a bone that will be a controller for the **Inverse Kinematic (IK)** constraint of the leg. We add this to the ankle and align it with the floor. It's important that this bone is disconnected for now. We rename it as **LegIK.L**.

2. Under the **Bone** tab of the **Properties** editor, we will uncheck the **Deform** checkbox so that our bone does not deform our geometry later.

What is an IK constraint?

Usually, when you manipulate bones in the **Pose Mode**, you rotate each one in order to pose your object, and this method is called **FK (Forward Kinematic)**. The role of an **IK constraint** is to let Blender calculate the angle between a minimum of two bones according to a target. To better understand what this does, imagine that your foot is a 3D object and you can move it where you want in space. As you can see, your thigh and lower leg will automatically bend with an appropriate angle and direction. That's the whole point of **IK**!

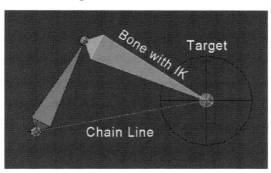

3. Now we are going to tell Blender that this new bone is the target that will control the IK constraint. To do this, we will first select it in the pose mode (*Ctrl + Tab*) and then select the lower leg bone to make it the active bone. Now we can use the *Shift + I* shortcut to create a new IK constraint. As you can see, the lower leg bone turns yellow.

4. Now we will change the settings of the constraint. The bone Constraints panel is located in the **properties** editor (a bone with a chain icon) in the **Pose Mode**. If we select the lower leg bone, we can see our IK constraint located here. As we've used the *Shift + I* shortcut, all the fields are already filled. The setting that we will change is **Chain Length**. We set this to two. This will tell Blender to calculate our IK constraint from the bone where the constraint is on the tip to the next bone in the leg chain.

5. We can now go back to the **Edit Mode** (*Tab*) and add a new floating bone in front of the knee location. This bone will be the target of the knee. Rename it as **PollTargetKnee.**L.

6. Back in the **Pose Mode** (*Ctrl + Tab*), we will set this new bone as the **Pole Target** bone for the IK constraint. We will first select the **Armature** object and then the bone. After this, we will adjust **Pole Angle** to reorient the IK constraint so that the leg points to the knee target. In our case, it's set to **90°**.

7. The next thing to do is to uncheck the stretch option so that the leg can't be longer than it already is.

8. Now that we've rigged the leg, it's time to rig the foot. We are going to make an easy foot rig here. But note that a foot rig can be much more complex with a foot roll. In our case, we will first remove the **Foot.L** parentation. To do this, we go into the **Edit Mode**, select the parent, press *Alt + P*, and select **Clear parent**.

9. Now we want to switch the direction of the bone so that its root is located at the toes. To do that, we will select the bone in the **Edit Mode**, press *W*, and select **Flip Direction**. Remember that a bone rotates around its root, so this will give us the ability to lift the foot up on the character's toes.

10. Now we can connect the IK target to the foot bone. To do this, we will simply select the child (**LegIK.L**), select the parent (**Foot.L**), press *Ctrl + P*, and select **Connected**. So now, when we rotate the foot in the **Pose Mode**, the IK target is going to lift up and the IK constraint will do its job.

11. The last thing that we will need to do is create a master bone that will move all our foot bones. In the **Edit Mode**, we will add a bone that starts from the heel to the toes and rename it as **FootMaster.L**. We will then parent the toes to this with the **Keep Offset** option. Then we will parent the foot to the toes with the **Keep Offset** option. As you can see, if you move the master bone in the **Pose Mode**, all the bones will follow this. We are done with the foot and the leg rig!

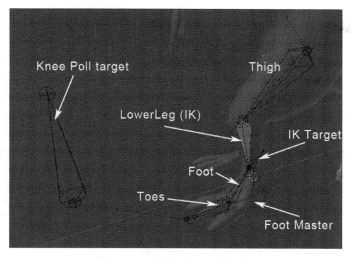

The rigging of the foot and the leg

The arm and the hand

The next important part to rig is the arm. In many rigs, you will have a method to switch between FK and IK for the arms. In our case, we are only going to use IK because it will be quite long and boring to teach how to create a proper IK/FK switch with snaps. When animating the arm with IK, you will have to animate arcs by hand, but this will allow you much more control if you don't have an FK/IK switch.

1. We will create a new floating bone that will become our IK target for the arm by duplicating the bone of the hand and clearing its parent. Remember that the target of an IK switch needs to be freely movable! We will rename this bone as **HandIK.L**.

2. Then we will set up our IK constraint by first selecting the target, then the forearm, and then pressing *Shift + I*. Now, we can change the chain length to two as we did for the leg.

3. The next thing to do is add a poll target for the orientation of the elbow. To do this, we will create a floating bone behind the elbow of our left arm, we rename this as **ElbowPollTarget.L**, and we set this as the poll target of the IK constraint. Also, we will change the **Poll Angle** to match the correct orientation of the elbow.

4. Both the target and the IK target need to have the **Deform** option turned off.

5. The animator will only want to manage one bone for the hand. The bone that will deform the hand is not the target as it needs to be connected to the arm, so we will need to find a way to tell the hand-deforming bone to follow the IK target rotation. If this happens, the animator will only control the target for both arm placement and the hand rotation. To do this, the IK target is going to transfer its rotation to the deform bone. So, we will first select the **HandIK.L** bone, then the **Hand.L** bone, and then press *Ctrl + Shift + C* to open the constraint floating menu and select **CopyRotation**.

6. We are now going to rig the fingers again with a **Copy Rotation** constraint. The motion that we want to achieve is that, when the base of the finger is rotated around the X local axis, the finger curls. To do this, we will indicate to the mid bone of the finger to copy the rotation of its parent (the top bone) and the tips to copy the rotation of its parent too (the mid bone). We will show the process for the index finger and let you do the rest for the others.

7. We will select the **Finger1Top.L** bone, then the **Finger1Mid.L** bone, press *Ctrl + Shift + C*, and select **CopyRotation**. After this, we will select the **Finger1Mid.L** bone, then the **Finger1Tip.L** bone, and create a copy rotation constraint. If we rotate **Finger1Top.L** on the X local axis, we can see that the finger bends.

8. In order to finish the hand, we will disable the **Y** and **Z** local rotations of the mid and tip bones of each finger. To disable a rotation on a particular axis, we will open the right panel of the 3D view (*N*) and change the rotation type from **Quaternion** to **XYZ Euler**. Then we can use the lock icon on a particular axis.

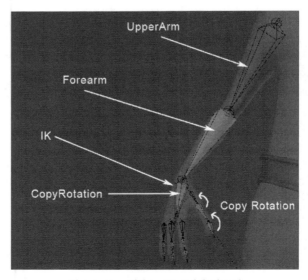

The rigging of the arm and the hand

What is a Copy Rotation constraint?

As its name implies, the copy rotation constraint will tell an entity to copy the rotation of another entity. The settings of the constraint allow you to choose in which space the rotation will be. The often used spaces are **World** or **Local**.

The **World** space has its axes aligned with the world (you can see them in the left corner of the 3D view).

The **Local** space has to do with the orientation of an object. For instance, if an airplane has a certain direction, but when it rotates around its fuselage, this takes into account its orientation.

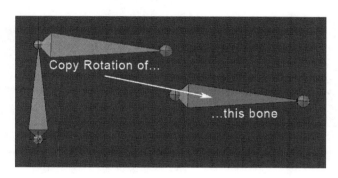

The hips

Now it's time to do the hips motion so that it is easier to control for animation. You have done a lot of work until here. Have yourself a cookie, you deserve it!

1. To create our hips motion, we will duplicate the hip bone. Also, remember to uncheck the **Deform** option. We will rename it as **HipsReverse**.

2. Now, we are going to flip the direction of this bone so that the hip deforming bone rotates around its tips (because the root of the hip's reverse bones will be here).

3. Now you can test in the **Pose Mode** that, when you rotate the **HipsReverse** bone, the hip's deform bone rotates with it.

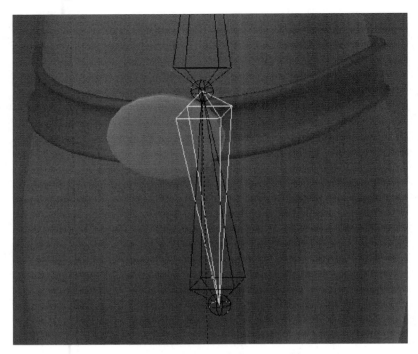

The rigging of the hips with the reversed bone

The tail

A rat without a tail is pretty strange, so we will take some time to rig his tail. The technique that we will show here is quite simple but very effective:

1. In order to rig the tail of the Rat Cowboy, we will need to add a new bone that controls this in the **Edit Mode**. To do this, we will extrude the last **Tail07** bone so that it is placed at the right location, and we will un-parent it with *Alt + P* and select **Clear Parent**. Rename this as **TailIK**.

2. We will now need to create an IK constraint. We will first select the target, then the **Tail07** bone (the last in the chain), and press *Shift + I*.

3. Now in the IK constraint settings, we will change the chain length to **7** (to let the IK constraint solve the angles from the tip to the last bone of the tail chain).

4. We will check the **Rotation** option, too. Now, as you can see, the tail is fully rigged and can be placed and rotated through the tail target:

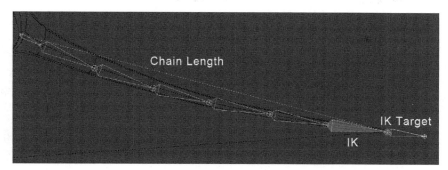

The rigging of the tail with a chain length of 7

The head and the eyes

In order to control the head, we will only manipulate the bone of the head, so we will directly begin the rigging of the eyes. We will ensure that the eyes are two separated objects and they have their pivot points at the center to make for good rotation. In our case, we have two half spheres, so we don't waste performance with hidden geometry:

1. We will select one of the eyes, and in the **Edit Mode** (*Tab*), we will select the outer edge loop. We will press *Shift + S* to open the *Snap* menu, then we will select the **Cursor to Selected** option, and then, in the **Object Mode** (*Tab*), we will press *Ctrl + Alt + Shift + C* and select **Origin to 3D cursor**. The pivot point must be at the right location. Do not hesitate to test this with a free rotation (**R x 2**) in the **Object Mode**. We must repeat the same process for the other eye.

2. In the **Object Mode**, we will select the eyes and the teeth, and then we will parent them to the head bone, but not with the usual method of parenting the bones that we saw earlier. To do this, we will first select the eyes and the teeth, and then the head bone (the armature must be in the **Pose Mode**). We will press *Ctrl + P*, and we will select the **Bone** option.

3. We now want to create a controller bone for each eye. We will select the armature, and in the **Edit Mode** (*Tab*), with the 3D Cursor in the middle of the eye, we will create a bone (*Shift + A*). In the Orthographic (*5*) left (*3*) view, we will move the controller bone in the front of the character. We need a small distance between the head and the bone controller. We will repeat the same process for the other eye, and we will rename them as **EyeTarget.L** and **EyeTarget.R**.

4. We will set the eyes to look at their controllers with a **Damped Track** constraint (**Properties | Constraint**). We will start with the left eye. We must select the Armature as **Target** and **EyeTarget.L** as the bone. Now, we must adjust the rotation by tweaking the **Z axis**.

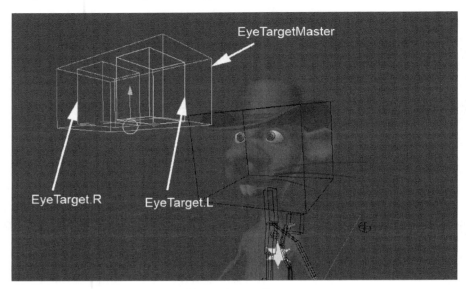

The eyes' controllers

The Damped Track constraint

This allows us to constrain a 3D object to always point towards a target on an axis. The 3D object doesn't move, it just rotates on its pivot point depending on the location of the object.

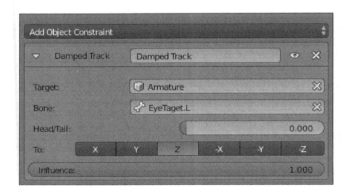

Both the eyes must now follow the **EyeTargetMaster** movements. Do a test by pressing G.

Mirroring the rig

In order to save time, as in the modeling or the sculpting process, it is often very useful to work with symmetry. There are three ways to do this in an armature.

The first method consists of checking the **X-Axis Mirror** option in the **Armature Options** tab in the left panel of the 3D Viewport (*T*) that allows us to directly create the bones in a symmetry. We must extrude the bones by pressing *E* while also pressing *Shift*. This solution doesn't copy the constraints.

The second method is efficient even if it requires some manipulations to get a perfect mirror. Until then, we will place the bones of the arms and legs on the left-hand side with all the constrains that we need and the appropriate names:

1. We will select the armature in the **Edit Mode**, and we will align the 3D cursor at the center (*Shift + S* and select **Cursor to Center**).

2. In the **Header**, we will put the **Pivot Point** options on 3D Cursor.

3. Then, we will select every bone of the arm and the leg on the left-hand side.

4. We will duplicate them (*Shift + D*), and we will mirror them by pressing *S + X + 1* on the numeric keyboard. Then we will press *Enter*.

5. In the **Edit Mode**, we will select the bones of the arm and the leg on the right-hand side and flip the names (**Armature | Flip Names**). This renames all the bones of the left-hand side with the **.R** termination.

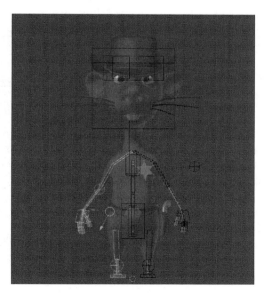

Mirroring the bones with their constraints from the left to the right side

The third method is very interesting. It has been available since Blender 2.75.

Once we have placed and named all the bones with the **.L** termination and have all the constraints, we will select them in the **Edit Mode**, and then we will press *W* and select Symmetrize. This will automatically rename the bones of the right-hand side and the constraints will be copied.

Let's now focus on the gun for a rig.

Rigging the gun

In order to easily animate the gun, we will need it to be able to follow the hand of our character when the Rat Cowboy uses it, and the gun must be able to follow the holster all the time. To do this, we will use a bone and a **Child Of** constraint.

The Child Of constraint

This constraint allows us to make an object a parent of another object by weighting their influences. This allows the animator to animate its influence in order to change its parent. This is much better than a classical parentation. This is very useful to make an object follow different objects one after another like a character driving with one hand on the steering wheel and the other hand on the speed box. You can also combine multiple children of the constraints.

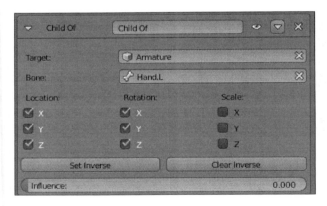

1. We will begin by taking care to apply the rotation of the gun (press *Ctrl + A* and select **Scale and Rotate**).

2. We will select our Armature, and in the **Edit Mode**, we will place the 3D Cursor at the location of the hammer; then we will create a bone (*Shift + A*) that follows the length of the gun. We will rename this new bone as **Gun**.

3. We will make the gun the parent of the bone by first selecting the gun in the **Object Mode**, then the **Gun** bone in the **Pose Mode**, and then we will press *Ctrl + P* and select **Bone**.

4. We will then modify the appearance of the bone in B-Bone (**Properties | Object Data | Display | B-Bone**). We will scale it to make it easier to rig (*Ctrl + Alt + S*).

5. We will check the **X-Ray** option.

6. We will move the gun in the holster by moving and rotating the Gun bone. You can also directly rotate the gun a little bit in order to get the best position.

7. We will add two **Child Of** constraints to the Gun bone. We will uncheck the scale option of both the constraints.

8. We will decrease the influence to **0** on both the **Child Of** constraints.

9. With the first **Child Of** constraint, we will put our Armature as Target with the **Hand.L** bone in the bone option. We will press the **Set Inverse** button.

10. For the second **Child Of** constraint, we will put the **Holster** object as Target, and we will press the **Set Inverse** button again.

Now, when we place the left hand with **HandIK.L** near the gun and put the influence of the first **Child Of** constraint at **1.000** (the influence of the second Child Of constraint must still be at **0**), the gun joins the **HandIK.L** bone and follows it. In order to reposition the gun in the holster, it must be very near to the holster. The influence of the first Child Of constraint must be at **0,** and the influence of the second one must be at **1.0** (reversed influences).

The gun bone

Rigging the holster

Now we are going to rig the holster. As you can see, it is a separate object. We will need to pin it to the belt. In this section, we won't use bones, but they are still a part of the rigging process.

1. First, what we are going to do here is create an empty object that will be the parent of the holster. To create an empty object, press *Shift + A* and select **Empty | Plain Axis**.

2. Now we will select the empty object, and while holding *Shift,* we will select the belt. We can now enter the **Edit Mode** of the belt and choose a vertex near the pin of the holster. We can press *Ctrl + P* and choose **Make Vertex Parent**. Now when we move the vertex, it moves the empty object!

3. The last thing that we need to do is make the holster the parent of the empty object, and the trick is done! Of course, we could have made the holster object a parent of the vertex directly, but it's always nice to have an empty object in between in this kind of situation.

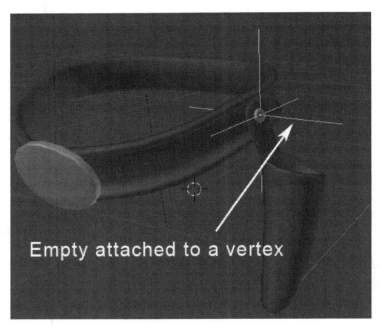

The rigging of the holster

Adding a root bone

The root bone is also called the master bone; it is the bone that will control the entire skeleton and is the top parent. With this, it is very convenient to place our character and animate it anywhere.

1. We will select the **Armature,** switch in the **Edit Mode** (*Tab*), place the Pivot Point at the center of the world (press *Shift + S* and select **Cursor to Center**), and then we will add a bone (*Shift + A*).

2. We will make this bone bigger (*Ctrl + Alt + S* in the **B-Bone** mode) because it represents the central control element of the **Armature**. We will flatten it by selecting and moving the tip of the bone. We will rename it as **Root**.

3. In the **Edit Mode**, we will select the IK bone controllers of the **hands, feet, tail, EyeTargetMaster** that controls the **Eyes, Hips,** and **Pole Targets** at the location of the knees and the elbows; finally, we will select the master bone (so that it is the active selection).

4. We will make them parents (press *Ctrl + P* and select **Keep Offset**).

5. Remember to uncheck the **Deform** option (Properties | Bone | Deform).

6. You can see all the bones follow when you move the **Root Bone**.

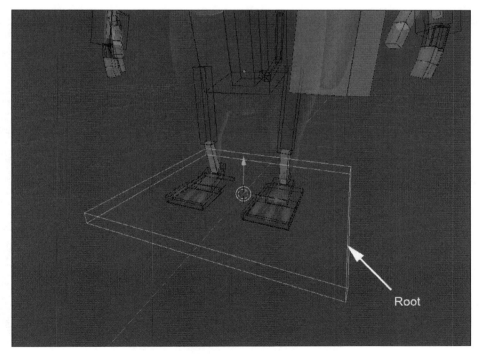

The root bone at the center of the world

Skinning

Skinning is a very important step in the setup of a character for animation that will allow us to deform a mesh parented to a rig. It should be noted that the term skinning is not directly used in Blender. In Blender, you will generally find the term "Weight" designating the influence that a bone has on the geometry. It is often a long and delicate step, but fortunately, Blender allows us to perform an automatic skinning that is already very clean and quick. This is one of the most efficient skinning algorithms.

Before skinning our character, just as a reminder, we must determine which bones will deform the mesh and which not. This will be done as follows:

1. We will verify whether the **Deform** option is unchecked for all deforming bones (**Properties | Bone | Deform**).

2. In the **Object Mode**, we will select the mesh of the **Rat Cowboy**, then the Armature, and we will make them child and parent (press *Ctrl + P* and select **With Automatic Weight**).

A nice skinning has been done for us. You can make a few rotations on the rig in the **Pose Mode** to visualize the result.

However, we must do a few adjustments to improve this. Let's dive into the tools that we have at our disposal.

The Weight Paint tools

If we select our mesh and observe the **Data** menu of the **Properties** panel, we can see **Vertex Groups** that matches the bones of the Armature. This menu, in **Weight Paint** mode, allows us to select and view the influence of each bone. The **Weight Paint** mode could be activated directly on the object. If the armature is in the **Pose Mode**, it is possible to select the bones by a RMB click as well while we are in the **Weight Paint** mode of the object.

In the **Weight Paint** mode, we can view the influence that each bone has on the geometry with a color play. Blue means a 0% influence, a greenish-blue color means 25%, green means 50%, yellow means 75%, orange means 85%, and red means 100%.

In order to modify the influence, we have several brushes that can be used exactly in the same manner as **Texture Paint** and **Sculpt Mode** in the left panel of the 3D viewport. These brushes allow us to paint bones influence directly on the mesh. In our case, we will use only three brushes. The brushes that will serve us for sure will be the **Add**, **Subtract**, and **Blur** brushes.

- The Add brush allows us to increase the weights

- The Subtract brush allows us to reduce the weights
- The Blur brush allows us to soften and mix the weights

The options of the brushes are exactly the same as with **Texture Paint** and **Sculpt Mode**. We can change the radius of the brush by pressing *F* and moving the mouse. Also, we can change the strength of the brush that will completely modify the impact of the brush. You can change the curve, too.

We can paint the weight in symmetry. To do this, the mesh must be perfectly symmetrical. We will check the **X-Mirror** option in the **Option** tab of **Left Panel** (*T*).

There are also a few useful options in the **Weight Tools** menu. For example, **Mirror**, to make a symmetric skinning and **Invert**, to invert the influence of our bones.

For more information, you can have a look at the official Blender manual at this address: `https://www.blender.org/manual/modeling/meshes/vertex_groups/weight_paint_tools.html`.

The weight paint of the Rat Cowboy (here the head influence is shown)

Manually assigning weight to vertices

Weight Paint is a very useful technique, but sometimes it is not very accurate. It can be useful to assign weight precisely on some geometry components.

To do this, we must be in the **Edit Mode** and select the vertices to which we want to assign a weight. Then we can go in the **Vertex Group** menu (**Properties | Data | Vertex Groups**). There will be a **Weight bar** from which we must select the desired weight and click on **Assign**. If you don't have any group, you can click on the **+** icon.

Another nice feature is located in the **Right Panel** (*N*). There the **Vertex Weight** menu allows us to visualize the bones that influence the selected vertex and adjust the vertex directly. We will notice that the total weights assigned to a vertex group may exceed **1.000**. In fact, Blender will add the total of influences and make an average.

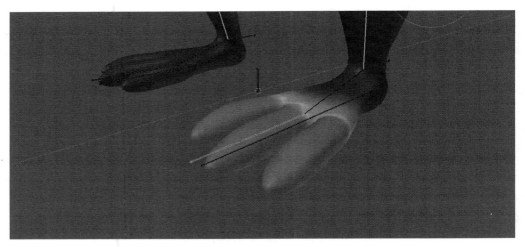

Correcting the weight paint of the toes.

Correcting the foot deformation

If you have used the **With Automatic Weight** option, you should have a very few things to change. The arms, legs, and head deformations should be quite good.

However, the toes aren't working well because there isn't a bone for each toe. So we will fix this as follows:

1. We will check the **X-Mirror** option, and we will select **Toe bone**.

2. Now, we can paint with **Add Brush** to add some weight to the toes until we get a red color (100%).

3. Then, we will need to remove the influence that the foot bone has on the toes. To do this, we will use the subtract brush. Now the foot shouldn't affect the toes.

Stick Display for Weight Paint

To easily edit a skinning, it is advised to change the appearance of the bones to **Stick Mode** with the **X-Ray activated** option. You will get better visibility.

Correcting the belt deformation

Let's do the skinning of the belt. It is not a particularly easy element to skin because of its thickness and possible interpenetration with the body, but do not be discouraged. In this case, we will manually assign the weight to the vertices. This is shown in the following steps:

1. We will start by selecting the belt, then select the Armature, and we will make them child and parent (*Ctrl* + *P* and select **With Automatic Weight**).

2. In the **Vertex Groups** menu (**Properties | Data | Vertex Groups**), we will remove all the vertex groups except these: **Hips**, **Thigh.L**, and **Thigh.R** with the - button.

3. First, we will assign a weight of **1.000** to the **Hips** vertex group, so the hips bone deforms all the belt.

4. Then, we will select the vertices on the right half of the belt in the **Edit Mode**, and we will assign a weight of **0.2** to the **Thigh.R** group.

5. We will do the same thing for the vertices on the left half of the belt but with **Thigh.L**.

6. Then we will check the rotations of the **Belt** bone to verify some of the potential problems of transition. We will adjust the weight of a few vertices. The goal here is to create a gradient of weight at the center according to each thigh bone so that the thigh "attracts" some part of the belt in a smooth manner.

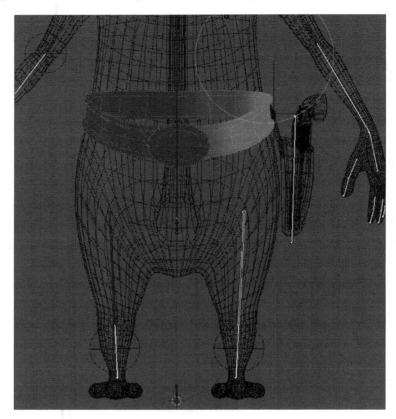

The weight of the left-hand side of the belt

Custom shapes

Now that our rigging is almost finished, we can opt for custom shapes. These are 3D objects that can replace the usual look of bones. The purpose is primarily aesthetic, but functional as well. We can make bone shapes that will go around the mesh and allow us to uncheck the X-ray option. Also, it will allow us to manipulate bones more easily.

We can hide the bones that do not require manipulation, such as the arms that are in fact only controlled by **HandIK.L** and **HandIK.R**.

To implement a custom shape, we must first to create a form, usually from a circle. We are going to make the custom shape of the **Neck** bone together and let you do the rest as this is very repetitive:

1. We will add a circle (eight sides is enough) to the scene (press *Shift + A* and select **Mesh | Circle**).

2. In the **Edit Mode**, we will select the opposite vertices on the Y axis, and we will connect them (*J*). This connection in the custom shape allows us to visualize the orientation of the bone better.

3. We will rename this object as **SHAPE_Circle_01**.

4. Now we will select the neck bone and **SHAPE_Circle_01** in the **Custom Shape** option (**Properties | Bone | Display | Custom Shape**).

5. There is often a problem with the axis of rotation and the scale. These must be adjusted in the **Edit Mode**. We can work on **SHAPE_Circle_01** again in the **Object Mode** without modifying the custom shape applied to the neck bone.

6. Once the custom shape is adjusted, we don't have to see the **SHAPE_Circle_01** object, so we move it to another layer (*M*). We will choose the last layer to the right in our case. This layer is usually used as a garbage layer where we put unwanted objects.

We redo the same process for almost every controller bone. Some shapes are very often used, such as glasses for the eyes, but try to find custom shapes that fit your needs. They must be explicit and made of very few vertices.

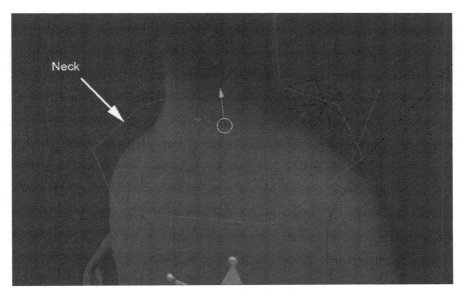

The custom shape of the neck bone

The shape keys

In the following sections, we are going to learn about shape keys and drivers. This will help us to create some very basic facial controls that we will use in the next chapter. Facial rigging is a long process, so we are not going to create a fully functioning facial rig here, but you will have all the tools needed to create your own if you want to.

What is a shape key?

A shape key is a method to store a change of geometry in a mesh. For instance, you can have a sphere object, add a shape key, move your vertices so that the sphere looks like a cube, and the shape key will store the changes for you. A shape key is controlled by a slider. The value of the slider corresponds to the distance each vertex has to move to get to the stored positions. As you can imagine, shape keys are very useful for facial rigging as they allow us to create different expressions and turn them on or off.

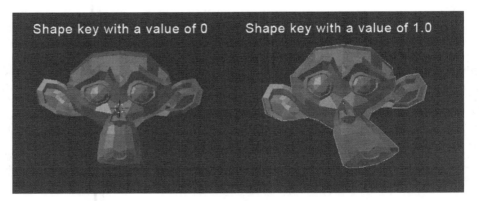

Example of a shape key with Suzanne

Creating basic shapes

In this section, we will create five basic shape keys. They are eye blink left and right, smile left and right, and frown. This will be done as follows:

1. First, we will need to select the object that will receive the shape keys. Then we will go to the **Object Data** tab of the **Properties** editor, and we will open the **Shape Keys** subpanel.

2. When creating the shape keys, we always need to have a reference key that will store the default position of each vertex. To do this, we will click on the + button. It is called **Basis** by default.

3. Now we can add a new shape key with the **+** icon and name it as **EyeBlink.L**. As you can see in the following, there is a **value** slider. At **0**, the shape key is turned off, so change the value to **1.0** in order to view your changes in the **Edit Mode**.

4. Now in the **Edit Mode**, we can change the left eye geometry to close the eye. You can use the **Connected Proportional Editing** tool (*Alt + O*) in order to smoothly move each eyelid to the center of the eye. Beware, you only want to move the eyelid's geometry, otherwise any other changes done will be part of the shape key.

5. Next, we will mirror the shape key without tweaking our geometry on the right side again. We can do this because our mesh is perfectly symmetrical. We are going to create a new shape key based on the one that is currently active in the shape key stack. The value of **EyeBlink.L** is still at 1.0, so we can click on **black arrow** under the **–** icon and choose **New Shape From Mix**. Now, we have a new shape key with the same information as **EyeBlink.L**, but this not what we want. We will need to mirror this to the other side. To do this, we will again click on **black arrow,** and we will press **Mirror Shape Key**. We can also rename this as **EyeBlink.R**. Now if you change the value of **EyeBlink.R**, you can see that the right eye of the Rat Cowboy is closing perfectly. What a huge time-saver!

6. The next two keys, **Smile.L** and **Smile.R**, are created using the same method. What you need to do is create a nice smile on one side and mirror it using **New Shape From Mix** and **Mirror Shape Key**.

7. The last key to be created is a frown. To do this, we are just going to create a new key with the **+** icon and move the geometry between the eyebrows. There are tons of other things to know about shape keys, but for now this is all we are going to need.

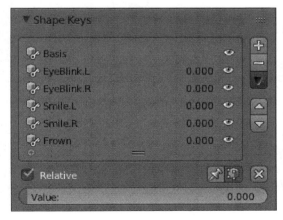

Our facial shape keys

Driving a shape key

You might be thinking that animating directly shape key from the sliders is not very practical, and you are right! This is why we are going to use drivers. It is a method to indicate to an entity (object, bones, and so on) to control another value. In our case, we are going to tell Blender that the sliders of our shape keys are going to be controlled according to the transformations of the bones located on the face. This will give an impression that we are directly manipulating the head of our Rat Cowboy.

1. The first thing to do is add three new bones to our **Armature** object in the **Edit Mode**. The first one will be located between the two eyebrows, and this will control the frown. The others are going to be near the mouth corner and will be symmetrical. They are called **Frown, Smile.L,** and **Smile.R** respectively. In order to control the eyes, we are going to use the bones we've used previously as targets.

2. Now we will add a driver to the **EyeBlink.L** shape key by right-clicking on the value slider. Note that the value slider is now inaccessible, so it will be driven by another entity.

Adding a driver to a shape key

3. Now split your view in a new editor of the **Graph Editor** type. Switch the mode from **F-Curves** to **Drivers** in the Graph Editor's header. As you can see, if you still have the rat mesh selected, you will have a new key on the left-hand side of **Graph Editor**. We can click on the white arrow on the left-hand side to unfold the group of keys, and we can select the **EyeBlink.L** one.

4. Now we will open the right panel of **Graph Editor** (*N*), and under the **Drivers** subpanel, we can change the different settings. First, if you have an error, you can go to the user preferences under the **File** tab and check **Auto Run Python Scripts**. Drivers work with Python internally, so you must accept that it runs scripts. But don't be afraid, we are not going to code here!

5. The first thing that we will change in our settings is the **Ob/Bone** field. We are going to choose the **EyeTarget.L** bone. So first choose the **Armature** object and then the bone. This will tell Blender that the target will be the bone that affects the driver.

6. Now we are going to set **Type** to **Y Scale** and **Space** to **Local**. This means that, when we scale our target, the value of the variable called **var** in the upper field will take the value of **Y Local scale** of the bone.

7. Now you need to imagine that the field called **Expr** is directly linked to the value slider of the shape key. You can even test this. If you enter 0, the eye will open, and if you enter 1, the eye will close. So now what we can do is replace this field with the **var** variable that holds the value of the y local scale. You can now see that the Rat Cowboy's eye is closed. But if you scale it, it will open. We are close to the required result.

8. The last thing to do is change the expression so that it is open by default. We know that the **Y local scale** of our bone is **1** by default and that the "open state" of the eye corresponds to the **0** value of the shape key slider. So we can add the **1-var** expression to the **Expr** field. If the Y local scale of the bone is 1, we will have **1-1 = 0** and the slider value will be 0, so the eye will be open. If the **Y local scale** of the bone is 0, we will have **1-0 = 1 and** the slider value will be 1, so the eye will be closed. Done!

9. We can replicate the same process with the other eye. In order to save time when creating the driver, you can simply right-click on the **EyeBlink.L** value slider, press **Copy Driver**, right-click on the **EyeBlink.R,** and choose **Paste Driver**. At this point, you just need to change which bone is controlling the key in the driver settings.

10. For the smile driver, we will do a similar thing. But instead of feeding the variable with the Y local scale of the eye target bone, we are going to use the local Y location of the **Smile.L** bone. If you see a need to move the bone a lot in order to change the shape key, you can simply multiply **var** time a scalar in the **Expr** field. In our case, the expression will be **var * 5**.

11. We can do the same thing for the other **Smile.R** bone and for the frown. The expression of **Frown** is **-var * 10** in our case. As you can see, we have negated the **var** variable because we want to move the **Frown** bone down in order to control the shape key.

12. As a bonus, we are going to lift the hat with the frown. To do this, we will copy our Frown driver to the X rotation of the hat object in the right pane of the 3D view (*N*). We will adjust the expression. In our case, the expression is simply **-var**.

13. We will need to add a **Limit Location** constraint to the Frown bone as well. This will provide the animator with the ability to lift the hat high or low by locking the bone between a minimum and a maximum value on the Y axis in local space. To do this, we will change the settings of the constraint. We will check **Minimum Y** and set the value to **-0.115**, and then check **Maximum Y** and set its value to **0**. Also, we can provide moves on the X and Z location by checking the other check boxes and setting their value to **0**. Then we will need to select the **Local Space**.

14. Now, we have minimum control over the Rat Cowboy's face in order to start animating our character. We advise you to go further yourself in order to gain experience with shape keys and drivers. For instance, you could add cheek puff or eyebrow shape keys.

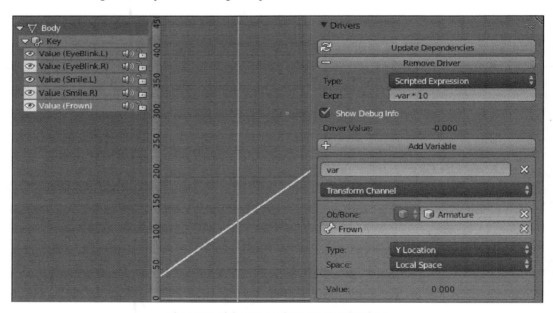

The setup of the Frown driver in Graph Editor

Summary

In this chapter, you've learned how to create a simple bipedal rig. All the knowledge that you've acquired could be used to push this further. For instance, you can add an FK/IK switch slider for the arms and the legs, add more facial controls, or create a more complex foot roll. If you want to see or use a more complex rig, you can check the rigify add-on (integrated in Blender by default). However, this rig will be quite interesting for animation. Talking about animation, let's start using our rig in the next chapter!

Rat Cowboy – Animate a Full Sequence

9

This chapter will be devoted to the animation of a full sequence. We will begin our journey by discovering the 12 animation principles. Then, we will learn more about the preproduction stage that is all the things that we need in order to prepare the animation such as the writing of a script and the creation of a storyboard. After this, we will learn some important tools in order to animate in Blender such as the Timeline, Dope Sheet, Graph editor, and NLA. Next, we will create a layout that is a rough 3D visualization of the sequence without animation. After we've done all this, it will be time to start animating our shots. We will first learn how to animate a walk and use the NLA in order to mix actions together. We will then animate a close shot and a gunshot inspired by old western movies. The graph editor will be used extensively in order to animate a trap. Finally, we will learn how we can render a playblast of our shots. So let's dive into the wonderful world of animation where things start to move!

In this chapter, we will cover the following topics:

- Learning the principles of animation
- Preparing our animation with a script, storyboard, and layout
- Using the Blender animation tools
- Animate different shots
- Render a playblast

Principles of animation

In order to start to animate with Blender in the best way, it is important to understand some basic principles defined in the 80's by Ollie Johnston and Frank Thomas. These principles are inherited from the 2D animation art called "traditional animation". Animation involves recreating the illusion of motion by a sequence of images. Most of these principles also work for 3D animation. Here, they have been developed for a cartoon style, quite far from realistic movements. So, we don't have to apply them to any situation, but they still contain the secrets of animation.

Squash and Stretch

This is one of the common principles that applies to cartoon-style animation. The goal is to over-exaggerate the effect of inertia and elasticity on a particular object. From a 2D perspective, it's quite hard to manage because the object doesn't need to lose its volume, so we need to judge the shape by eye, but in 3D this is just a matter of a good rig.

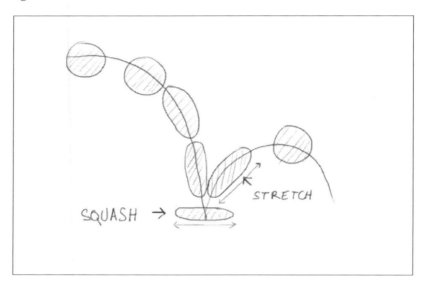

Anticipation

The principle of Anticipation describes the anticipation before an action. For example, a character ready to jump is going to bend the knees, the back, and the arms before the actual jump. It is important in order to add realism to the action you want to depict through your animation. To better understand this principle, try punching with your hand, you'll see your hand going back first.

Staging

This principle is applied in cinema and theater to retain the attention of the spectator on specific elements and remove every useless detail from their view. This is useful to communicate a perfectly clear idea. This may include many areas of animation such as lighting, acting, or camera positions.

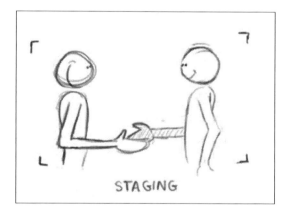

Straight Ahead Action and Pose to Pose

These are two different approaches while animating. The **Straight Ahead Action** method consists of making an animation gradually frame by frame from the beginning to the end. With 2D animation, this is especially useful to create special effects such as fire and water, and this allows improvisation.

The **Pose to Pose** method allows us a much better control of the timing and is easier to manage. This is often much more efficient when we animate characters. For this method, we start by adding the **Key Poses**. They are the main keys that indicate the action. Then comes the **Extremes** that we add to the extremities of motions that exaggerate the action between two key poses. Then, there are the **Breakdowns** that are the main intermediate keys of the action between the extremes. These add more fluidity to the action. A mix of the both methods is often used.

Follow Through and Overlapping Action

Follow Through and Overlapping Action techniques being very close consist of giving some inertia to an animated object and add a better sense of realism. **Follow Through** consists of continuing the movement of a part of an object after it has stopped moving. This can be applied to a tail, for instance. **Overlapping Action** consists of creating an offset between a movement of an object and a part of this object. For example, long hair moves at a different speed than the head.

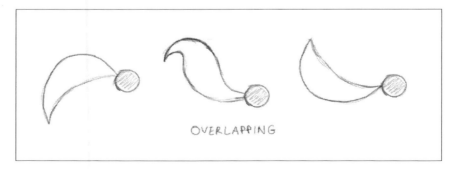

Slow In and Slow Out

These are two effects that consist of attenuating the speed of a moving object around the extreme keys. A Slow In effect is a deceleration at the beginning of an action, and a Slow Out effect is a deceleration at the end of an action. In Blender, these effects can be seen in the form of Bezier curves and are controlled by their handles in the Graph Editor.

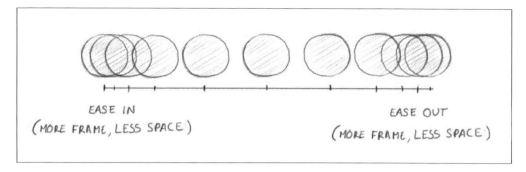

Arcs

This is a principle that consists of creating movements that follow an arc trajectory. Almost every motion follows this principle. For instance, when a character throws a ball, his or her hand follows an arc trajectory. If you take a pendulum and fix the ball, you will see that it follows an arc.

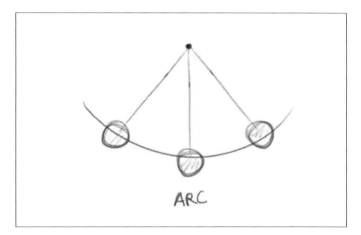

Secondary Action

The Secondary Action principle is about how every little action adds dimension to the main action. For example, in the case of a facial expression, a blink of the eyes can add more expression to the character. Another example could be the ears of a dog that hangs when he turns his head.

SECONDARY ACTION

Timing

The number of frames between the beginning and end of an action directly affects the speed of the action. Timing is related to a physical consistency respecting certain laws of physics. In order to animate a character, timing defines its personality and emotions. For example, if a character is sad, timing is going to be definitely slower.

24 images per second

The frame rate in cinema is 24 images per second, and this is enough for the eye to have an impression of fluidity. This frame rate is used in the basic parameters of Blender.

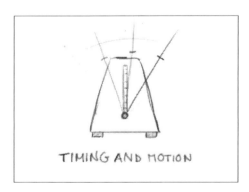

TIMING AND MOTION

Exaggeration

The exaggeration principle is used when you want to accentuate the action that you are transmitting to the viewer. The action can be a pose, a gesture, or an expression. Sometimes it is better to slightly get away from realistic animation to get a better impact. For instance, if you want to accentuate a punch, you can exaggerate the proportions of the arm of a character.

Solid drawing

This principle mostly applies to 2D animation. It consists of ensuring certain realism in drawing regarding volume, weight, and balance. This advocates paying attention to volume and perspective in order to avoid a flat render. A character must be possibly seen from any angle of view. In 3D animation, it is a bit different. Even for a 3D animator, drawing can be seen as a strength, because it allows to quickly put the poses you have in mind on paper, but this is not going to be your main tool.

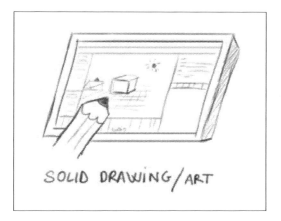

Appeal

This principle is mainly about the interest and appearance of the characters you will animate. It means making a dynamic design through shapes, colors, proportions, gestures, and personality. It can be a hero or a villain, whatever.

Animation tools in Blender

Now that you understand a little bit more about what animation involves, we are going to dive into the different tools that we are going to use when animating our sequence. In order to test these tools, we are going to use the default cube of a new .blend file.

The timeline

The timeline editor gives us a lot of information about the animations of our file. The timeline represents each frame as you can see in its lower part. You can navigate to any frame by dragging the green bar. Using the Left and Right arrows, we will move one frame at a time. Using *Shift* and Up or Down arrows, we will move by an increment of ten frames. In the header we have two sliders, Start and End, which respectively represent at which frame the animation starts and ends. As you can see, we have dark grey parts in the timeline that visually shows this range. If you want, you can set the start and end frame by placing the timeline bar where they need to be and by pressing *S* and *E* respectively. You can quickly move the timeline bar to the start and end frame by pressing *Shift* and left or right mouse buttons. You can also zoom in to the frame with the Mouse Wheel. You can use the well-known play, rewind, and pause buttons in order to play the animation. The shortcut to play the animation is *Alt + A*.

The timeline

What is a keyframe?

Now it's time to learn how to set keyframes. But wait a minute, what is a keyframe? It is used to store the state of an object (or any other animatable thing) at a certain frame. Let's add a keyframe to our default cube:

1. We will open a fresh new blend file, and we will select the default cube.

2. We will then place the timeline bar at frame 0 and press *I* to open the **Insert Keyframe Menu**. We can now choose between many options, but we are going to choose the **LocRotScale** one because we are going to keyframe the location, rotation, and scale of our object.

3. Now we will go to frame 20 (remember the *Shift* + Up arrow shortcut of the timeline), and we will move, scale, and rotate our cube. Now we can add a new key to store the current state of the cube, press *I* and select **LocRotScale**.

4. If you move the timeline bar or play the animation, you can see that Blender automatically interpolates the motion for you! You can clearly see that you have two keyframes represented in yellow. Congratulations, this is your first animation in Blender.

The AutoKey option

In the timeline header, we have a nice little red circle button that allows us to automatically create a keyframe as soon as we change the location, rotation, or scale of our selected object. Thus we don't have to call the Insert Keyframe menu every time.

The Dope Sheet

The timeline is great but is not very useful when we want to manipulate our keys. To do so, we can use a more robust editor called **Dope Sheet** (as always you can split your view and select the editor type that you want on the left-hand side of the header). On the left-hand side, we can see every object that has keys on it. In the header, we have many important options such as the **Show only selected** button (a mouse pointer icon) that tells Blender to only show the keyframe of the selected objects. The keys are represented by a diamond shape and can be selected with by right-clicking on them or by using the *B* key for the box select tool. Of course, you can select all the keys by pressing *A*. You can move the keys with *G*. You can also scale a group of keys with *S*. In this case, the timeline bar will be the pivot point. The **Dope Sheet Summary** row enables us to select every key that is below the corresponding key.

For instance, if we select the dope sheet summary key at frame 0 by right-clicking on it, we will automatically select every key on frame 0.

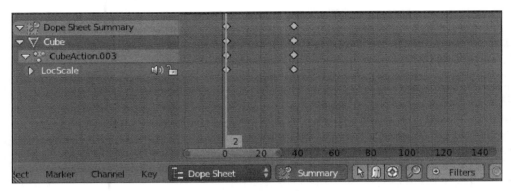

The **Dope Sheet** editor

The Graph editor

Now we will learn a little bit more about curves with the **Graph** editor. This is a really important editor to learn in order to become a good animator. It mainly allows us to control the interpolation between the keys. It looks like graph paper with the *y* axis corresponding to the value of the key and the *x* axis to the time. We can select the keys in the same way as the Dope Sheet. As you can see on the left-hand side, we still have the objects on which we added the keyframes. We can also see that we have the type of the keyframe that we've placed; **LocRotScale** in the case of our cube. If we open this with the white arrow, we can see each transformation and its corresponding curve on the right-hand side. Each frame has a handle type that you can change with the *V* key. It looks a little bit like the curve handles that we saw in the Haunted House project. We can set them as **Vector** to have a linear interpolation, for instance. We can also change the interpolation type of each frame by pressing the *T* key. This is a very useful menu that we are going to use in order to quickly animate the bounce of our trap. If you press the *N* key, you will see a bunch of options. You can even see modifiers that allow us to add procedural effect to our curves, for instance, noise. Note that you can use the *Ctrl* + MMB shortcut to squash the graph.

Default interpolation setting

In **User preferences**, in the **Editing** tab, we have the ability to choose the default type of interpolation that we want between two keys. Many animators like to set it as constant so they don't have any interpolation. When the animation plays, it looks like stop motion. After they have the right poses, they select all their keys in the graph editor, and they press *V* to set the Bezier interpolation type back in order to polish the animation.

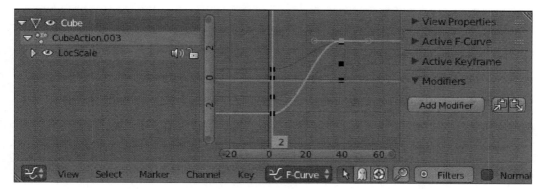

The Graph editor

The Non-Linear Action editor

The **NLA** or **Non-Linear Action** editor is a huge time-saver tool! It allows us to edit actions. Similar to doing video editing, you will edit tracks on which there are actions. You can see an action like a box of keyframes that represent a certain motion of an object. Actions are located in the **Dope Sheet** editor. In its header, we can see a drop-down menu. We can change it from **Dope Sheet** to **Action Editor**. Near this drop-down menu, we have a text field with the name of our action. We can create multiple actions by duplicating them with the **+** button. Each action has its own set of keyframes. So, for instance, you could animate the walk of a character in a specific action, its displacement in another action, and mix them back together in the NLA editor. Back to the NLA editor, we can press *Shift + A* in order to add a new action to a specific track. Tracks are represented on the left-hand side. We can add new tracks by going to the **Add** menu in the header and by choosing the **Add Tracks** option. We can open a hidden panel by pressing *N*. In this panel, you will have many options concerning the selected action.

For instance, we can repeat the selected action by changing the **Repeat** value under the **Action Clip** subpanel. We can also move actions by pressing *G*. This also allows us to move an action from one track to another.

The NLA editor

Preparation of the animation

Before starting the creation of the sequence, it is important to plan what we are going to do.

Writing a short script

We start by organizing our ideas with some brief writing work. We must describe the scene to be animated shot by shot. We can be creative at this moment of the process and imagine any kind of place and situation.

In the first part, we will put some useful information such as the title, exposure (for instance, Out-Day in order to indicate that the action happens outdoors during the day), and the number of the sequence. In our case, there is only one sequence, so we call it **Sequence 1**. This kind of information is usual in a movie script.

The action of the sequence is in the desert. In a very warm and dangerous place, our rat sees a trap after a very long walk. This trap seems to be there for him.

We will follow a rather traditional script structure. There is an initial situation, a disruptive element that happens, and then the fall. In the case of a short animated film of one minute, there is no time to introduce and develop the characters and an enigma. We must go straight to the point.

For our short film, we will do a staging composed of different camera shots, which will require an editing step later. But we must conceive it now. Maybe you know that cinema has a visual grammar that is expressed by editing. It allows us to make sense of the different shots. It is something that you can learn, and there are certain rules to understand. Going deep in this area can only be a huge advantage for your 3D projects.

In order to write a script, we must describe our shots. There are different types of information. These are the field sizes of a shot:

- **The extreme long shot**: This is used for panoramas.
- **The long shot (or establishing shot)**: This allows us to introduce a situation.
- **The full shot**: This frames the characters entirely. It is great for large movements.
- **The medium shot**: This frames the chest and the head of the character.
- **The American shot (or ¾ shot)**: This frames a character from the thighs to the head. It is close enough to a medium shot.
- **The close-up shot**: This frames the face of the character, and it allows us to perceive emotions better.
- **The Italian shot** (or extreme close up): This frames the eyes of the character.

There are also the angles of a shot:

- **The low angle shot**: The camera is low and the frame upwards. This will enhance the character.
- **The high angle shot**: The camera is high and the frame downward.
- **The aerial shot**: This frames the scenery viewed from the sky.

The camera can also rotate with a pan or be mobile. We often speak of a **tracking shot**. In cinema, the camera is often mounted on a camera dolly or a steady cam for a perfect smooth shot. There are other types of shots and framing, but these are the main types you should know in order to express yourself.

```
Title : Rat Coybow

Outdoor Day

Sequence 1 :

Shot 01 : Long shot of the background.  The character moves forward and
the camera makes a lateral tracking shot. The character stops walking in
front of the camera. He frowns and seems to observe something away.

Shot 02: Medium shot of the cheese placed on a trap.

Shot 03 : Full shot on the side. We see the position of the rat and the
trap.

Shot 04 : Close up of the eyes of the rat.

Shot 05 : Close up of the cheese. slight zoom.

Shot 06 : Close up of the hand preparing to take the gun located above
the holster.

Shot 07 : Close up of the cheese with the trap.

Shot 08 : Italian shot on the side. The rat waits a moment and shots with
his gun.

Shot 09 : Full shot. The cheese is projected behind the trap that closes.
Tracking shot focus on the rolling cheese.

Shot 11 : Close up of the eyes of the rat. He is smiling.
```

The storyboard

Making a storyboard

After this first reflection of writing the script, we can start making a storyboard. It is a technical document that the areas of animation films have been using since the 30's. A storyboard allows us to describe the action with drawings, but it also to goes further than the text in the design of the shots. In the case of teamwork, it is a very useful tool to communicate the work, and it gives a comprehensive view of a project.

Seeing that the storyboard allows us to save a huge amount of time and money, it is a practice that has gradually extended to the field of cinema (classical movies, but mostly special effects movies), theater, clips, and commercials. Even if we are very far from making a blockbuster, and have no team to communicate our work to, a storyboard is a very important step to make a good animated short film.

Don't worry if you are not very gifted in drawing. Many storyboards are very simple and schematic. The most important thing is to clarify your ideas of staging. It must be easy to understand with the indications of stage direction such as camera and character motion.

For our storyboard, we draw the different shots referring to the script that we have done previously. Continuity is from left to right like a comic. To describe a shot, we can make several drawings. For shot 1, three drawings are used to describe the movement of the camera and the character. In order to avoid getting lost, we mark the number of the matching shot at the bottom left of each thumbnail.

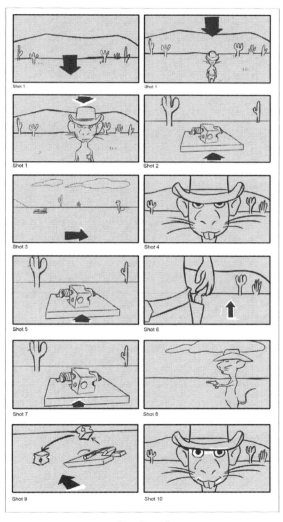

Storyboard

Finding the final camera placements and the timing through a layout

The layout is an animated version of the storyboard. It is sometimes called an "Animatic". We don't need to animate our character at this stage. We simply need to visualize the shots that we imagined previously with the script and the storyboard. We can then verify if this works and get a better idea of the time we need for each shot.

The process is as follows:

1. We will import the character in Blender by simply copying it from the `RayCharacter.blend` file to a new file.

2. We will save the scene as `RatLayout.blend`.

3. We will start outlining very simple scenery with a few low poly 3D models. We will use a plane for the floor and an extruded cube for the mountains beyond.

4. We will model a simple cactus and duplicate it pretty much everywhere on the floor.

5. We will also make a simple model of the trap and the cheese. We only need to get the basic shape.

6. To be more comfortable with this, we will organize the environment by dividing it in several parts. It is much better to display the **Dope Sheet**, **Graph** Editor, and camera view in a little window (0 of the numeric keyboard).

7. For each shot, we will create a new scene by clicking on the + button in the main menu bar, and we will select the **Full Copy** option.

8. The placement of our character, the trap with the cheese and making a few tests with the camera are still remaining.

This is the step where we can still make a few changes and test movements and timings.

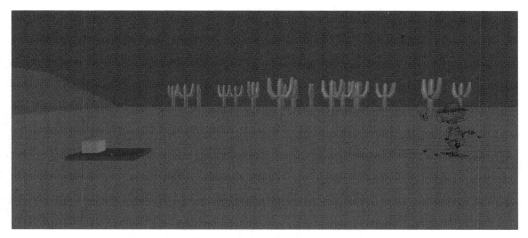

Screenshot of the layout shot 03 with the rough modeling

Animation references

While animating, it is important to have as many references as you can so that you can have the perfect shot. Many computer animators have a folder with videos of themselves acting the shot. Recording yourself is one of the best ways to understand the gesture of a character. This way you will be able to catch many unconscious movements that you do when you look at the video. It is also a way to improvise different acts. Other reference materials such as character poses or animation cycle images are very interesting. Apart from this, paper and pencil are often useful in order to grasp some poses that you have in mind. You don't need to draw in detail, as a simple stick figure will suffice in order to put the poses ideas on paper.

Organization

Before starting to animate our shots, we will introduce to you how to organize yourself for the whole sequence. The different assets have been created in different `.blend` files. What's neat about this is that we are going to link them all in one final file for each shot. The benefit of this is that if we want to change the look of one of the assets, we can do it in the original file and it will replicate in the master file. For the rig of the rat cowboy, we are going to create a proxy.

In our case, we have ten shots, so we will create one .blend file for each of them. All these files will be placed in a Scene folder and will reference files that are placed one folder up in the folder hierarchy. Let's create our files:

1. We will first create a new blank file in Blender and save it as 01.blend in a new folder named Scene. Note that you can create a new folder in the file browser with the *I* key.

2. Now let's open the terrain file and select everything that needs to be linked in the shot file. We are only selecting the mesh type objects here. We are going to group our selection with *Ctrl + G* and rename the group as Terrain in the last tool option subpanel.

3. We will then repeat the same process with the other asset files. For the cactus file, you can create one group for each cactus.

4. Now the different groups are ready to be linked in the shot file. In the 01.blend file, select the **Link** option in the **File** menu or press *Ctrl + Alt + O*. We can now click on the **Terrain** file and navigate to the **Group** folder in order to select the **Terrain** group that we've created within this file. We can validate by pressing **Link from Library**.

The Link and Append file structures

The structure of a .blend file is composed of different sections that represent the file. Each section is related to the entity it contains. For instance, in the **Group** section, you will find every group that has been created in the file, and in the **Nodes** section, you will every node that has been created in the file, and so on. This file format is quite nice because it's open and very well organized.

One very cool feature of Blender is the ability to mix files or parts of files together by linking or appending them. With the **Link** option, you keep a relation with the original file, so any modification will be replicated. The **Append** method creates a pure copy of what you want to mix.

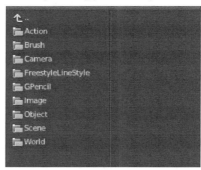

The structure of a blend file

---

5. The link should be done. You can test whether it works by saving the **01** file then tweaking the **Terrain** file, and going back to the **01** file to see whether the changes appear. Now we can repeat the same process with the other assets that need to be linked in the shot file. You can easily nest files by linking groups to files that are linked themselves as a group in another file.

6. Cactus, bones, and bush are linked in the terrain file and they are part of the **Terrain** group (remember to add them to this group, as it will be linked in each shot file). The terrain is linked in each shot file. The **Cheese** group is linked to the **Trap** file, and the **Trap** group is linked to the **02, 03, 05, 07,** and **08** files. We will not link the trap in the terrain file as it won't be needed for each shot. For the rat character, we will simply create a group with the **Armature** and **Mesh** object that we will link to the **01, 03, 04, 06, 08,** and **10** files.

7. In each file, we need to create a proxy for the rig of the rat. To do so, we will select the rig, and we will press *Ctrl + Alt + P* and click on the **Armature** object.

Proxy

You may have already seen that when you use the link option, you can't do any modifications in the linked file. This is a security guard, so you only manage your art in one file. But in the case of a rigged character, this could be embarrassing. That's why we create a local access of the rig called a **Proxy** in the linked file with *Ctrl + Alt + P*.

You can have a look at the structure of our project as follows:

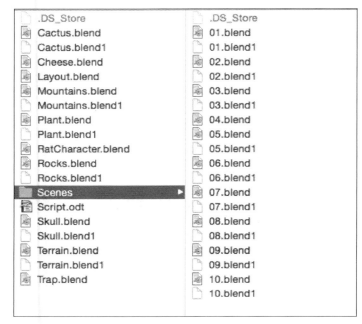

The architecture of our project

Animating the scene

Now that we have a story to tell, let's start to animate each shot using the tools that we saw previously.

The walk cycle

We are now going to learn how to create a walk cycle for the first shot. Why a cycle? This is because we are simply going to repeat the walk actions automatically later in order to save time. There are different types of walk that can express the actual feeling of the character. In our case, we are going to animate a cowboy walk, so this means our character will need a certain assurance. In order to be efficient, we are first going to "key" the three main poses of a walk as follows:

1. We will first open the 01.blend file and focus our view on the left-hand side view of the character. We will need to be sure that the **Auto Key** button is turned on, so any translation (grab, rotate, or scale) will create or override a key where the bar is located in the timeline. This button is located in the header of the **Timeline** editor and looks like a recording button.

2. Before creating our poses, we will have to select our armature in pose mode. We can then hide the **Master** bone by selecting it and pressing *H* because our walk will be animated onsite. Also, be sure that your timeline bar is at frame 0.

3. The first pose that we are going to create is usually called the "Contact pose" because both feet are touching the ground. From the side view, we will select the left foot bone, and we will move it in front of the character. We will then place the other foot bone in the opposite location. As you can see, because the legs are too far apart, the character isn't able to touch the ground (represented here by the Y world axis). So we have to select all the visible bones and move them down until the character is on the ground.

4. Now we will lift the front leg toes up a little bit on the local *x* axis (press *R* and then *X* twice).

5. We will then pose the back foot so that the rat stands on its toes.

6. From a front view, we will orient both legs outwards a little bit.

7. The arms need to follow the direction of their opposite leg. To move the arm, we will use the **HandIK** bone. We can also slightly bend the arms and rotate it, and then break the hand rotation a little bit.

8. From a front view, we can slightly put the right arm inward. The left arm will not rotate as much inward because of the holster.

9. In order to polish this pose, we will rotate the **Hips** bone down in the direction of the right leg and the **Spine01** and the **Neck** bone in the opposite direction of the hips. We will also rotate the head down so that the character looks at the ground. We will also pose the fingers so that the index finger is straighter than the others. We will also rotate the tail outward.

10. At this point it's a good idea to open a **Dope Sheet** editor. As you can see, we have small diamonds that represent the keys on each bone (described in the list on the left-hand side). For the main poses, it's always a good idea to have a key placed on every bone. To do so, we will select them all in the 3D view, and we will press *I* and choose the **LocRotScale** option.

11. In order to have a perfect cycle motion, the first and the last key of the walk needs to be the same. So in the dope sheet, we will select all the keys of our first pose by right-clicking on the **Dope Sheet Summary** corresponding to the key, and we will press *Shift + D* to duplicate this. We can move this to frame 24. You can clearly see that the keys are the same because of the dark lines that link them.

12. Now, we will copy this pose right between these two keys but in a mirror. To do so, we will select every bone in the 3D viewport, and we will store the pose with *Ctrl + C*. At frame 12, we can press *Ctrl + Shift + V* in order to copy the pose in the mirror, thanks to our bone naming convention with the **.L** and **.R** suffixes. If we scrub the timeline bar, we can see a preview of our walk. But there are still many things missing.

Congratulation, you have made the contact poses of the walk cycle! Now we will create the "Passing pose". This is done as follows:

1. To create our passing pose, we will use the same process as before. We will first create our pose between the 1 key and the 12 key, and we will mirror it between the 12 and 24 keys.

2. So we will place our timeline bar at frame 6. We will start creating our pose from the side view. The leg that was in the front of the character will be straight. So we will select the left foot controller, and we will align it horizontally with the rest of the body. As you can see, the leg can't be straight if the hips aren't moved up. We move the hips up. This is the key point of any walk: *the body always moves up and down.*

3. The other foot is bent. It is also placed slightly behind the straight leg, and the toes point downward.

4. At this point, the arms are almost straight and aligned with the rest of the body.

5. From the front view, **Hips**, **Spine01**, and **Neck** need to be aligned with the ground.

6. We can slightly rotate the head on the *z* axis to the left of the rat.

7. Now we ensure that we have keys on every bone. After this, we will copy our pose in the mirror on frame 18 with the same method seen previously.

8. A nice trick you can do is to change the visual look of your keys in the Dope Sheet by selecting them and by pressing *R*.

We now have the essential poses of a walk. The rest of our work will consist of exaggerating the motion by adding a "Down" and "Up" pose. This is done as follows:

1. The "Down" pose will be placed before the "Passing" pose. To create this, we will clear the toe rotation of the front foot.

   Then we will exaggerate the pose by slightly moving the pelvis down. The whole goal of this pose is to feel the weight of body on the ground.

2. The "Up" pose is placed after the "Passing" pose. This consists of lifting the character on his straight leg and toes.

3. After we have finished these poses, we can duplicate them in the mirror by following the same order according to the "Passing" pose.

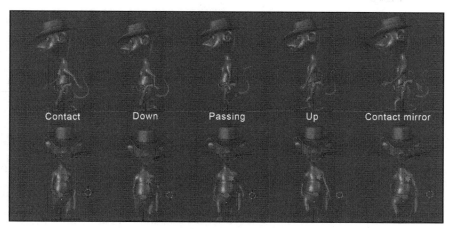

Walk cycle poses

The walk cycles is completed now! We can view it by scrubbing on the timeline or simply by changing the end frame to the 23 frame in the timeline header and by playing the animation with *Alt + A*.

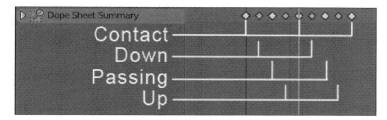

The Dope Sheet for our walk cycle

Mixing actions

We are now going to create three new actions that we will blend in with the NLA editor. One will be in charge of moving the character from its current location to the front of the camera. One will represent the character lifting his head up, and the last one will contain a mix of the others. This is done as follows:

1. The first thing to do is to copy the camera from the Layout blend file. To do so, we will simply copy the camera of the first scene in the corresponding file with *Ctrl + C*, and we will paste it with *Ctrl + V* in the **01.blend** file. If you have any other cameras in the scene, remove them and be sure that the copied one is the active one by selecting it and pressing *Ctrl + 0* numpad key.

2. In order to create our new actions, we will need to open the **Action Editor** from the Dope Sheet editor. As you can see, our walk cycle has been already placed on the default action. By the way, we can rename it `Walk`.

3. We can now click on the **+** button in order to create a new action. This new action will be a copy of the walk action, so we can delete all the present keys and rename the action `Move`.

4. Now we can start to animate the character displacement on this action. To do this, we will simply use the **Master** bone of our rig. In our case, we have added two keys at frame 0 and 225.

5. The problem now is that the rat seems to accelerate at the beginning and decelerate at the end. To solve this, we are going to use the graph editor and change the shape of the Y location curve. So in the graph editor, we select the keys for the Y location, and we press *V* and **Vector**. Now, as you can see, the curve is linear. Remember to save your file!

6. Now we are going to mix the walk and the displacement together. To do this, we will create a new action that contains all the others. We rename it as `Final` and remove all the present keys.

7. In the NLA editor, we will ensure that we are editing on this action. We will then create a new track (**Add | Add tracks**) and press *Shift + A* to add the `Move` action to it.

8. We can then press *Shift + A* in order to add the **Walk** action under the **Move** track. Now we just need to repeat our walk cycle with the **Repeat** option located in the right menu (*N*) under **Animation Clip** (be sure that the walk action is selected in your track). The important thing here is that the cycle stops just before the **Move** action because we are going to animate be hand the end of the walk and the head in a new action.

9. We now need to copy the pose of the character when the walk cycle stops, so we can start with this pose in a new action. We will use *Ctrl + C* with all the bones selected.

10. Now we are going to create the next action. To do this, we will click on the **+** button again, delete the keys, and rename the action `End`.

11. We can now paste our pose (*Ctrl + V*) on the same frame where we copied it in the NLA in the **End** action. This is because of the camera motion.

12. Now we need to complete a half walk and animate the character's head. In our case the animation starts at frame 216 and ends at frame 248. We ensure the character stands on his feet correctly, and we can animate the head pointing towards the camera. We can also add an eye blink in the middle. We will also rotate the head to the left of the camera.

13. After finishing the animation of the action, we will need to reposition our keys so that they start at frame 0. In the **Action Editor**, we will press *A* in order to select all the keys, and with *G*, we will drag them until the first frame of our animation is on frame 0.

14. Now we can go back to the **Final** action and open the NLA editor. We will then place our **End** when the walk cycle ends.

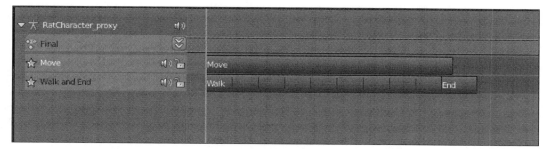

The NLA with our three actions mixed together in the **Final** action.

15. That's all! We have now blended our three actions with the NLA. Note that you can also rename your tracks on the left-hand side of the NLA by clicking on their default name.

One frame of the **End** action

Animation of a close shot

The close up of the face that we are going to do is directly inspired by Italian westerns of the 60's. A close up allows us to give a tension focusing on the eyes of our character. This is done as follows:

1. We will start by opening the **04.blend** scene.

2. We will need to place our character at the same place as in the **01.blend** scene, so we will also open the **01.blend** scene.

3. In the **Right Panel** (*N*) of scene **01**, we must copy the location information of the **Master** bone (Root) on the three axes, X, Y, and Z. In our case, **X: -1.19863, Y: 0,0,** and **Z: 12.29828,** and we will paste them on the location parameters of the **Master** bone in scene **04**. Our character is now in the right place.

4. We need to be sure that the **Auto Key** button is turned on, and we add the first key at frame 1 on the camera and all the bones of the character.

This animation will be in 50 frames.

1. We also need to place the camera in front of the face of the character.

2. We will move to frame 50 of the timeline, and we will slightly move the camera on the local *z* axis.

3. We can see a slow in and slow out effect of the camera, the keys are in Bezier interpolation mode. In order to change the interpolation mode, we must open the **Graph Editor**. We will select the keys of the camera and press V and select **Vector**. Now the camera is moving in a linear way.

Let's animate our character. He is watching the trap, so he doesn't move a lot. The animation is done as follows:

1. We begin by animating the head. We will move the cursor of the **Timeline** at frame 50, and we make a little rotation on the local *z* axis, a new key frame is added.

2. The Frown bone stays down to keep a serious look.

3. We can now animate the eyes. At frame 50, we will move down the **EyeTargetMaster** a little bit. He is still looking straight toward the camera.

4. We will now add a blink of the eyes to give more realism.

5. We will select the both **EyeTarget.L** and **EyeTarget.R**, and we will add a key at frames 16 and 23 (press *I* and select **Scale**). We will move then at frame 19, and we will scale the bone controllers to close his eyes.

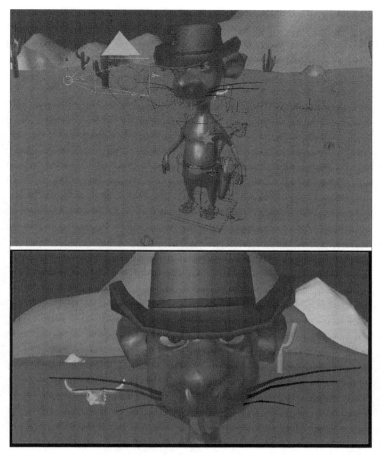

The close shot

This very short animation for shot 4 is finished. Shot 10 is almost the same but with a smile at the end. Let's start the animation of the gunshot!

Animation of the gunshot

The animation of shot 8 this time is a bit more complex. This will be done as follows:

1. We will start by opening the **08.blend** scene.

2. We will place our character at the same location as the **01.blend** file.

3. With the **Auto Key** button turned on, we will start placing the camera on the left-hand side of the character.

It is an animation in 30 frames.

1. We will put the camera on the left-hand side of the character, and then we will move it slightly to the left along the *y* axis to frame 30. We will change the keys of the camera in the **Vector** mode (V) in the **Graph** Editor.

2. We can now animate our character. We will start animating the hand. The hand must go straight to the butt of the gun to hold it. The position and the inclination of the hand are very important. It doesn't matter if there is a little interpenetration of the thumb. The animation is fast, and the point of view of the camera can hide small mistakes. The forefinger must be close to the trigger when he holds the gun.

The gun shot

3. To move the fingers, we must select the top bones and rotate them on the local x axis (press R and then press X twice). The **Copy Rotation** constraints will make the rest.

4. When the gun is caught, we must change the influence of the **Child Of** constraint of the gun bone. The influence of child of controlled by the holster is now at **0.000**, and the influence of child of controlled by the left hand is now at **1.000**. The gun is now following the hand. We can keep animating the left hand.

5. We will position the hand so that the gun gives the impression that it will shoot ahead. There is the recoil of the gun, so the hand makes a sudden rotational movement upwards.

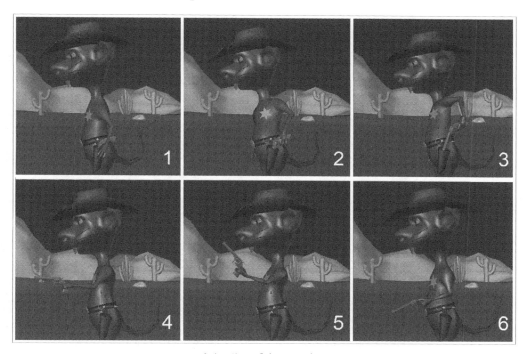

Animation of the gun shot

When the animation of the left hand and the gun is done, the largest part of the animation of the sequence will be done too, but we still need to polish this shot a little bit. The rest of the body must be animated and can't stay inert. This will be done as follows:

1. We need to make a rotation of the **Spine01** bone on the *z* and *y* local axis when the left hand catches the butt of the gun. Likewise, the left shoulder must rotate towards the top (refer to **2** and **3** in the preceding screenshot) at this moment.

2. As the rotation of the spine01 bone the head is inclined to the right, we will rotate it a little bit to adjust it. For the recoil of the gun, we will make a little rotation of the head.

3. The **HipsReverse** bone also makes a rotation on the local *z* and *y* axes to gives a more realistic feeling.

4. The right hand and the tail also make a little arc. In this case, they are quite important details.

So, the animation of the gunshot is now complete. Let's talk about the animation of the trap.

Animation of the trap

It's now time to animate one of the most technical shots of our sequence where the cheese gets shot on the trap. This will be done as follows:

1. We will start by opening the **09.blend** file. Then we can frame the trap with camera as done in the layout.

2. The first thing to do is to add a key frame on each bone of the trap only for rotation, so we select them and press *I* and select **Rotation**. We won't use AutoKey for now. Remember that the trap is linked. If you can't access the rig, it's simply because you don't have a proxy in order to manipulate it.

3. Now we can go to frame 13 and rotate the **TopStick** and the **TrapPlank** bone on the their *x* local axes as far as their can logically go.

4. The **Spring** bone animation will be shorter, though. We will key its extreme rotation on frame 7.

5. We can now test our animation to see what's wrong with it, but first we will hide the cheese with the *H* key. As you can see, the animation doesn't seem very natural. This is why we are going to tweak the curves in the graph editor.

6. We will open the graph editor and click on the **Show only selected** button in the header.

7. Now we can select the **TopStick** bone and unfold its **Rotation** values on the left-hand side of the **Graph** editor. We can even hide the other y and z rotations as we don't need them. To do so, we will use the Eye icon. As you can see, the curve has an ease in and ease out effect. We don't want this. We want a bounce effect. To do so, we can, of course, add more keys and waste time to animate it by hand, or we can use the power of the Dynamic effects of the interpolation menu. So we select our keys, and we press T and select **Bounce**. As you can see, the curve changes.

8. We can do the same with the **TrapPlank** and the **Spring** bones. For this, a later bounce will be more subtle. Now if we play our animation, everything looks more natural.

9. Now let's animate the cheese. First unhide it with $Alt + H$.

10. We can now reactivate the **AutoKey** option, it will be easier. Let's start by adding a key on frame 0 with press I and select **LocRotScale**. Now, because of autokey, we can move to frame 16 and move the cheese to its final destination.

11. We can now go to frame 5 and put the cheese in the air. This will change its Z location. We can also rotate it and scale it locally on its z axis (press S and then press Z twice).

12. The animation at this point is not very convincing. In order to add more realism to it, we can open the graph editor and change the curve of the Z location of the cheese, so it is much more like a "dome" at the beginning. To do so, we can set frames 0 and 9 to a vector type (press V and select **Vector**). We will need to change the handles of frame 5 too.

13. Next, we will change the end of the motion by adding two new keyframes on the Z location at frames 11 and 17. These keys will have a **Bounce** Dynamic effect. We will use the handles in order to smooth the curve as much as possible where it is needed. Remember that the animation process involves a lot of trial and error. You also need to constantly play your animation in order to know what you'll have to correct.

14. We can now reset the scale of the cheese at frame 11 by pressing $Alt + S$.

15. What we've done so far is the base of the cheese animation. Now we can polish the animation by changing its rotation here and there and by polishing the Y location curve.

16. We can now animate the camera. Between keys 0 and 16, the camera doesn't move, so we simply duplicate frame 0 to frame 16.

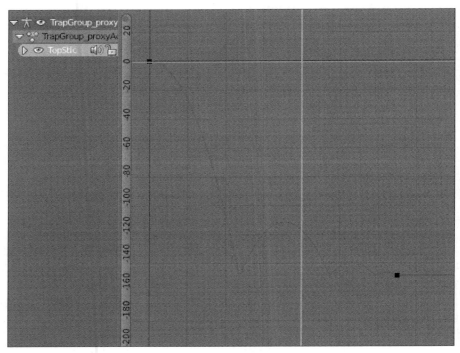

The **TopStick** X rotation curve

17. We can now place our timeline bar at frame 37 and focus on the cheese closely, so we can see the hole due to the gunshot. The key has been placed due to the AutoKey option.

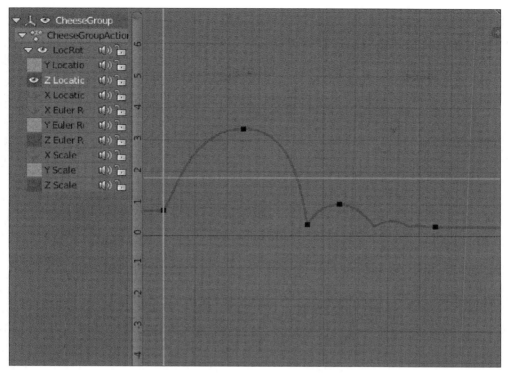

The cheese Z location curve

The animation of the 09 shot is now completed, congratulations!

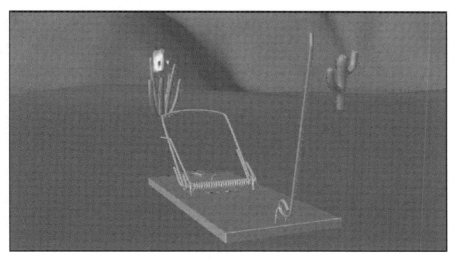

Frame 4 of the 09 shot.

Render a quick preview of a shot

The last thing we are going to do is render quick previews of each shot. This is often called a **PlayBlast**. This simply renders the animation of the viewport. In this section, we are only going to render the playblast of the first shot. So let's start:

1. We will open the **01.blend** file.

2. In the Properties editor, in the **Render** tab, we will go to the **Output** subpanel. Here we can choose the path where the render will be. To be well organized, let's create a **Playblast** folder in our **Scene** folder and set it as the output path.

3. Now we will need to choose the file format. By default, it will output a sequence of a PNG file. We change it to **H.264** in order to have a movie type file.

4. In the **Encoding** section, we can choose the extension of our movie, and we choose **Quicktime** to have a .mov file. Later, you'll see how to render the shots frame by frame in a non-video format, but for now in order to quickly see the result, we will use .mov.

5. Be sure that you are viewing from the camera by pressing the *0* numpad key. In order to render the playblast, we can press the **OpenGL Render active viewport** button in the header of the 3D View (a clap icon).

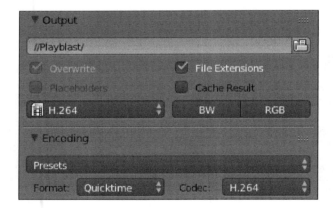

The **Output** option for the **Playblast** rendering

Summary

This was a very tough chapter, but we hope you have found it interesting. We covered a lot of things here, such as the principles of animation, the majority of the Blender animation tools, and how to prepare ourselves with a script, storyboard, and layout. We also learned how to animate a walk cycle and mix it with other actions using the NLA. We applied many of the 12 principles of animation such as pose-to-pose, squash, and stretch overlapping. Now, you should have all the knowledge to start telling your own stories with Blender. In the next chapter, we are going to finalize our sequence by rendering it with cycles and editing it with the VSE.

10
Rat Cowboy – Rendering, Compositing, and Editing

Welcome to the last chapter of the book. In this chapter, you will learn advance material creation in Cycles, such as how to use a skin shader or how to create a realistic fur. Next, you will learn about passes and how to do a raw render with the different passes. Then, you will receive an introduction to the nodal compositing so that you can enhance your shots. Lastly, we will talk about the Video Sequence Editor in order to edit the final sequence. Let's start!

In this chapter, we will cover the following topics:

- Creating advance material
- Creating fur particle systems
- Setting up Cycles for an animated scene
- Using passes
- Introducing nodal compositing
- Editing a sequence

Creating advanced materials in Cycles

We already covered material creation with Cycles in the Haunted House project, but now we are going to go further by creating a skin material using subsurface scattering, a complete fur, and an eye material. Let's start!

Skin material with Subsurface Scattering

The skin has a very translucent aspect. We can truly see this effect when we pass our hand in front of a lamp or in the thin part of the ear (the helix). So, when creating a skin material, we get this phenomena with a Subsurface Scattering node (usually abbreviated SSS). It is called this because the light rays are scattered through the geometry when intersecting the mesh. This is not the case with a diffuse shader, for instance, as the light rays are simply blocked. SSS often gives a reddish tint to the thin parts where light rays scatter a lot. So let's create the skin material of the rat.

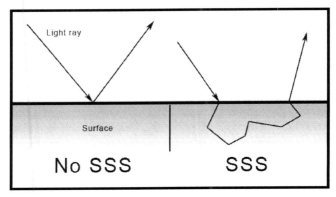

The way light rays react on SSS surfaces

1. We will open the `RatCharacter.blend` file and split our interface so that we have a second 3D view for the real-time renderer and a node editor. Note that the real-time renderer for the SSS shader will only work in the CPU mode or with the GPU in the experimental mode.

2. We will add a new slot in the material tab of the Properties editor and a new material that we name as **Skin**. We will press the **Use node** button in order to work in the node editor.

3. In the node editor, we will remove the default **Diffuse** shader by selecting it and pressing **X**. Then, we can add a **Subsurface Scattering** shader by pressing *Shift + A*.

4. We have some options to tweak for this shader. The first one is the **Scale option,** which corresponds to the amount of SSS that we want. In the case of the rat, we set it to **0.1,** but in order to have the correct value, you will need to perform a test. It's just a matter of placing a light in the back of the character and looking at the thin parts, such as the ears.

5. The next very important setting to tweak is the radius that corresponds to the predominant color that will result to the SSS effect. In many cases, we will let more red than green and blue because of the color of the blood that's under the skin. This is a set of three values that corresponds to R, G, and B, in our case, we set them to **1.0, 0.7,** and **0.5** respectively.

6. Now, we will plug our texture in the **Color** input. Finally, we can connect the shader to the output.

7. We will now add a reflection to our skin by mixing our SSS shader with a glossy shader. To do so, we append a **Mix Shader** on top of the SSS to the Material output wire.

8. In the second shader input, we can bring a **Glossy BSDF** shader and change the **Roughness** value to **0.392** so that the reflection is less sharp.

9. For the **Fac** input of the **Mix Shader**, we will add a **Fresnel** node. This skin shader will be sufficient for our needs, but note that we can go much deeper in the subject by creating a shader with multiple maps that corresponds to the different skin parts, such as sub-dermal and epidermal.

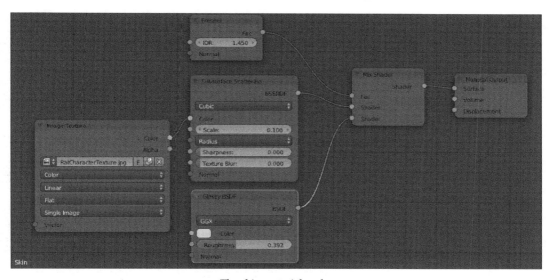

The skin material nodes

The SSS effect on the ears to the right and on the hand to the left in viewport rendered mode will look like the following:

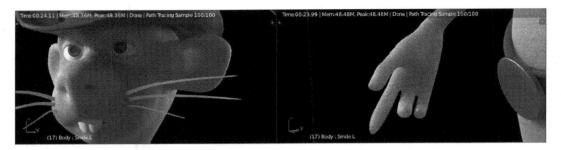

Eye material

We are now going to create a less difficult material, that is, the one of the eye corneas. This will be like a glass material, but we will optimize it a little bit because the default glass shader is so physically accurate that it also casts shadows of the glass itself. These take a long time to render and are rarely visible. In order to apply our material, we will model a simple cornea in the eye mesh itself. The front part of the cornea is extruded a little bit. This allows us to catch the reflections rays better:

1. We will first need to add another material slot and a material that we rename as **Cornea**. As you can see, we already have three slots that correspond to the white part and the pupil of the eyes. Feel free to replace it with one material with a texture.

2. Next, we can select the cornea piece of the mesh in the **Edit Mode** with the L key and press the **Apply** button in order to apply the cornea material on this part of the mesh.

3. In the node editor, we will replace the default Diffuse shader with a **Glass BSDF** shader.

4. We will now mix the **Glass BSDF** shader with a **Transparent BSDF** shader. A transparent shader simply lets every ray to pass through.

5. Now, in the **Fac** input of the **Mix** Shader, we will plug a **Light Path** node (press *Shift + A* and select **Input**) with the **Is Shadow Ray** output. This will tell the render engine to use the transparent shader for the incoming shadow rays and the glass shader for the others. At this point, we should have a nice reflecting eye.

The fur of the rat

Now, let's dive into a complex section about fur creation. In order to create a convincing fur, we will have to create a complex material, have a perfect hair particle combing, and correct lighting. If one of these three parameters is sloppy, it won't look great. Let's start with the particle systems:

1. In order to add more realism, we are going to create three particle systems. Let's first select the character in the **Edit Mode** and add the main particle system in the Particle tab of the Properties editor. We will name both the system and its settings **Basic_FUR**.

2. We will change the system's type from **Emitter** to **Hair**. In the **Emission** subpanel, we will change the **Number** to **500**, which correspond to the guiding hairs. We can also change the hair length to **0.140**.

3. In the **Children** section, we will choose the **Interpolated** method. The number of children that will follow the guiding hairs is too low. We will change the **Render** option to **600**, so each guide will have 600 children. We can also change the display option to **100** to preview the result in the viewport.

4. In the **Children** subpanel, we can change the **Length** setting to **0.640** and the **Threshold** to **0.240**. This will add some randomness to the length of the children.

5. Then, in the **Roughness** section, we can change the **Endpoint** value to **0.046** and the **Random** to **0.015**. **Endpoint** will spread the tips of each hair strand.

6. Now, we will create a Vertex group that will determine where the fur will be located on the rat. In the **Object data** tab of the Properties editor, in the **Vertex Groups** section, we will start by locking all our skinning groups by selecting the black arrow button and choosing the **Lock All** option. This will ensure that we don't change them inadvertently. We can now add a new group with the + button and name it **Fur**. In the **Edit Mode**, we can select the hands, nose, ears, tail, mouth, and eye contour. We invert the selection with *Ctrl + I* and press the **Assign** button with a weight of **1.0**.

7. Back in **Particle** tab, in the **Vertex Groups** section, we can set the **Density** field to our new vertex group. We should now only have hairs on the needed parts.

8. In order to improve our system, we will create a new vertex group named **Fur_Length** that will affect the length of the hair on certain parts. To create the group, we can duplicate the previous **Fur** group with the corresponding option in the black arrow drop-down menu. We can then use the weight paint tools in order to subtract weight from different parts. In our case, the head is green and the arms and the legs are orange and blue under the belt.

9. In the **Vertex Groups** section of the **Particle Settings** tab, we can change the **Length** field to this new group.

Now, we need to comb our particles as follows:

1. To do so, we can use the **Particle Mode** (located in the same drop-down menu of the **Object Mode** or **Edit Mode**). By pressing *T*, we open the **Brush** panel where we can use the **Comb** brush to comb the character's hair.

2. We will use the same shortcuts as the sculpt mode for the brush settings. The **Add** brush is nice in order to add new strands when you find some gaps. When using this brush, it's best to check the **Interpolate** option so that it smoothly blends with the others.

3. In the header of the 3D view, you have three new buttons (to the right of the layers) that allow you to select the particle in different ways. With the **Path** mode (the first one), you can only control them with brushes, while with the **Point** mode (the middle one), you have access to each point of the hair, and with the **Tip** mode (the last one), you only control the tip. With the last two modes, you can grab and rotate your character's hair with **G** and **R**. In the left panel, we can also activate the **Children** option in order to see the children.

4. Now let's add another particle system and name it **Random_FUR**. We can then copy the settings of the first one by choosing it in the **Settings** field and pressing the 2 button to make a unique copy of it. Now, we can safely change the setting without affecting the other system. We can click on the **Advanced** option.

5. We will start by changing the amount of guiding hairs to 50 and their length to **0.1**.

6. In the **Emit from** section, we will choose **Verts** and check the **Random** option.

7. In the **Physics** subpanel, we can change the **Brownian** value to **0.090** to add a little bit of randomness.

8. In the children section, we will change the **Render** and **Display** sliders to **50**.

9. We will then change the **Length** to **0.288** and the **Threshold** to **0.28**.

10. We will then ensure that the **Density** field still contains the **Fur** group, but we will remove the **Length** field.

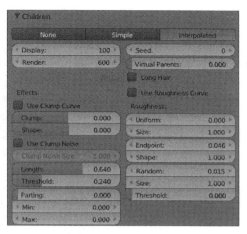

The children settings of the Basic_Fur system.

11. Just as we did for the first two systems, we will add a new system for the fur of the ears. This is very subtle. It has a short hair length and a vertex group for the **Density** field. It also has only 20 children.

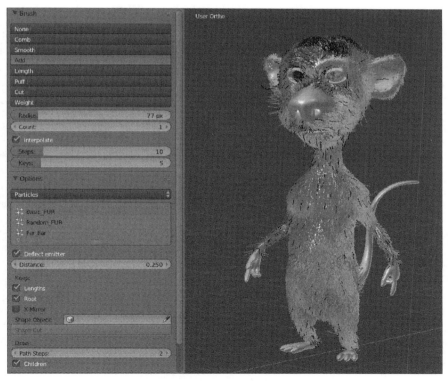

The Particle Edit Mode

You are now done with the particle systems. It's now time to create the materials and change the strand thickness and shape. This will be done as follows:

1. Let's add a new slot in the material tab and a new material named **Fur**.

2. In the node editor, we will delete the default **Diffuse** shader and add two **Hair BSDF** shaders. The first one will be of the **Reflection** type with **RoughnessU** and **RoughnessV** set to **0.500**, and the second will be of the **Transmission** type with **RoughnessU** to **0.1** and **RoughnessV** to **0.2**. We will mix them with **Mix Shader**. The **Fac** input will be plugged with the **intercept** output of a **Hair info** node.

3. We will then add **Musgrave Texture** node with a scale of **538**. We will add a **HueSaturationValue** node with the **Fac** output of the texture connected to the **color** input. We will then mix the result with a **MixRGB** node and **ColorRamp**. The **Fac** input of the color ramp is fed with the **intercept** output of a Hair info node. This will add a gradient map on each strand.

4. We will then plug the output of the **MixRGB** node into another **MixRGB** node. The second input of this node will be fed with a **HueSaturationValue** node. The **Hue** input will receive the color output of a **Musgrave** texture node. This will add color variety to the strand. But in order to lessen the coloring effect, we will change the **Fac** of the **MixRGB** node to **0.047**.

5. Finally, we can plug the result of the last **MixRGB** node in the **color** input of the first **Hair BSDF** node. Our hair material is now completed!

6. We now have to change the **Render** settings of each particle system. In the **Render** subpanel of the particle settings of each system, we will choose our fur material and activate the **B-Spline** option with a value of **4**. This will smoothen the render of the hairs.

7. Then, for the **Basic_Fur** system in the **Cycles Hair Settings** subpanel, we will change the root to **0.5** with a scaling of **0.01** and a shape of **-0.09**. We will use the same settings for the **Random_Fur,** except for the root that we set to **0.15**. Again, we will use the same settings for the **Ear_Fur** system, except for the root that we set to **0.05**.

8. We can now add temporary lights in our `RatCharacter.blend` file in order to do test renders. We will set our samples to 300 and render a preview of our rat.

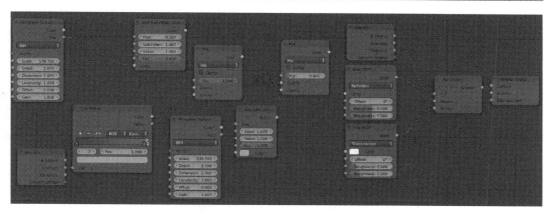

The fur material in the Node editor

The image with a preview render with low render settings is a follows:

Now you have the knowledge to create even more complex materials with Cycles! We are now going to show you how to render the first shot of the sequence, and what's nice with the link is that we will see our fur and materials in each shot file.

The Raw rendering phase

Previously, we have seen how to render an image in Cycles. It is quite different for an animation. It's best to first do a raw render of the shots with the following settings:

1. We will start by adjusting the device. If you have a good graphics card, remember to check the **GPU** device option.

2. Let's now adjust the samples in the **Render** panel (**Properties | Render | Sampling**). The skin needs enough samples to reduce a noisy effect. 100 or 150 samples are enough to have an idea, but consider setting a higher value for the final render.

3. Still in the **Sampling** tab, we will put **1.00** to **Clamp Direct** and **1.00** to **Clamp Indirect**. It allows us to reduce the noise, but you may lose a little bit of the bright colors.

4. We should remember to check the **Cache BVH** and the **Static BVH** options in the **Performance** tab. It allows us to optimize the render time.

5. You can make a test by just rendering a frame (*F12*). Pay attention to the time it takes to complete the rendering process for only one frame. Thus, you can calculate the time needed for a shot.

6. In the **Passes** tab (**Properties | Render Layers | Passes**), we will verify whether **Combined** and **Z** passes are checked.

Passes in Cycles

Passes are a decomposition of the 3D image rendered in Cycles. We can also render passes with Blender Internal but in a different way. Once the rendering calculation is over, we can combine these passes and combine each pass together to create the final image with directly compositing in Blender or another software. The passes allow us to get a control to considerably improve an image and make changes even after the image is rendered. So, it gives more fine-tuning opportunities and saves us a lot of render time.

If you want to explore all the passes of Cycles, visit this link:

`http://wiki.blender.org/index.php/Doc:UK/2.6/Manual/`
`Render/Cycles/Passes`

7. Now that the image quality parameters are set, we must choose an output format of our animation. In the **Output** tab, we will choose the **OpenEXR MultiLayer** format.

   This format has the advantage of containing all active passes with a lossless compression. The passes are a decomposition of the rendered picture (Diffuse, Shadows, Ambient Occlusion, and so on). In our case, we are going to save some time by only rendering the combined and the Z passes. The combined pass corresponds to the final image with all the different passes already combined, and the Z pass gives us a black and white image corresponding to the depth of the scene.

8. In the **Output** tab, we must choose an **Output** path. We will write the following address: //Render\01\. We will press *Enter* to validate the address. The // symbols create a file just next to the blend file.

9. It is a raw render, so we uncheck the **Compositing** option in the **Post Processing** tab (**Properties | Processing**).

OpenEXR

This is a high dynamic-range (HDR) image file format created and used for special effects in the VFX industry. It is now a standard format supported by most of 3D and compositing softwares. The OpenEXR Multilayer format is a variation. It can hold unlimited layers and passes.

If you want more information about OpenEXR in Blender, visit this link:

http://blender.org/manual/data_system/files/image_formats.html#openexr

You are now ready to render the animation. You can press the **Animation** button to start rendering. We must repeat this process for each shot.

Enhance a picture with compositing

Now that we have a raw render, it is time to learn how to improve it using the compositing tools of Blender.

Introduction to nodal compositing

Blender is a complete tool that also allows compositing. This is the ability to edit an image or a sequence after the rendering phase. You probably have already tried compositing, maybe unknowingly. For example, Adobe Photoshop© is a software that allows us to composite a single image. Unlike Adobe Photoshop©, Blender uses a nodal system that provides a great flexibility. We can make changes at any point without the loss of information. Let's try this:

1. For a first approach of nodal compositing, let's open a new Blender scene.

2. In order to access the compositing mode, you must open the **Node Editor**. This is the same as the Node Editor for materials.

3. We must then check the **Compositing** button near the **Shader** button in the **Header** options. It is a small icon button symbolizing an image over another.

4. We must also check the **Use Nodes** button.

We have now two nodes, a Render Layer node and a Composite node.

1. We can split our scene to open the 3D View and make a render of the cube in the middle of the scene (**F12**).

2. We can also add a **Viewer** node (press *Shift* + *A* and select **Output | Viewer**). This node will allow us to visualize the compositing result directly in the **Node Editor**. You only need to connect the **Image** output socket of the **Render Layer** node to the **Image** input socket of the **Viewer** node and check the **Backdrop** option of the **Header**.

Now the render image appears behind the nodes. It will be pretty useful to do compositing in full screen. If you want to move the render image, use *Alt* and MMB. Two other interesting short keys are *V* to zoom in and *Alt* + *V* to zoom out.

1. We will add a **Color Balance** (press *Shift* + *A* and select **Color | Color Balance**) and connect it between the **Render Layers** node (to the **Image** output socket) and the **Viewer** node (to the **Image** input socket).

2. If we change the lift color, the render image is directly updated.

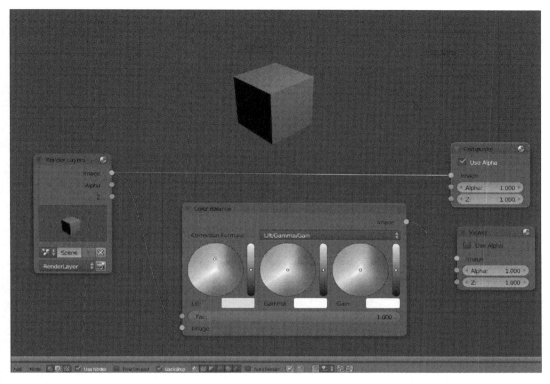

3. We can also replace the render of the cube by any other picture, by adding an **Image** node (press *Shift + A* and select **Input | Image**), and connecting the **Image** output socket to the **Image** input socket of the **Color Balance** node.

> **Looking at a texture node through the Viewer**
>
> There is a node that can help you to better visualize what the compositing looks like at a certain point. You can press *Ctrl + Shift* and right-click on any node to append a ViewNode and connect to it.

The possibilities of compositing in Blender are enormous. For instance, you can easily use keying techniques that are often needed in the movie industry. It consists of replacing a green or a blue screen behind an actor by a virtual set. Compositing is an art and it take too long to explain everything, but we will see some of its basic concepts so that we can improve the shots of our sequence.

Now, we are going to work on the first shot of the sequence:

1. As with any other image file, we must add an **Image** node (press *Shift + A* and select **Input | Image**) and connect it to the viewer.

2. We press the **Open** button of the **Image** node, and we take the corresponding OpenEXR Multilayer file. We also check **Auto-refresh**.

Depth Pass

The following is the combined output socket of the Image node, and there is a Depth output socket. This pass will allow us to simulate an atmospheric depth. It is an effect that can be observed when we look at a distant landscape and a kind of haze is formed. The Depth pass is a visual representation of the Z-Buffer on a grayscale. The objects near the camera will have a gray value close to black, unlike the distant elements, which will have a value close to white. This pass could serve for other things such as masking or blurring the focal depth. It all depends on the context. A controlled atmospheric effect may bring realism to the image.

1. We will start by adding a **Normalize** node (press *Shift + A* and select **Vector | Normalize**). This allows us to clamp all pixel values between 0 and 1. We cannot visualize the Depth pass without a Normalize node.

2. We will add **RGB Curves** (press *Shift + A* and select **Color | RGB Curves**) to change the contrast of the ZDepth pass and control its strength effect.

3. We will then add a **Mix** node (press *Shift + A* and select **Color | Mix**) with a **Mix** blend mode.

Now that we have added the nodes, we are going to connect them as follows:

1. We will need to connect the **Z** output of the **Image** node to the input of the **Normalize** node and the output of the **Normalize** to the **Image** input of the **RGB Curves** node.

2. We will also connect the **Image** output of the **RGB Curves** node to the **Fac** input of the **Mix** node and the **Combined** output socket of the **Image** node to the first **Image** input socket.

3. We must adjust the RGB Curves node by adding another point to the curve. The point is located at **X: 0.36667** and **Y: 0.19375**.

4. We will also need to change the color of the second **Image** input socket of the **Mix** node. The hex code of the color is **D39881**. It will color the white pixels.

A render before and after the ZDepth pass

Color correction of the shot

One of the most important aspects of compositing is color calibration. Fortunately, there are easy-to-use tools in Blender to do that.

1. In order to quickly change the hue, we will add a **Color Balance** node (press *Shift +A* and select **Color | Color Balance**). The hue corresponds to the color tint of the image.

2. We must be very careful to slightly change the value of **Lift**, **Gamma**, and **Gain**. They become strong quickly. The RGB values of Lift are **R: 1.000, G: 0.981**, and **B: 0.971**. The RGB values of Gamma are **R: 1.067, G: 1.08**, and **B: 1.068**. The RGB values of Gain are **R:1.01, G: 0.998**, and **B: 0.959**.

There are two correction formulas: **Lift/Gamma/Gain** and **Offset/Power/Slope**. These are the two ways to get the same result. For each one, there are three color wheels and a value controller (**Fac**). You can modify the darker, the mid-tone, and the highlight values separately.

If you want more information about the color balance node in Blender, visit this link :

```
https://www.blender.org/manual/composite_nodes/types/
color/color_balance.html
```

A render image with an adjustment of the **Color Balance** node will look like this:

Before finishing the compositing, let's add a few effects.

Adding effects

We will add a **Filter** node (press *Shift + A* and select **Filter | Filter**). We must connect the **Image** output socket of the **Mix** node to the **Image** input socket of the **Soften** node, and we will connect the image output socket of the **Soften** node to the **Image** input socket of the **color balance** node. We will keep the filter type to **Soften** with **Fac** of **0.500**. This blends the pixels so that the image is less sharp. A photo is never perfectly sharp.

We will add then a **Lens distortion** node (press *Shift + A* and select **Distort | Lens Distortion**). We must connect the **Image** output socket of the **Color Balance** to the **Image** input socket of the **Lens Distortion** node and the **Image** output socket of the **Lens Distortion** node to the **Image** input socket of the **Viewer** node. We will check the **Projector** button. The **distort** option is at **0.000,** and the **dispersion** option at **0.100.** This node usually allows us to make a distortion effect such as a fish eye, but in our case, it will allow us to make a chromatic aberration. This adds a soft and nice effect.

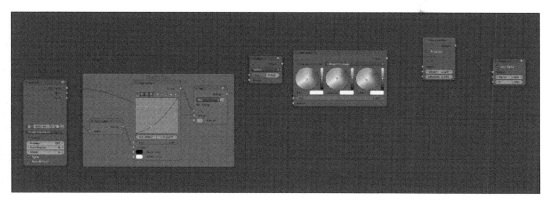

The nodes of compositing

We have now completed the appearance of the shot.

A render with final compositing

Compositing rendering phase

We are now ready to make the render of our compositing:

1. In the **Output** options (**Properties | Render | Output**), we must change the Output path. We will write the following address: //**Render\01\ Compositing**. We will press *Enter* to validate the address.

2. We will also change the Output format to **TGA**.

3. It is a compositing render, so we will check the **Compositing** option in the **Post Processing** tab (**Properties | Processing**).

4. Now, we are ready to render the scene. We will use the same process for each scene.

Editing the sequence with the VSE

Now that we've rendered and done some compositing on each shot, it's time to bring back the whole sequence in one final place. In this section, we are going to do a basic video editing with the VSE.

Two VSE, one is set to the Image Preview (top), the other to the Sequencer (bottom)

Introduction to the Video Sequence Editor

The **VSE** or Video Sequence Editor is a method of video editing in Blender. It is really simple to use and could be very powerful. The best way to use it is to use the **Video Editing** layout located in the menu bar. We usually don't use the Graph editor here, so we can join it back. We have now an interface with two Video Sequence Editors and the Timeline at the bottom. On the head of the VSE, we have three icons that are used to display **Sequencer**, the place where we edit strips, and **Image Preview,** where we see the result of our editing, or both. In Sequencer, we can add different types of strips with *Shift + A*. We are mainly using **Image, Movie**, or **Sound**. We can import Image Sequences with the **Image** option. You can select a strip with RMB and move it with *G*. When you have a strip selected, you have access to two buttons to the left and right represented with arrows that define the start and the end of the strip. You can cut a strip by placing the timeline where you want the split to be and pressing *K* (for knife).

We are not going to go deep into every setting of the VSE, but for each selected strip, you have some options in the right panel of the editor (*N*), such as the **opacity** of an image or movie strip or the volume of an **audio** strip. Of course, you can animate each option by right-clicking on them and choosing the **Insert Keyframe** option, or by simply pressing *I* while hovering over them. You can press *Ctrl* to snap a selected strip to another strip. You can also use the *Shift + D* shortcut in order to duplicate a selected strip.

Edit and render the final sequence

Let's now create the editing of our sequence with the shots that we've composited and rendered before:

1. In order to edit our sequence, we will open a new fresh file. We will also change the layout of our interface so that we have two **VSEs**, one with **Image Preview** and the other with **Sequencer**.

2. Now, we can add our first shot by pressing *Shift + A* in the sequencer and by choosing **Image**. In the file browser, we will go to the **Render** folder and select the **01-compositing** folder in order to select every `.targa` file with *A*. We will now have a new strip that corresponds to the first shot. We will repeat the same process with the other shots.

3. Now, we can move each shot one after the other to create continuity. Be sure that each strip is snapped to the previous one by pressing the *Ctrl* key while moving them.

4. We will also need to readjust the animation start and end in the timeline from the beginning of sequence to its end frame.

5. If you want, you can add **Sound** strips in order to add music or sound effects.

6. We are now ready to render our final edited sequence. To do this, we will change the **Output** path in the **Render** tab of the Properties editor, and we will choose the **H.264** file type. In the **Encoder** section, we will use the **Quicktime** type, and we will, finally, press the render button.

Summary

First, congratulation for arriving at this point of the book; we hope you've learned a lot of things and that you can now realize all the ideas that you ever dreamed about. In this last chapter, we learned how to finalize our sequence by creating advance materials. We also learned how to use the particle system to create a complex fur. Then we set up our render with the OpenEXR MultiLayer format and discovered what passes are. After this, we saw the power of nodal compositing by changing the color balance and adding effects to our shot. As a bonus, we learned how to use the VSE in order to edit our full sequence. Be aware that we didn't explain a lot of things, and you can go deeper into each subject. We recommend that you practice a lot and skim the web and the other books of the PacktPub collection in order to extend your knowledge. Remember, you can learn a tool, but creativity is one of the most important things in this field. We wish you a successful continuation.

Index

Symbols

3D scene
  anatomy 2-5
3D workflow
  3D scene, anatomy 2-5
  overview 1

A

add-ons
  about 13
  searching, on hard-disk 14
  using, in Blender 13
advanced materials, Cycles
  creating 283
  eye material 286
  fur, creating 287-291
  skin material, with Subsurface Scattering
    node 284
  skin material, with Subsurface Scattering
    node 285
Alien Character
  about 14
  retopology, creating 94
Alien Character retopology
  creating 94
  environment, preparing 94, 95
alpha 58
Alt key 55
ambient occlusion
  about 119
  bake, creating 120
  baking 119
  colors, multiplying 119
  displaying, in viewport 121

animation, preparing
  about 258
  final camera placements, searching 262
  final camera timing, searching 262
  organization 263-266
  references 263
  short script, writing 258-260
  shot, angle shot 259
  shot, field sizes 259
  Storyboard, creating 260
animation principles
  about 248
  anticipation 248
  appeal 254
  arcs 251
  exaggeration 253
  Follow Through 250
  Overlapping Action 250
  Pose to Pose 249, 250
  Secondary Action 252
  Slow In 251
  Slow Out 251
  solid drawing 253
  Squash and Stretch 248
  staging 249
  Straight Ahead Action 249, 250
  timing 252
animation tools, Blender
  about 254
  Dope Sheet 255
  Graph editor 256
  keyframe 255
  Non-Linear Action editor 257
  timeline editor 254
Anticipation principle 248
appeal principle 254

D

Damped Track constraint 228
Depth pass 296
Dope Sheet 255
Duplicate Linked tool 41, 130
Duplicate Object 41
Dyntopo
  first touch 61
  versus Multires modifier 60

E

edge loop 23
editor
  about 8
  anatomy 8, 9
  detaching 9, 10
  Header 8
  Join Area button 9, 10
  layout presets 11
  Split Area 9, 10
environment
  cliff, modeling 139, 140
  modeling 139
  scene, enhancing with barrier 144-149
  scene, enhancing with carts 144-149
  scene, enhancing with rocks 144-149
  tree with curves, modeling 140-144
environment preparation, Alien Character
    retopology
  arms 106, 107
  F2 add-on 97
  hands 106-108
  head 95-102
  legs 108, 109
  neck 103-105
  polygon pairs 96
  smooth option 101
  steps 94, 95
  torso 103-105
exaggeration principle 253
Extremes 250
extrusion tool 22

F

Fac input 196
Fill brush 164
Flatten/Contrast brush 85
Follow Through principle 250
fork, Robot Toy
  modeling 41- 43
  protections, modeling 44
Forward Kinematic (FK) 221
Fresnel 197

G

Gizmo tool 21
Grab brush 71
Grab tool 20
Graph editor 256
groups
  using 150

H

Haunted House
  about 15
  bases, blocking 125-128
  blocking 124
  element geometry, working on 135, 136
  stack simulation of wooden planks,
    adding 137
  stack simulation of wooden planks,
    creating 137-139
  world scale, working on 124, 125

I

IK constraint 221
Image Base Lighting (IBL)
  painting 191-195
  using 191-195
Inflate/Deflate brush 78
inset 24
Inverse Kinematic (IK) 221

J

join tool (J) 31

K

keyframe 255
Key Poses 250
knife tool (K) 31, 51
Knife Topology tool (K) 37
Krita 54

L

lattice 143
Left Mouse Button (LMB) 10
light path settings, Cycles
  Filter Glossy 183
  Max and Min Bounces 183
  reflective and refractive caustics 183
lights
  about 184
  IBL, painting 191-195
  IBL, using 191-195
  testing material, creating 184
  types 184-188
  using, in scenes 189, 190
light types
  about 184
  area 187
  hemi 187
  point 186
  spot 187
  sun 186
Link and Append file structures 264
LoopCut tool 28
low poly mesh 110

M

mask 95
Mask brush 84, 164
Matcap
  using 66, 67
materials
  creating, with nodes 195
  mask, adding for windows 199, 200
  Normal Maps, creating in Cycles 202-204
  of house, creating 195-198
  of rock, creating 195-198

of tree, creating 195-198procedural
  textures, using 200, 202
metric system 124
Middle Mouse Button (MMB) 7
mirror modifier 33
mist pass
  compositing 212
modeling tools, Robot Toy
  extrusion 22, 23
  using 21
modifier 27
Multires modifier
  about 60
  first touch 60

N

navigation, Blender
  editors 8
  of 3D Viewport 6, 7
  preferences, setting up 11
  using 6
navigation preferences
  add-ons, using in Blender 13, 14
  default navigation style, customizing 12
  Preferences window 11
  setting 11
N-Gon 25
nodal compositing 294
Non-Linear Action editor 257
normal map
  about 117
  baking 117
  creating, with bake tools 117, 118
  displaying, in viewport 118, 119

O

OpenEXR
  about 293
  URL 293
origin/pivot 43
outliner 33
Overlapping Action principle 250

P

pen tablet
  using 55
performance settings, Cycles
  Tiles 183
  Viewport BVH Type 183
picture
  Depth pass 296, 297
  effects, adding 298
  enhancing, with composing 293
  nodal compositing 294, 295
  rendering phase, compositing 300
Pinch/Magnify brush 76
PlayBlast 280
Plugins 13
poly modeling 55
Pose to Pose principle 249, 250
Preferences window 11
Project From View 153
projects
  about 14
  Alien Character 14
  Haunted House 15
  Rat Cowboy 15
  Robot Toy 14
Proportional Editing 36
proxy 265

R

Rat Cowboy
  about 15, 217
  arm 224
  arm, rigging 223-225
  deforming bones, placing 217-220
  Display options 220
  eyes, rigging 227, 228
  foot, rigging 221, 222
  gun, rigging 230, 231
  hand 224
  hand, rigging 223-225
  head, rigging 227, 228
  hips, rigging 225
  holster, rigging 232
  leg, rigging 221, 222
  rigging 217
  rig, mirroring 229, 230

  root bone, adding 233
  tail, rigging 226
raw rendering phase 292, 293
realistic grass
  creating 205
  grass, generating with particles 205, 206
  grass shader, creating 207, 208
retopologized mesh 116
retopology
  creating 90
  creating, best practices 92, 93
  of Alien Character, creating 94
  polygon density 94
  polygons arranging, possibilities 90-92
Return key 26
rigging process 216
Robot Toy
  about 17, 18
  antenna, modeling 24-27
  arm, modeling 47-51
  buttons, modeling 40, 41
  chest, modeling 34-38
  Edit Mode, versus Object Mode 20, 21
  eyes, modeling 34
  fork, modeling 41-44
  head, modeling 22, 23
  image reference, adding for preparing
    workflow 18, 19
  main wheel, modeling 47
  modeling 18
  naming shortcuts 20
  neck, modeling 38, 39
  rendering, with Blender Internal 51
  thunderbolts, modeling 30-33
  torso, modeling 39, 40
root bone 233

S

sampling, Cycles
  Preview samples setting 182
  Render samples setting 182
scene animation
  about 266
  actions, mixing 269, 270
  close shot animation 272, 273
  gunshot 273-275

U

UVs
about 111
island adjustment 115
island placement 115
layers 160
layers options 161
seam placement 111-114
textures, baking 116
tiling 160
tiling, goal 160
unwrapping 110, 154
UV unwrapping process
about 111, 154
environment objects, unwrapping 159
Project From View, using 154
remaining house components 155-157
tree, using with Smart UV project 158, 159

V

Vertex Connect Path tool 51
Video Sequence Editor (VSE)
about 301
final sequence, editing 301
final sequence, rendering 301
used, for editing sequence 300

W

Weight Painting stage 216
Weight Paint tools
about 234
skinning, editing 237
URL 235

Thank you for buying
Blender 3D By Example

About Packt Publishing

Packt, pronounced 'packed', published its first book, *Mastering phpMyAdmin for Effective MySQL Management*, in April 2004, and subsequently continued to specialize in publishing highly focused books on specific technologies and solutions.

Our books and publications share the experiences of your fellow IT professionals in adapting and customizing today's systems, applications, and frameworks. Our solution-based books give you the knowledge and power to customize the software and technologies you're using to get the job done. Packt books are more specific and less general than the IT books you have seen in the past. Our unique business model allows us to bring you more focused information, giving you more of what you need to know, and less of what you don't.

Packt is a modern yet unique publishing company that focuses on producing quality, cutting-edge books for communities of developers, administrators, and newbies alike. For more information, please visit our website at www.packtpub.com.

About Packt Open Source

In 2010, Packt launched two new brands, Packt Open Source and Packt Enterprise, in order to continue its focus on specialization. This book is part of the Packt Open Source brand, home to books published on software built around open source licenses, and offering information to anybody from advanced developers to budding web designers. The Open Source brand also runs Packt's Open Source Royalty Scheme, by which Packt gives a royalty to each open source project about whose software a book is sold.

Writing for Packt

We welcome all inquiries from people who are interested in authoring. Book proposals should be sent to author@packtpub.com. If your book idea is still at an early stage and you would like to discuss it first before writing a formal book proposal, then please contact us; one of our commissioning editors will get in touch with you.

We're not just looking for published authors; if you have strong technical skills but no writing experience, our experienced editors can help you develop a writing career, or simply get some additional reward for your expertise.

Blender 3D Basics
Beginner's Guide

Second Edition

ISBN: 978-1-78398-490-9   Paperback: 526 pages

A quick and easy-to-use guide to create 3D modeling and animation using Blender 2.7

1. Explore Blender's unique user interface and unlock Blender's powerful suite of modeling and animation tools.

2. Learn how to use Blender, and also the principles that make animation, lighting, and camera work come alive.

3. Start with the basics and build your skills through a coordinated series of projects to create a complex world.

Blender 3D Cookbook

ISBN: 978-1-78398-488-6   Paperback: 608 pages

Build your very own stunning characters in Blender from scratch

1. Establish the basic shape of a character with the help of templates, and complete it by using different Blender tools.

2. Gain an understanding of how to create and assign materials automatically, working in both the Blender Internal engine as well as in Cycles.

3. Familiarize yourself with the processes involved in rigging, skinning, and finally animating the basic walk-cycle of the character.

Please check **www.PacktPub.com** for information on our titles

Blender Cycles: Lighting
and Rendering Cookbook

ISBN: 978-1-78216-460-9   Paperback: 274 pages

Over 50 recipes to help you master the Lighting and
Rendering model using the Blender Cycles engine

1. Get acquainted with the lighting and rendering
    concepts of the Blender Cycles engine.

2. Learn the concepts behind nodes shader system
    and get the best out of Cycles in any situation.

3. Packed with illustrations and a lot of tips
    and tricks to make your scenes come to life.

Blender Cycles: Materials and
Textures Cookbook
Third Edition

ISBN: 978-1-78439-993-1   Paperback: 400 pages

Over 40 practical recipes to create stunning materials
and textures using the Cycles rendering engine with
Blender

1. Create realistic material shaders by
    understanding the fundamentals of
    material creation in Cycles.

2. Quickly make impressive projects production-
    ready using the Blender rendering engine.

3. Discover step-by-step material recipes with
    complete diagrams of nodes.

Please check **www.PacktPub.com** for information on our titles

58290073R00186

Made in the USA
Lexington, KY
07 December 2016